Lincoln and McClellan at War

LINCOLN

· AND ·

McCLELLAN

AT

WAR

CHESTER G. HEARN

LOUISIANA STATE UNIVERSITY PRESS

BATON ROUGE

Published by Louisiana State University Press
Copyright © 2012 by Louisiana State University Press
All rights reserved
Manufactured in the United States of America
First printing

DESIGNER: Michelle A. Neustrom
TYPEFACE: Ingeborg
PRINTER: McNaughton & Gunn, Inc.
BINDER: Dekker Bookbinding

Maps by Michael G. Marino

LIBRARY OF CONGRESS CATALOGING-IN-PUBLICATION DATA

Hearn, Chester G.
     Lincoln and McClellan at war / Chester G. Hearn.
       pages cm
     Includes bibliographical references and index.
     ISBN 978-0-8071-4552-4 (cloth : alk. paper) — ISBN 978-0-8071-4553-1 (pdf) — ISBN 978-0-8071-4554-8 (epub) — ISBN 978-0-8071-4555-5 (mobi)
       1. McClellan, George Brinton, 1826–1885—Military leadership. 2. Lincoln, Abraham, 1809–1865—Military leadership. 3. United States—History—Civil War, 1861–1865—Campaigns. 4. Command of troops—History—19th century. I. Title.
     E467.1.M2H45 2013
     973.7′3—dc23

                                                                    2012004477

To my wife, Ann,
and to all the years she has given me

CONTENTS

Lincoln and McClellan at War

Introduction

FOLLOWING THE SURRENDER of Fort Sumter on April 14, 1861, Abraham Lincoln began searching for advisors to aid him at the outbreak of war. His seven-man cabinet, composed partly of Whigs and partly of former Democrats, provided little help because they understood politics without understanding warfare. On matters concerning how the conflict should be prosecuted, the cabinet also held differing opinions, most of which at the outset of war were delusionary and wrong.

Lincoln also relied for advice on septuagenarian Brevet Lieutenant General Winfield Scott, the venerable hero of the War of 1812 and the war with Mexico, who for the past twenty years had been the nation's general-in-chief. Being a year older than the United States Constitution, Scott had witnessed a great deal of war without keeping current on advances in military technology. Most of his sixteen thousand–man regular army, composed of northerners and southerners, were on the frontier keeping peace with the Indians while trying to enforce harmony between militant proslavery and antislavery settlers intent on exterminating each other. The army had not been modernized, nor had its officers been exposed to European advancements in war fighting. Even when he was twenty years younger, Scott might never have been capable of commanding the huge armies formed during the Civil War. The Army of the Potomac became ten times larger than the little army Scott took to Mexico. Now too old and sick to retain his ceremonial post as general-in-chief much longer, Scott admitted that his infirmities, which included vertigo, gout, and obesity, prevented him from ever taking command in the field. In late April Secretary of State William H. Seward visited army headquarters to speak with the general and remarked: "We are gathering a large army. What I do not see is how it is to be led. What are we to do for generals?" Scott paused before replying. "That is a subject that I have thought much about. If I could only mount a horse," he lamented then, checking himself, added with a shake of his head: "But I am past that. I can only serve my country as I am doing here now, in my chair." Three months later, after Robert E. Lee rejected the top U.S. Army command post and joined the Confederacy, Scott brought thirty-four-year-old Major General George Brinton McClellan to Washington to organize what one month later became the Army of the Potomac.[1]

McClellan's arrival in Washington marked the beginning of the president's relationship with the young general, whose credentials included graduation from West Point second in the class of 1846, distinguished service with three brevets during the Mexican War, a year in Europe studying foreign military methods, and a recent successfully led campaign in western Virginia, after which he took credit for defeating Robert E. Lee. In addition to being one of the most thoroughly prepared military scientists of his generation, McClellan radiated tireless energy and brought fresh ideas to Washington, which is what Lincoln wanted. Although McClellan's background looked impressive by American standards, it was also limited by his study of engineering and fortifications at West Point, which with mathematics formed the major focus of the army's curriculum because no officer at the academy anticipated a prolonged war from within the sprawling boundaries of the nation. McClellan concentrated most of his time in Europe on the same subjects—engineering and fortifications—and returned home having learned little about formulating strategy, directing staff, or how top European generals organized and led large armies in combat. His own generals could not help him, having been indoctrinated in the same West Point courses of study, and it is likely he would not have listened to their advice if given.

McClellan accumulated a vast knowledge of military history by studying the brilliant battles of Napoleon at the turn of the eighteenth century. He became the great Corsican's disciple, and this affinity would become one of McClellan's greatest handicaps because Confederate generals threw away their West Point textbooks and developed new tactics. Before contemplating an expedition, McClellan first asked himself what Napoleon would have done. Napoleon had never seen rifled muskets, rifled artillery, repeating carbines, or Virginia mud. McClellan could recite the military maxims of Jomini and Vauban, which he tenaciously adopted, but he could not fight successfully by following them. The realities of warfare in Virginia puzzled and paralyzed him, and though Lincoln eventually characterized the general's indecisive movements as "the slows," the president may never have completely understood why. Confederate general Robert E. Lee attributed McClellan's deliberateness to the latter's West Point training as an engineer. Lee, being one himself, knew that army engineers typically insisted on having everything precisely and methodically organized to ensure a predictable outcome—an unlikelihood on any mid-nineteenth-century battlefield. In this regard McClellan stumbled into the Civil War somewhat less a novice in modern military warfare than Lincoln.

Over time there would never be a commander of the Union army with whom Lincoln would become more closely associated than McClellan. He tried to establish a close and trusting friendship with the general but never succeeded. Lincoln needed McClellan. Being a total novice on military matters, the president sought knowledge, and his training began—for better or worse—on the day he first met the general. Over a period of a year and a half, while McClellan commanded the Army of the Potomac and served for several months as general-in-chief, Lincoln discovered, without knowing the reasons why, that his general, who excelled at organizing armies, inexplicably avoided fighting. During those months Lincoln learned a great deal about military strategy, partly because of what McClellan did well and partly because of what McClellan did poorly. As Lincoln acquired military knowledge, his working relationship with the general deteriorated because of growing differences between the two over strategy and political doctrine. Reunification of the nation became the only war aim on which the two men concurred, but they often disagreed on the methods for accomplishing that objective. As Hugh McCullough, who later became secretary of the Treasury under Lincoln, observed: "When General McClellan issued his first order, as commander-in-chief, his star was in the zenith. Its decline was rapid."[2]

McClellan constantly frustrated Lincoln, who at times humbled himself to placate his egotistic general because he, as president, admitted ignorance in organizing an army and making it fight. His inept secretary of war, Simon Cameron, distinguished himself by his uselessness. When Lincoln decided to replace enfeebled Winfield Scott with young George McClellan, he admitted to being uncertain whether there should be any such officer as general-in-chief, so he asked Edwin Bates, his attorney general. Bates replied: "The *General in chief*—or *chief General*—is only *your lieutenant*. You are Constitutional 'Commander in chief,' and may make any general you please." Six months later, when in December 1861 Lincoln became perplexed by McClellan's stalling, Bates questioned whether having a general-in-chief added anything to the war effort. After holding another session with Lincoln, Bates noted in his diary: "I insisted that, being 'commander in chief' by law, he [Lincoln] must command—especially in such a war as this. The Nation requires it, and History will hold him responsible." Lincoln had not taken executive control of the army, and Bates pointed to the deficiency, writing, "If I were President, I would command . . . and I would know what army I had, and what the high generals (my Lieutenants) were doing with that army." While admitting "the Presdt. is an excellent man, and, in the main wise," he chided Lincoln for lacking "*will* and *purpose*" and professed, "I greatly fear he has not *the power to command*." Bates was not alone in this assessment. Lincoln felt the same way about himself regarding military matters, which was the reason he needed McClellan.[3]

Because McClellan regarded Lincoln as an inferior made the relationship tedious and insufferable at times. As the president acquired military knowledge, he became more assertive. He developed his own ideas about how the war should be fought, and such intrusions by the president understandably and often justifiably upset the general. McClellan believed the army was not the president's business, and in the early months of the war Lincoln let the general have his way. Both men were still in the learning process, but the president learned quickly. The general resented suggestions and disliked being questioned. He always countered with his own plan any the president suggested. McClellan could capably develop good strategies but not carry them out, partly because he preferred fighting defensively and partly because of the president's interference. All of McClellan's strategies required going on the offensive, which was inconsistent with the general's preference to build forts and earthworks to fight defensively. McClellan had become so steeped in the knowledge of defensive tactics that he disliked attacking an enemy in defensive works. He also disliked bloodshed, which is partly why he never clearly won a battle. Nor did he have a field general's quest to defeat an enemy he considered to be his southern brothers, which led to moderation in his tactics and a series of lost opportunities. McClellan never recognized this weakness; Lincoln eventually did. Lincoln also came to realize that he must stop interfering with his generals. Congressman John B. Alley wrote after reflecting on a conversation with the president, "He himself was not a military man—did not pretend to be—and yet I never found any one of the leading generals, or any civilian, who had such a clear and accurate knowledge of all the movements of the army, and who conceived and understood so perfectly their strategic movements."[4]

Attorney General Bates summed up the situation on April 9, 1862, after wondering why Lincoln allowed McClellan to take the Army of the Potomac to the Peninsula: "I do believe the Genl. has such a morbid ambition of originality that he will adopt no plan of action suggested by another— He must himself invent as well as execute every scheme of operations. And yet it seems to me that he has but small inventive faculty—Hence his inevitable failure." During his entire career McClellan would never have, and by a wide margin, fewer troops than his Confederate opponent.[5]

McClellan always found a way to argue against doing something suggested by someone else or by blocking something he was instructed to do. He gave credible, but not always accurate, reasons for ignoring his instructions. This habit came close to driving some who dealt with him, such as Secretary of War Edwin McMasters Stanton and General-in-Chief Henry W. Halleck, insane. Yet there were many supporters, especially among the Democrats, who praised the general. "The Army of the Potomac was composed of men of unusual intelligence," wrote Hugh McCullough, a more passive observer. "There were hundreds in the ranks who were fitted to be captains; scores who were fitted to be colonels and generals. The manner in which McClellan was received by such men—the men whom he had trained, under whom they had fought in the desperate battles on the Peninsula—was not only a compliment to him as a man, but a strong testimony to his merit as a commander."[6]

McCullough's assessment of General McClellan's abilities was partly right and partly wrong. The general excelled at building an army but failed to fight it effectively, often because of poor staff work. When General Scott brought McClellan to Washington in July 1861, he probably picked the best man available at the time. No other officer had the training or the knowledge to build a large army and prepare it for battle. Lincoln tried to help McClellan but never knew quite how. Both men struggled to put armies into the field without knowing what those armies required to be effective. Fighting Indians provided no insight into the problems of staffing a large army. McClellan's first battles occurred on the Virginia Peninsula. The learning curve for both men had already begun back in Washington. One man grew immeasurably during those eighteen months. The other man grew slowly, barely at all.

1

• •

"It is impossible for him to lead"

T HE CIVIL WAR BEGAN DISASTROUSLY for Abraham Lincoln.
He hoped to reunify the country without an armed conflict,
but measures he took after becoming president hurried the
war. Lincoln did not understand warfare. His only military
experience traced back to April 16, 1832, when Governor John Reynolds
of Illinois called for volunteers to repel an incursion of Black Hawk's so-
called British Band into the Rock River area, located in the northwestern
part of the state. The force consisted of about five hundred Sauk and Fox
warriors and a thousand old men, women, and children.

Lincoln joined the Sangamon County militia company as a volunteer
because Denton Offutt's general store, where he clerked, was closing, thus
depriving him of a job. He had also put himself before the public as a candidate for the state legislature and believed a war record would increase
his popularity at the polls. Friends from Sangamon elected him as their
leader, and the unit became "Captain Abraham Lincoln's Company of the
[Fourth] Regiment of the Brigade of Mounted Volunteers commanded by
Brigadier-General Samuel Whiteside." The Mounted Volunteers had no
horses, so at first they walked. They knew nothing about fighting Indians,
but state law compelled every able-bodied man between the ages of eighteen and forty-five to drill twice a year or pay a one-dollar fine. Nobody
had a dollar to spare, so everyone drilled.[1]

Captain Lincoln had no experience giving orders, nor had he become
handy with firearms. His first official order, given to an independent-
minded volunteer, drew the response "Go to hell." As an officer, Lincoln
carried a pistol and a sword. He accidently fired the weapon in camp,
which was forbidden, and served one day under arrest for violating regi-

mental rules. A few days later hungry men from his company raided the officers' supply tent, stole several few jugs of whiskey, and went to bed dead drunk. When they appeared intoxicated at morning roll call, Abe paid the price for his men's misconduct. General Whiteside held court-martial proceedings, stripped Lincoln of his weapons, and ordered him to carry a wooden sword for two days. Colonel Zachary Taylor arrived to take command of the regiment and in a speech told sixteen hundred volunteers, including the Sangamon men, that as citizens of Illinois there "would probably be congressmen [among them who would] go to Washington" someday. Lincoln took notice and decided to become a better soldier.[2]

On May 27, because of poor discipline in General Whiteside's command, Governor Reynolds mustered the Sangamon men out of the service. With no job waiting at home, and because Colonel Taylor's words suggested a possible political career for men who served, Lincoln and his friends reenlisted for thirty days in General Robert Anderson's brigade as privates. Anderson would later become distinguished as the Union officer who defended Fort Sumter in 1861. He assigned Lincoln to Captain Elijah Iles's company of Independent Rangers, a mounted unit engaged in carrying messages and reconnoitering Black Hawk's movements. Because the volunteers had no camp duties and drew rations as they pleased, Lincoln found serving as a private more agreeable than shouldering a captain's responsibilities.[3]

On June 16 Lincoln reenlisted for another thirty days and joined Captain Jacob M. Early's Independent Spy Corps. A Methodist minister from Springfield, Illinois, Early had previously been a private serving under Lincoln. The nearest Lincoln came to participating in a skirmish occurred on June 25 at Kellogg's Grove on the upper Rock River, where he arrived in time to bury five men who had been scalped during a surprise attack. The company pursued Black Hawk into the Michigan Territory (later Wisconsin), which Lincoln recalled as the hardest march of his life. When provisions gave out on July 10, three weeks before the last battle, Early disbanded the company and sent the volunteers home. Someone stole Lincoln's horse, so he walked with friends as far as Peoria, bought a canoe, paddled down the Illinois River to Havana, and walked the rest of the way home to New Salem. Years later he joked about his seminal military experience as thrashing about in swamps and sinkholes and recounted bloody struggles with mosquitoes while leading dashing assaults on onion patches.[4] By all accounts Lincoln survived the short campaign without ever seeing action. He learned nothing of tactical value from his experience, and his war record failed to launch his career as a Whig. On Election Day, August 6, Lincoln won his hometown vote but lost his bid for the state legislature, finishing seventh among a field of twelve. The defeat did not wrench Lincoln from politics. Six weeks later he filled a local post as clerk of the September election.[5]

Although Lincoln may have heard of General Winfield Scott, who arrived with U.S. Army regulars to participate in the Black Hawk War, or of Jefferson Davis, who conducted Black Hawk to prison, he learned nothing about fighting or military leadership. He did learn something about sloppy logistics because he and his friends sometimes went days without rations. Lincoln never intended to become a military man, but after becoming president in 1861and suffering several avoidable military disasters, he developed rapidly into a strategist.

DURING THE TWENTY-EIGHT YEARS between the Black Hawk War and the presidential election in 1860, Lincoln became a lawyer, a politician, but never again a soldier. Elected in 1834 to the state legislature, he served continuously for four terms as a Whig and became the unelected but accepted speaker of the lower house by caucus affirmation. In 1841 he left office to concentrate on law, but five years later Illinois voters sent him to Congress. He served one term, from 1847 to 1849, but never took part in the great 1850 debates over slavery. While serving as a U.S. representative he did work on the Wilmot Proviso, which prohibited slavery in the territories acquired from Mexico, and he backed the prohibition of slavery in the District of Columbia, a piece of legislation that came to the floor for a vote during his term. Lincoln's efforts were among his first toward emancipation on a limited scale and were radically different from those of Democrats, who sanctioned slavery, and Republican radicals, who demanded immediate abolition. Lincoln believed masters should be paid for freeing their slaves, and he still felt the same way when he became president. Had legislation passed in 1849, following Lincoln's statesmanlike approach to applying gradual solutions to the slave problem, the South might have retained confidence in Lincoln as president, and South Carolina might not have been so hasty to secede from the Union on December 20, 1860.[6] Lincoln's congressional term brought him no particular distinction, and with Democrats running Illinois, he returned to Springfield with few aspirations of a political career and resumed his practice of law. As Whigs gradually lost power in the North, Lincoln observed the early formation of the Republican Party while remaining circumspect. He refused to join the Know-Nothings, an emerging political coalition promoting prejudice against non-American racial groups, which in 1856 nominated former president Millard Fillmore as their candidate. Democrats nominated James Buchanan of Pennsylvania, partly because he abhorred abolition and partly because he disliked the divisive antislavery policies espoused by the emerging Republican Party. Republicans nominated John C. Frémont, the nationally acclaimed "Pathfinder" who during the Mexican War once contrived to become dictator of California. Senator and former governor William H. Seward of New York would have been a better choice for the ticket, but Seward's mentor, Thurlow Weed, restrained him from seeking the nomination until 1860.[7]

In 1856 Lincoln suddenly found himself back in politics when he discovered his name had been placed on the ballot as Frémont's running mate during the Republican National Convention in Philadelphia. Although he personally distrusted Frémont and never intended to run for vice president, Lincoln received 110 votes during an informal ballot. Senator William L. Dayton of New Jersey won the nomination with 259 votes. Lincoln received the news while attending court in Urbana, Illinois. He brushed off the information, remarking that the votes were probably meant for "the other *great man* of the same name from Mass[achusetts]." That his name had been put forward at the national convention served as a stimulant, and Lincoln began to reconsider a political career more seriously.[8]

In 1854 Lincoln had already begun easing back into politics by making speeches on issues of national interest, such as the Kansas-Nebraska Act. He had been reelected to the Illinois legislature but resigned his seat to run for the U.S. Senate. After failing in 1854, he waited until 1858 to run against Senator Stephen Douglas, an Illinois Democrat with whom he had differentiated himself politically through four years of public speaking appearances. Although the famous Lincoln-Douglas debates took place in 1858, they actually began in 1854, when the two rivals first took opposing positions on state and national issues. On June 16, 1858, the Republican State Convention at Springfield granted Lincoln's wish by nominating him as their candidate for the Senate. Lincoln responded to the honor by delivering his famous "House Divided" speech, which differentiated him from Douglas's "popular sovereignty" doctrine. The speech launched Lincoln's Senate campaign and made him a contender for the presidential nomination in 1860.[9]

The 1858 debates with Douglas took place during a time when Lincoln represented the Illinois Central Railroad in several legal cases. At the time former U.S. Army captain George Brinton McClellan served as the railroad's vice president. As a conservative Democrat, McClellan staunchly supported Douglas and admitted having nothing in common with Lincoln. During the summer and fall campaign of 1858 he made his private car available to Douglas. On one occasion he accompanied the senator to a debate and tidied him up after a night of hard drinking. According to a statement in Stephen W. Sears's biography, McClellan wrote, "Douglas' speech was compact, logical & powerful—Mr. Lincoln's disjointed, & rather a mass of anecdotes instead of arguments. I did not think there was any approach to equality in the oratorical powers of the two men." McClellan's handiwork also appeared on Election Day, when he issued orders to the railroad's superintendent to have a specially chartered locomotive filled with Lincoln voters break down in some remote area until the polls closed. The two incidents marked McClellan's first encounters with Lincoln. He never changed his political views or his early impressions of Lincoln. Both men would one day work together to save the Union, each in his own way, but in 1858 Lincoln had no inkling that McClellan had lurked in the background manipulating the outcome of the election and stigmatizing him as inferior. After Lincoln became the president-elect, McClellan did not disagree when in January 1861 he received a letter from John M. Douglas, a fellow director on the Illinois Central, who wrote, "I tell you it is impossible for him to lead," a conviction they shared and one that McClellan accepted without reservation.[10]

Douglas won the Senate race, but Lincoln won national visibility by defining the differences between Democrats and Republicans. Without the debates Lincoln would not have become a presidential candidate. He espoused a mild antislavery position because he believed the institution would, over time and with gentle nudges, self-destruct. He managed to convince northern moderates without repelling radical abolitionists. Douglas paid dearly for his stand on popular sovereignty, which favored freedom only where people wanted it. Oddly enough, Lincoln did not fundamentally disagree with Douglas but made it seem so. The debates put Lincoln before the public. Invitations to speak on national issues came from other states, in particular New York and Ohio. He promoted his position of resisting popular sovereignty as a means of appeasing slave interests as he done during the Douglas debates. In 1859 friends began urging Lincoln to consider running for the Republican presidential nomination, but it was not until April 29, 1860, that he admitted to Senator Lyman Trumbull, "The taste is in my mouth a little." By then he had finished a tour of the East, made his Cooper Union speech on February 27, 1860, and began to differentiate himself from Seward, the Republican frontrunner from New York, and Ohio governor Salmon P. Chase, Seward's main competitor.[11]

When delegates to the Republican National Convention met in Chicago on May 16, 1860, Lincoln had established himself as a serious presidential contender. Although he did not directly participate in the convention, his political handlers, Judge David Davis and Leonard Swett, made several deals to bolster his nomination. After Lincoln won the presidential election in November 1860, one of those deals brought Simon Cameron, a corrupt powerbroker from Pennsylvania, into the cabinet as secretary of war. Cameron knew nothing about running the War Department and filled it with political friends. On military matters he relied on seventy-five-year-old Brevet Lieutenant General Winfield Scott, a venerable general-in-chief smitten by age, gout, dropsy, and vertigo. When young, Scott had distinguished himself during the War of 1812 and again during the Mexican War. He still carried two British bullets in his ponderous frame, but age had sapped his energy and blunted his interest in the expansion of military technology. Having lately acquired the sobriquet "Old Fuss and Feathers" because of his passion for red tape, Scott could no longer mount a horse, though he continued to be the most celebrated soldier in America. When not asleep on a sofa at army headquarters, he spent his wakeful hours conducting business from a huge armchair. In early 1861 Scott still functioned as the foremost military authority in the country, and Edwin McMasters Stanton, who had previously served as President James Buchanan's attorney general, wrote, "He is, in fact, the Government."[12]

Lincoln also created problems for himself in attempting to balance his cabinet by filling it with four former Democrats and three former Whigs, with himself as the fourth Whig. Of the seven cabinet members only Postmaster General Montgomery Blair, who had graduated from West Point in 1835, had military training. After serving one year fighting Seminoles, he had resigned to study law. Seward occupied the top post in the cabinet as secretary of state and espoused strong views on running the administration, which irritated other members of the cabinet. As secretary of the Treasury, Chase reigned over the number-two post in the pecking order. Seward and Chase had been competing presidential candidates in 1860. They held different views on abolition and secession and disliked each other. Their personal rivalry created two mini–political factions in the cabinet, which provided Lincoln with little help, either militarily or politically. Gideon Welles, the secretary of the navy and a former Democrat, disliked Seward's efforts to upstage Lincoln and remained one of the president's staunchest supporters. Welles's involvement with naval affairs during the Mexican War gave him a small amount of helpful administrative experience. Edwin Bates, also a presidential candidate and former Democrat, provided reliable legal advice as attorney general and on occasion sound political advice. Caleb Smith of Indiana became secretary of the interior because of another deal made by Lincoln's managers during the presidential nominating convention. Smith sided with Seward on every issue and, next to Secretary of War Cameron, contributed no useful political or military advice. With seven of eleven southern states having already seceded when Lincoln took office on March 4, 1860, rifts within the cabinet provided the president with little consensus and many months of frustration.

During the first weeks of his presidency Lincoln invited comments from the cabinet on the relief of Fort Sumter. Major Robert Anderson, who had first appeared in Lincoln's life during the Black Hawk War, commanded the fort. Sumter represented the only fully functional Federal fort still in Union possession in Charleston, South Carolina's harbor, and no provisions or supplies had been delivered to the isolated garrison for several months. On requesting opinions from cabinet members, Lincoln said he was anxious to avoid offensive measures and to forbear suggesting acts of aggression. Seward opposed relieving the fort because he erroneously believed a strong pro-Union sentiment still existed in the South. General-in-Chief Scott, an old Whig, sided with Seward, but with a standing army of only sixteen thousand regulars, mainly on duty in the West, he hoped to avoid war. Cameron agreed with Seward because Scott did. This became one of the rare moments when Chase agreed with Seward and suggested the South should be allowed to go its separate way. Bates and Smith also agreed with Seward and said an expedition would be unwise. Only Postmaster Blair advocated the immediate relief of Fort Sumter.[13]

Lincoln eventually turned the majority of the cabinet's thinking toward provisioning rather than abandoning the fort and ordered Welles to do it. Although Seward opposed the relief of Sumter, he urged the reinforcement of Fort Pickens in Florida. He never explained why strengthening Pickens would not provoke war while the relief of Sumter would. Meanwhile, South Carolina batteries fired on the fort a few hours before Union relief ships appeared offshore. In the first official military engagement of the Civil War, Major Anderson surrendered Fort Sumter on April 13, 1861. Although some said the president provoked the South into starting the war, Lincoln insisted the Sumter expedition was purely humanitarian. He also claimed that no reinforcements reached shore at Fort Pickens until after Sumter surrendered, therefore implying the South had started the war.[14]

FOLLOWING THE SURRENDER OF FORT SUMTER, Lincoln issued a proclamation on April 15 calling for 75,000 ninety-day militia for national defense. He also called for a special session of Congress to convene on July 4. Four more southern states seceded, including Virginia, bringing the total to eleven. The South had already begun to mobilize after the formation of the Confederate States of America in February 1861. President Jefferson Davis called for 82,000 volunteers for one year, many of whom were already available from organized militia companies. Davis blamed Lincoln for being the aggressor and continued to up the ante by increasing the size of the Confederate army. Lincoln responded on May 3 and called for another 42,034 volunteers to serve three-year enlistments as infantry and cavalry, after which military escalation expanded both North and South.

At first Lincoln ignored the advice of General Scott, who asked for three hundred thousand troops. By the time Congress convened in July, Lincoln decided he needed at least four hundred thousand three-year volunteers and $400 million to pay for the force. Congress responded by authorizing a volunteer army of five hundred thousand men. Lincoln was undecided about how to employ his original call-up of seventy-five thousand troops but knew he must put them to work before their enlistments expired. He did not expect a long and protracted war, but he wanted it quickly settled, the nation restored, and a permanent understanding that no state could "withdraw from the Union, without the consent of the Union."[15]

After the surrender of Fort Sumter, followed by the April 17 secession of Virginia, General Scott's widely spread army of regulars suffered a rapid reduction when 313 officers defected to the South, followed by hundreds of enlisted men. Among the regular army officers joining the South were some of General Scott's most trusted and talented officers, including Ambrose Powell Hill, Joseph E. Johnston, Robert E. Lee, James Longstreet, and James E. B. "Jeb" Stuart. So many southerners with West Point educations and years of active experience resigned to join the Confederacy that Scott could not find among the faithful remnants enough capable officers to organize, train, and lead the rapidly assembling Union army. When Lincoln prodded the secretary of war for solutions, Cameron complained that General Scott's infirmities prevented him from taking field command and admitted being distressed by the situation.

The problem intensified when pro-secessionists occupying Federal positions in Washington engaged in slurs and fistfights with pro-Union employees. Federal regulars posted in the capital were too few to control the turmoil, and though Scott declared the city safe, others predicted a large Confederate force from Virginia would pounce on Washington at any hour. The tension diminished after militia from Massachusetts and New York began appearing on the streets of Washington.[16]

While concerned for the safety of the city, Lincoln became personally involved in efforts to keep the border slaveholding states of Delaware,

Kentucky, Maryland, and Missouri from joining the Confederacy. Should Maryland be lost, Washington would be sandwiched between two southern states and the government forced to abandon the national capital. Lincoln worried constantly about Kentucky, his native state, but hesitated to apply military force. Being close to Washington, Lincoln believed Delaware and Maryland could be coaxed away from Confederate influence, but Kentucky and Missouri required delicate handling. Although Lincoln's April 19 proclamation blockading southern ports infuriated the Confederate administration, nothing irritated border state governors more than Secretary Cameron's imposed quota system for raising troops.[17]

Governor Claiborne F. Jackson of Missouri took exception to Cameron's demand for troops, writing, "Your requisition, in my judgment, is illegal, unconstitutional, and revolutionary in its object, and cannot be complied with." Cameron admitted having no clue how to respond to Jackson's rejoinder and pitched the problem of Missouri to Lincoln. The president conferred with Bates and Blair, who both understood conditions in Missouri, and decided that Brigadier General William S. Harney had enough troops to keep the situation under control and safeguard the St. Louis armory, which the governor wanted. Lincoln believed the status of Missouri depended on keeping Kentucky in the Union, so his efforts reverted to his home state.[18]

The military frontier west of the Allegheny Mountains remained in turmoil, which resulted from the absence of a military presence. One of the hotspots occurred along the Ohio River, already severely complicated by conflicting pro-secession/pro-Union scuffles in Kentucky. To Cameron's request for militia, Kentucky Governor Beriah Magoffin curtly declared he would "furnish no troops for the wicked purpose of subduing her sister Southern States."[19]

Illinois, Indiana, and Ohio all depended on the Ohio River for transporting goods to Kentucky and Missouri as well as to Arkansas and Tennessee, which on May 2 still belonged to the Union. When Arkansas seceded on May 6, Cameron established a checkpoint at Cairo, Illinois, to search for munitions aboard all traffic entering the Mississippi River from the Ohio River. Orders went to militia general George B. McClellan, who had resigned as a railroad executive and on May 3 took command of the Department of the Ohio. Although McClellan's initial responsibilities pertained to Ohio, on May 13, after expressing great confidence in the former captain of cavalry, General Scott expanded the Department of the Ohio to include Illinois and Indiana. McClellan had previously served under Scott, managing engineering projects for the general.[20]

McClellan understood the political situation and recommended a system of defense with two or three regiments of infantry and a few gunboats posted at Cairo to deter incursions from pro-secessionists in Kentucky. When Governor Oliver P. Morton of Indiana suggested placing batteries across the Ohio River from Louisville, McClellan wisely vetoed the suggestion, writing: "I cannot permit this, it would only serve to irritate . . . The moral effect of the presence of troops at Cairo, Evansville, and Camp Dennison [near Cincinnati] ought to be sufficient to reassure Union men in Kentucky." Lincoln must have been aware of McClellan's effective vigilance along the Ohio because on May 14, 1861, he removed Joseph K. F. Mansfield's name from a list of appointments to major general and replaced it with McClellan's. Lincoln knew very little about his new general and signed the memorandum on Scott's recommendation. The one-time railroad executive, known to others as "Little Mac," was now officially back in the U.S. Army, although the commission still required the approval of the Senate, scheduled to convene in July.[21]

McClellan quickly became thoroughly involved in both the military and the political situation along the Ohio line. His efforts won praise from Cameron, Scott, and the governors of Illinois, Indiana, and Ohio. His railroad experience gave him excellent knowledge of the area and the leadership problems in Kentucky. For the moment Kentucky's legislature assumed a position of neutrality, declaring, "The present duty of Kentucky is to maintain her present independent position, taking sides not with the Administration, nor with the seceding States, but with the Union against them both; declaring her soil to be sacred from the hostile tread of either; and, if necessary, to make the declaration good with her strong right arm."[22]

For the time being Lincoln accepted Kentucky's statement of neutrality because it served his purpose of keeping an important border state in the Union. McClellan believed neither Cameron nor Lincoln fully understood the volatile situation in Kentucky. He had spoken with Garrett Davis, a Unionist in Kentucky, who said, "We will remain in the Union by voting if we can, by fighting if we must, & if we cannot hold our own we will call on the General Government to aid us." McClellan promised to support Garrett Davis with forty thousand men, if necessary, and to support the pledge, he began pressing the War Department for more men, more batteries, and more cavalry. His initial requests were modest, but they never ended.[23] Thus began a relationship between the president, the general, and the War Department that evolved into some of the most engrossing incidents of military mismanagement in the annals of modern warfare.

2

"Come hither without delay"

BORN IN PHILADELPHIA on December 3, 1826, the son of a distinguished surgeon, George Brinton McClellan received an education in the city, entered West Point in 1842 at the age of fifteen, and graduated in June 1846 second in a class of fifty-nine. He believed he should have graduated first and blamed the oversight on faculty injustice—a trait developed at an early age of always reproaching someone else for his own limitations. During the years at West Point his closest friends were southerners, which included, among others, roommates Ambrose Powell Hill from Virginia and James Stuart from South Carolina. The opinions of his southern friends influenced his own. As McClellan's biographer Stephen W. Sears observed, "Like most of McClellan's views, which, once fixed in his mind, rarely changed, his sympathy with Southern attitudes would remain constant—with the singular exception of the matter of secession." Upon graduation McClellan joined the Corps of Engineers as a second lieutenant and in September went to Mexico with the army. Instructors at West Point had already marked Little Mac among those in the class of '46 for high command.[1]

As the third-ranking officer in a company of engineers, McClellan shipped out of New York and reached the mouth of the Rio Grande in mid-October. He noted that General Zachary "Old Rough and Ready" Taylor, having defeated the Mexicans at Palo Alto and Resaca de la Palma, was already being courted as the Whig's presidential candidate to unseat Democrat James Polk in the 1848 national election. As Lincoln had observed during the Black Hawk War, McClellan came to appreciate how military service might lead to a brilliant career in politics. Transferred to a new expedition commanded by General Winfield Scott, McClellan sought swift promotion. Using his father's influence, he tried to obtain a captaincy but learned every position had been filled for ten new regiments being formed at Washington. The officers lacked military training but had political connections. The incident gave McClellan a lifelong aversion to politically appointed officers, many of whom had never performed the basic manual of arms.

McClellan's group of engineers consisted of men who would one day become adversaries as well as comrades at arms. While serving under Colonel Joseph G. Totten's Corps of Engineers, young George McClellan fought beside Pierre G. T. Beauregard, Thomas J. (later "Stonewall") Jackson, Joseph E. Johnston, Robert E. Lee, John Bankhead Magruder, George G. Meade, and Gustavus W. Smith. During Scott's brilliant overland march from Vera Cruz to Mexico City, McClellan earned brevets to first lieutenant for bravery at Contreras and Churubusco and to captain for meritorious conduct at Chapultepec. Although McClellan fought bravely, one can speculate on what men such as Beauregard, Johnston, and Lee might have observed about Little Mac's conduct on the battlefield.[2]

After the Mexican War, McClellan returned to West Point and served as an instructor of practical engineering. He became bored, quarreled with the academy's superintendent, and finally in 1852 liberated himself from the stifling restraints of West Point by accompanying Captain Randolph B. Marcy, his future father-in-law, on an exploration of the Red River. While the mission incorporated a survey of a proposed route for a transcontinental railroad, the tedious task provided no stimulation, just hard work. During the assignment McClellan met Ulysses S. Grant, who was serving as quartermaster at Fort Vancouver, Washington, and considered him a hopeless drunk. Little Mac wrote glowing reports of his own achievements, but his engineering was slipshod—partly from disinterest and partly from laziness.

Facing a dull career with little opportunity for promotion in the peacetime army, McClellan began considering his options when in 1855 Secretary of War Jefferson Davis, who had taken personal interest in Little Mac, sent a three-man commission to observe and report on military organizational and tactical developments in Europe. Davis wanted to enhance his personal knowledge of military administration, modernization, and warfare. Little Mac had just received the permanent rank of captain in the regular army and, as junior officer, accompanied two majors. He disliked being subordinate to stodgy officers perceived as being over the hill and had already developed the habit of airing grievances while corresponding with friends and family. To John, his brother, he wrote: "These d____d old fogies!! I hope I may never be tied to two corpses again—it is hell upon earth." McClellan's personal traits began to evolve through his ever-increasing private correspondence, which eventually became the basis for solidifying his opinions about everything from war and politics to personalities with whom he disagreed.[3]

McClellan spent a year in Europe with the "d____d old fogies" studying army organization, methods for transporting men and horses, how to embark and disembark troops, field equipment and clothing, arms and ammunition, fortifications for seacoast defense, siege operations, boats, wagons, and other topics pertaining to the art of war abroad. As guests of the British government, the commission observed the Crimean War. Leaving the Crimea in November, McClellan toured military posts, fortresses, and defensive sites throughout Europe. He collected an enormous amount of information and on April 19, 1856, sailed for home with a huge library of books and manuals covering every aspect of European war fighting. Being fluent in French and German and having learned the Russian language while in Europe, McClellan built his theories on how to conduct war on this library.[4]

On returning to America, McClellan obtained permission from Jefferson Davis to remain at the family home in Philadelphia to prepare his report. When published as a congressional document in 1857, militarists hailed the report as "a model of conciseness and accurate information." McClellan also translated several European manuals, some of which were adopted by the army. He also designed what became known as the McClellan cavalry saddle, copied somewhat from the Hungarian pattern. Although praised for his cavalry manual and his saddle, McClellan never actually served in the cavalry, though he had been posted to it as a captain.[5]

Of the many activities observed in Europe, those McClellan ignored were among the most important. He took no interest in top generals and the techniques and methods they applied to command large armies. As a consequence, he gained no insight into how to utilize a staff to prepare and manage field operations, which became one of his gravest shortcomings during the Civil War. He also blundered by overlooking the first use of rifled muskets. A rifled (spiral-grooved) barrel charged with Claude Minié's bullets could be fired with more velocity and hit distant targets far more accurately than the smoothbore muskets still used by the army. Although he observed rifled muskets and rifled cannons in use in Europe, he seemed to overlook the tactical impact of rifled weapons on casualties.

After winning praise from Congress and the War Department for his report, McClellan reconsidered his future when assigned to a remote post in Kansas to keep peace between the proslavery element and the Free-Soilers fighting each other over the future of slavery in the territory. At the age of thirty he announced his intention to resign and seek more lucrative employment as a civilian. McClellan could never have withstood the stuffy old officers in charge of the territory. He probably made the right decision to resign while he still had a first-rate reputation as being among the best and the brightest in the army.[6]

McClellan never completely explained his decision to quit the service, but while writing his report during the summer of 1856, he looked for engineering work through army friends holding good civilian positions. Gustavus Smith, who had gone into construction work as a civil engineer, helped position McClellan as chief engineer for the Illinois Central, a railroad on the verge of bankruptcy. Little Mac doubled his income by accepting the position and nearly doubled it again the following year when he became vice president of the railroad. Meanwhile, he began a regular correspondence with the daughter of his old commander, Major Randolph Marcy. One of his competitors for the hand of Mary Ellen Marcy had been Ambrose P. Hill, his former roommate at West Point. After Major Marcy discouraged his daughter from marrying Hill, Ellen transferred her affections to McClellan. She soon became the devoted recipient of all his aspirations, disappointments, and grievances during the Civil War and his most steadfast supporter and sympathizer.

In 1858, during McClellan's career as vice president of the Illinois Central, he staunchly supported Stephen A. Douglas's reelection to the Senate and opposed Lincoln's efforts to unseat the man who had become known in politics as the "Little Giant." During the debates McClellan decided that Lincoln, one of the railroad's attorneys, was intellectually and socially inferior to Douglas and unfit for public office. He had not completely disconnected himself from military matters and accepted a commission in the Chicago Light Guards, a local militia company. When the Illinois Central needed a cashier, he hired an old friend from West Point, Ambrose Burnside, who had graduated in 1847. He also came to respect the work of Allan Pinkerton, whose detective agency protected the railroad's property, passengers, and freight. Burnside and Pinkerton would later play a critical role in McClellan's generalship during the Civil War.[7]

McClellan could not work for anyone without engaging in personal conflict, and by the spring of 1860 his relationship with the Illinois Central's president, William Osborn, set him on a collision course. Little Mac's hands-on approach to effective railroad management, however, soon became known to others in the industry. In June 1860, a month after marrying Mary Ellen Marcy, McClellan doubled his income by joining the Ohio and Mississippi Railroad, also in receivership, with the understanding he would be advanced to president. In August 1860 he moved with his wife to Cincinnati and enjoyed a few months of wedded bliss before engaging in a rift with the railroad's superintendent. The firing on Fort Sumter eventually led to McClellan's resignation, although he continued to receive pay as the railroad's president until early 1862.[8]

McClellan detested the secession of South Carolina. He never wavered from his loyalty to the North and blamed South Carolina for initiating the secession movement. He also blamed Massachusetts, which he regarded as the center of the radical abolition movement. He later told Secretary of the Navy Gideon Welles that both states should be "extinguished" and if he ever had the opportunity to capture Charleston, South Carolina, he would demolish it. He made this statement somewhat recklessly in September 1862 while placing dozens of Massachusetts regiments into the Army of the Potomac.[9]

A few days after the surrender of Fort Sumter on April 13, 1861, William C. "Baldy" Smith and Major Fitz-John Porter, two friends from West Point, told McClellan the president had called for seventy-five thousand volunteers and urged him to apply for a generalship. Letters later arrived from Governor Andrew G. Curtin and Governor Edwin Morgan, offering him command of Pennsylvania troops and New York troops, respectively. Meanwhile, McClellan spoke with Governor William Dennison and on April 23 accepted command of Ohio troops as major general of militia.

Little Mac immediately contacted General Scott and, though allocated only ten thousand troops, asked for muskets and camp equipment for twenty thousand men and five million cartridges. He also established a training camp near Cincinnati and requested that two friends from West Point, Fitz-John Porter and John Reno, along with his father-in-law, Major Randolph Marcy, and Ohio legislator Jacob D. Cox be part of his senior officer corps. Scott vetoed the transfer of Porter and Reno, which resulted in one of the first disagreements between Little Mac and the general-in-chief. During the organization cycle Ulysses S. Grant stopped at McClellan's Cincinnati headquarters to apply for a commission. The general remembered Grant as a hard drinker and refused to see him. After waiting two days for an audience, Grant returned home and eventually obtained a colonelcy in an Illinois regiment.[10]

At Cincinnati the public received their first glimpse of thirty-four-year-old George B. McClellan as a commanding general. Cox described McClellan as "rather under medium height, muscularly formed, with broad shoulders and a well-poised head, active and graceful in motion. His whole appearance was quiet and modest, but when drawn out he showed no lack of confidence in himself." McClellan had not acquired a uniform and arrived in his business clothes, wearing a narrow-rimmed soft felt hat. His methods for training officers and men in Cincinnati were much the same as the techniques later used when building the Army of the Potomac. He put the recruits through intensive drills and completely indoctrinated them into the routine and discipline of military life. He appeared regularly on the field riding Dan Webster, his favorite horse—a large dark bay presented by Cincinnati friends. When in his office he wrote a profusion of letters consisting of orders, reports, requisitions for more men and military equipment, and his own views on strategy. This routine established the mode in which McClellan conducted his affairs throughout the war.[11]

This period also marked the resumption of McClellan's differences with higher military authority and his displeasure at being partly under the thumb of General-in-Chief Scott. Little Mac revealed his biases and private opinions through his letters to his wife, but Ellen was with him in Cincinnati, which left voids in his otherwise copious correspondence. Any instructions restricting his efforts or differing from his own views, especially when coming from Scott, met with outbursts of criticism shared with only his family and closest friends. One week after assuming command of the Department of the Ohio, McClellan did not believe he had enough men and asked Scott for twenty thousand more, bringing the total to thirty thousand. He also asked for eighty thousand arms, foreshadowing his plans to raise a large army. He then grumbled when Scott refused to authorize cavalry and artillery on the assumption "neither . . . would be needed!" Nor did Scott yield to McClellan's request to build a staff of personal friends.[12]

Early differences with Scott eased on April 27, when McClellan presented his grand scheme to end the war. He believed the rebellion would cease after one massive thrust under his personal leadership. He proposed using a force of 80,000 volunteers against Richmond, soon to become the Confederate capital. He accurately predicted that western Virginians would side with the Union if his Ohioans marched on Richmond. He also proposed using water transportation down the Ohio and Mississippi to attack rebel cities along the river, claiming he would save time and money by avoiding the cost of marching by land. He then contradicted himself by suggesting he cross through Kentucky by rail with another 80,000 men to capture Nashville. To do all this would require about 240,000 volunteers, and crossing through Kentucky would certainly be resisted by the state's pro-Confederate governor. The secession of Kentucky and Missouri would likely follow, neither of which would have been agreeable to Lincoln. "I think to lose Kentucky is nearly the same as losing the whole game," the president confided to Orville Browning. Little Mac then suggested moving on Montgomery, Mobile, and New Orleans without explaining how 80,000 or any number of troops could achieve this strategy without first having several bitter battles with the enemy. T. Harry Williams, commenting on McClellan's brainstorms, wrote, "He could conjure up a grandiose design based on conditions that existed mainly in his own imagination, and at the same time devote serious attention to a thimble-sized matter." Nevertheless, McClellan's plan did make sense with respect to western Virginia: his force consisted of only 10,000 men.[13]

At this early juncture in the planning cycle, Scott wanted to minimize bloodshed by using blockades and economic strangulation. He endorsed part of McClellan's plan, such as adding eighty thousand men for a movement down the Mississippi, and told Little Mac he "may be invited to take an important part." The proposed campaign echoed a strategy Scott had introduced to Lincoln. When leaked to the public, the scheme was dubbed by the press the "Anaconda Plan," partly because Scott intended to constrict the South into submission without much fighting. McClellan also wanted to avoid bloodshed and, like Scott, believed strong Unionist sentiment still existed in the South and would bring the disaffected element back into the Union. Lincoln, however, wanted not to irritate the border states and preferred, like McClellan and most northerners, to end the war with one decisive battle in Virginia. Nevertheless, Scott established November 10 as the date for the Mississippi campaign, thus giving himself ample time to raise a fleet of gunboats and transports.[14]

After ingratiating himself with Scott, McClellan's businesslike approach to mobilizing an army also impressed Lincoln. Secretary of the Treasury Salmon P. Chase, former governor of Ohio, habitually lobbied for the promotion of Ohio men and convinced Secretary of War Cameron to press for McClellan's promotion. When on May 3 Scott recommended that his protégé be raised to full major general in the regular army, Lincoln agreed, and the promotion took effect on May 14, pending the approval of the Senate. After Scott, Little Mac became the ranking general in the Union army.[15]

McClellan contented himself temporarily with the problems of training his Ohioans, but he hired Allan Pinkerton to send spies into Kentucky, Mississippi, and Tennessee. With Kentucky directly across the Ohio River from Cincinnati, he also sent members of his staff into the state to assess Union sentiment and root out politicians fostering secession. From this enterprise McClellan received lengthy reports, not all of them accurate, on secessionist activity, and he used the opportunity to skirt Scott and communicate his findings directly to Lincoln.[16]

McClellan also kept Scott regularly informed using language suggesting a bold and aggressive drive into the South. Although no fighting had yet occurred on any front, it was McClellan's way of lobbying the War Department for an 80,000-man army. Referring to political instability in Kentucky, Little Mac said that though he would "refer to General Scott for orders," if an emergency occurred, he would "cross the Ohio with 20,000 men. If that were not enough with 30,000, and if necessary with 40,000;

but . . . would not stand by and see the loyal men of Kentucky crushed." McClellan did not have 20,000 men and began building a case for getting them. His department was huge, his army small, and his persistent demands on Washington began to pay dividends. After expanding McClellan's Department of the Ohio on May 3 to include Indiana and Illinois, the War Department later added Missouri, western Pennsylvania, and part of western Virginia. Bedazzled by McClellan's demands for more manpower, on May 21 Scott asked, "Would 80,000 men be sufficient to conquer its way to New Orleans and clear out the Mississippi to the Gulf?" In a postscript Scott added a caveat: "The friends of the Union in Kentucky, Tennessee, and Missouri" must not be left without protection.[17]

While Scott and McClellan ruminated over an expedition down the Mississippi, focus rapidly shifted to western Virginia, where people opposed Virginia's ordinance of secession passed on April 17 in Richmond. McClellan negotiated a détente while western Virginians decided how to vote on the May 23 secession referendum. The Baltimore & Ohio Railroad served as a crucial main link between the East and the Midwest and passed through the northern tier of western Virginia. Scott could not afford to lose control of the railroad and on May 24 telegraphed McClellan, warning that several companies of Virginia troops had reached Grafton for the purpose of occupying western Virginia. "Can you counteract the influence of that detachment?" he asked. "Act promptly." McClellan replied he would "make it a clean sweep" if Scott told him to. He returned immediately to Cincinnati from a conference of governors in Indiana and dispatched four Ohio regiments and one western Virginia regiment to protect the bridges of the railroad.[18]

Little Mac issued two proclamations, one to the troops and one to "the Union Men of Western Virginia." He ordered the soldiers to maintain discipline and protect the rights and property of the inhabitants, but he also ordered them to interdict any armed opposition. He appealed to western Virginians for support, informing them that troops had been sent to counterbalance "factious rebels" who had come to "deprive you of the expression of your dearest rights." He pledged to preserve the rights of slaveholders, which at the time coincided with Lincoln's views, and vowed to crush "with an iron hand" any attempted slave insurrection. After outlining the aims of the government, he asked western Virginias to "sever the connection that binds you to traitors" and "proclaim to the world . . . that you remain true to the Stars and Stripes."[19]

After releasing the two proclamations, McClellan realized he may have overstepped his authority and wrote a letter to the president explaining why he believed it necessary to act swiftly. A clue to Little Mac's personal views, which never changed during the Civil War, was when he publicly promised to use Union forces to protect slavery as private property. There is no record of a presidential response, but an enraged antislavery coalition took vocal exception to McClellan's decree, objecting to the general formulating political policy instead of adhering to military affairs. Had Lincoln not been so busy with other matters, he might have settled the issue of presidential prerogatives regarding policy-making and prevented more trouble later. At the time, however, McClellan's proclamation fully agreed with Lincoln's position on slavery. The president wanted western Virginia to renounce secession, and McClellan's proclamation supported that goal. Admitting it should have been first cleared with the White House probably set Lincoln, who inadvertently opened the door to more of the same, at ease. Lincoln had little reason to object to the manner in which McClellan handled the slavery issue other than the general's pledge to use the army to support the institution. If Lincoln did have concerns, he failed to mention them.[20]

McClellan abandoned his grand plan to invade the South after receiving Scott's authorization to move into western Virginia. A force of Confederates under the command of Colonel George A. Porterfield had seized Beverly and Grafton and began destroying Baltimore & Ohio bridges. When Ohio and Indiana troops began moving into western Virginia, Porterfield fell back from Grafton to Philippi. Union forces converged on the Confederates on June 3 and in the first land battle of the war routed the enemy in what local observers called the "Philippi races." From Cincinnati McClellan used the excuse for not pursuing the enemy on bad roads, poor transportation, and the lack of cavalry; issues similar to those he would press ad nauseam for the next seventeen months.[21]

On June 20 McClellan departed for western Virginia to assume personal command of the summer campaign. During the same period General Robert E. Lee, writing from Richmond, ordered Brigadier General Robert Garnett to destroy the Baltimore & Ohio bridge over the Cheat

River east of Grafton. McClellan arrived in the area on June 22 and began organizing twenty-seven infantry regiments, four batteries of artillery, and two cavalry companies for offensive operations. His whole force consisted of about twenty thousand men, including five thousand assigned to guarding some two hundred miles of railroad. McClellan informed Scott he would concentrate his army at Buckhannon, near Rich Mountain, by June 25 but did not reach the position until a week later. He estimated the Confederate force at six thousand and later at ten thousand. Garnett never had more than forty-five hundred men and spread the force over thirteen miles, with three thousand on Laurel Hill and the others with Lieutenant Colonel John Pegram at the southern end of Rich Mountain. McClellan had about twelve thousand troops available for fighting.[22]

On June 25 McClellan issued another in a series of Napoleonic manifestos, closing with: "Soldiers! I have heard that there is danger here. I have come to place myself at your head and to share it with you. I fear now but one thing—that you will not find foemen worthy of your steel. I know that I can rely upon you." This pronouncement occurred as he prepared to advance from Grafton to Buckhannon, after which he intended to cross through a gap in Rich Mountain and occupy Beverly on the Parkersburg branch of the main turnpike.[23]

McClellan moved slowly and deliberately. On July 10 he split his force, sending Brigadier General William S. Rosecrans's nineteen hundred–man brigade toward the gap near the southern end of Rich Mountain and positioned Brigadier General Thomas A. Morris's three thousand–man brigade defensively on the Philippi road north of Laurel Mountain. McClellan kept the bulk of his force in reserve near Buckhannon, intending to reinforce Rosecrans. When Morris asked for more men, McClellan replied: "You have only to defend a strong position . . . I propose taking the really difficult and dangerous part of this work on my own hands. I will not ask you to do anything I would not be willing to do myself . . . If you cannot undertake the defense of Philippi with the force now under your control, I must find someone who will . . . Do not ask for further reenforcements." Over the coming months Little Mac might have improved his generalship had he followed the same advice he gave to Morris.[24]

As McClellan explained to Lieutenant Colonel Edward D. Townsend on July 5, he planned to repeat General Scott's maneuver at Cerro Gordo in 1846, and in many respects he did. He held Colonel Pegram's troops in check on Rich Mountain with Rosecrans's brigade, while Morris contained Garnett's force on Laurel Hill. On July 11 Rosecrans began closing the pincers. He drove Pegram's small force out of the gap in Rich Mountain and up the Tygart River valley. McClellan planned to move quickly to reinforce Rosecrans, but the sound of heavy artillery fire worried him. Fearing Rosecrans was being whipped by a superior force, McClellan hesitated. When Garnett learned Pegram had been defeated on Rich Mountain, he withdrew from Laurel Hill and retreated to Carrick's Ford, where he died leading a rearguard action. Had McClellan not held the main force in reserve before joining the pursuit, Garnett would have been surrounded. McClellan's behavior foreshadowed an unfortunate trait that became prevalent as he later faced major battles. His tactics also manifested a preference for maneuver when opposing a force of uncertain strength. He lost only 12 killed and 59 wounded. Although Pegram surrendered 553 officers and men, Confederate casualties were also light, marking efforts on both sides to minimize bloodshed. McClellan's success at Rich Mountain secured western Virginia for the Union and brought Little Mac instant fame. No observers from Washington were present to analyze missed opportunities or assess what actually happened.[25]

On July 16, after McClellan received the thanks of Congress, he issued another exaggerated manifesto to his troops, writing: "I am more than satisfied with you. You have annihilated two armies, commanded by educated and experienced soldiers, intrenched in mountain fastnesses fortified at their leisure." He credited his men with taking a thousand prisoners and killing more than two hundred and fifty Confederates, none of which was true. In a closing remark he said, "Soldiers! I have confidence in you, and I trust you have learned to confide in me." McClellan forwarded similar but slightly modified claims in his official battle report to Scott, who had no way of verifying the accuracy of the account or any reason to do so.[26]

The minor battle came on the heels of Major General Benjamin Butler's defeat on June 10 at Big Bethel, Virginia, and gave the Union army its first victory. McClellan's success brought praise from General Scott, who wrote: "The General-in-Chief, and what is more, the Cabinet, including the President, are charmed with your activity, valor, and consequent success of Rich Mountain . . . We do not doubt that you will in due time sweep the rebels from Virginia." Little Mac's fame spread rapidly throughout the North. The war's first hero had emerged. He had once spoken of plunging through western Virginia's great Kanawha River valley and striking Richmond. He might well have been given the green light had Brigadier General Irvin McDowell's Federals not been defeated at First Bull Run on July 21, eight days after the Rich Mountain campaign officially ended.[27]

On the day after the Bull Run catastrophe Adjutant General Lorenzo Thomas, complying with General Scott's instructions on orders from the president, dispatched a telegram to McClellan: "Circumstances make your presence here necessary . . . come hither without delay."[28]

3

"The people trust him"

NTIL THE BATTLE OF FIRST BULL RUN on July 21, 1861, fighting had nowhere reached the magnitude of a major engagement. There had been civil disobedience in Maryland and Missouri, incidents at Harpers Ferry, a heavy skirmish at Big Bethel, and McClellan's broadly advertised minor accomplishments in western Virginia. After Congress convened in early July, Lincoln asked for four hundred thousand three-year volunteers, and they began pouring into the capital before arrangements could be made to accommodate them.[1]

In June those in government with the least military understanding became the most insistent that a rapid military expedition be launched before the ninety-day enlistments of more than a hundred thousand volunteers expired. "On to Richmond" became the battle cry of the press. Beset by streams of bad advice, Lincoln rejected Scott's Anaconda plan of subduing the South by economic and military strangulation, believing it would take too long. He also questioned Scott's claim the war might be won with one big battle but hoped the venerated general might be right. Other differences existed between civilian strategist Lincoln and military strategist Scott. The president understood the South's determination for independence better than the general or the cabinet, and he believed many efforts of many kinds would be necessary to reunify the country. One element Lincoln saw clearly after studying the Anaconda plan was the importance of controlling the Mississippi River, which also formed part of McClellan's strategy. Little Mac's next assignment might well have been his proposed descent of the Mississippi had not the Battle of Bull Run shifted military emphasis to Virginia.[2]

Seward and Cameron supported Scott, who thought the South should not be attacked. They believed a strong underlying Unionist sentiment would force Confederate authorities to seek peace and reunify. Together they urged Lincoln to wait because any military effort would exasperate southern Unionists and prevent the rebellion from being reversed without bloodshed. Lincoln rejected the premise as well as Scott's one big battle hypothesis. The president became conflicted between doing nothing until Federal troops were trained and ready to fight or bending to pressure from radical Republicans, jingoists, and newspapers preaching "On to Richmond!" One matter impossible to ignore was the expiring ninety-day enlistments beginning in late July.[3]

At first neither Lincoln nor Scott could do more than discuss plans. Despite calling himself general, Cameron contributed nothing to the discussions because of his vast deficiency concerning military matters. When Secretary of the Treasury Salmon Chase began meddling in War Department affairs, Cameron tuned to him for advice. After recommending McClellan to command the Department of Ohio, which Scott and Lincoln approved, Chase pointed to another Ohioan, Irvin McDowell, as the best man to organize and lead some thirty thousand troops camped outside Washington.

A forty-three-year-old graduate of West Point, McDowell had won a brevet in the Mexican War but afterward spent the majority of his time serving on Scott's staff in the adjutant general's office. Like McClellan, he had studied in France and understood European tactics. He excelled at staff work, a skill few army professionals understood. Six feet in height and strongly built, McDowell wore his beard in classic French military style. Friends knew him as a voracious eater, which became one of his distinguishing personal characteristics. His career changed drastically after being elevated to brigadier general and put in charge of the ill-prepared Department of Northeastern Virginia—forerunner of the Army of the Potomac—before his troops were trained. Grant later referred to McDowell as one of those generals who got started wrong and never recovered.[4]

McDowell had neither led an army nor expected to fight that summer. No American had ever commanded an army of thirty thousand men, which by July had grown to fifty thousand. Troops were inexperienced, maps of Virginia were old and inaccurate, and Scott's small staff lacked the experience necessary to prepare and implement a battle plan. McDowell completely agreed with Scott, who insisted the army was unready to fight and feared bloodshed would reverse the illusionary strong Unionist sentiment in the South.[5]

Despite opposition from army headquarters, Lincoln insisted on driving the Confederates out of Manassas—twenty-five miles southwest of Washington—and forcing them back to their secondary defensive line at Fredericksburg. Lincoln made the decision because he believed thirty thousand untrained Union troops could defeat twenty thousand untrained Confederate troops, and he wanted a campaign during the summer, before the South became stronger. Lincoln expected McDowell's hurried plan, formulated with help from Scott and Chase, to succeed, and the cabinet predicted the South would quit after the first major military defeat.[6]

During a meeting with Scott and McDowell, Lincoln arbitrarily designated July 9 for the advance on Manassas. McDowell protested, arguing it was wrong for the president to demand that he organize, discipline, train, march, and fight all at the same time. New regiments arrived with men who did not know how to load and fire a musket. Planning outpaced logistics, and wagon shortages impaired the army's ability to transport ammunition and supplies. Lincoln finally agreed to a one-week delay but said, "You are green, it is true; but they are green, also, you are all green alike." He told McDowell to stop stalling. Leaks in the War Department appeared in the press, tipping off Major General Pierre G. T. Beauregard's army at Manassas of McDowell's plans. Beauregard began drawing reinforcements from Major General Joseph E. Johnston's army in the Shenandoah Valley. Scott expected Major General Robert Patterson's Pennsylvania militia to prevent this from happening by fighting and holding Johnston's force in the valley. From Lincoln's perspective, if McDowell defeated the Confederates at Manassas, he could dispose of the remaining rebel forces in Virginia, capture Richmond, and shorten the war. Although the South might not collapse, Lincoln believed the effort would be both militarily and politically sound.[7]

After much delay McDowell crossed Bull Run on July 21 and in torrid heat assaulted the left flank of Beauregard's army. Washington sightseers neglected services that Sunday to watch McDowell whip Beauregard. McDowell drove the Confederates back until the enemy formed a strong position on nearby hills. During the morning thousands of troops from Johnston's Shenandoah Valley army disembarked from trains at Manassas Junction and poured onto the field. Beauregard's force swelled, equaling the size of McDowell's army, and counterattacked. The Federals, having exhausted their ammunition and stamina, fell back, creating the first signs of alarm. Panic intensified with every backward step. McDowell tried to check the stampede, but it swept around and through him. In desperation he tried to get the army safely back to Washington, but carriages and civilians jammed the roads. McDowell almost achieved the victory Lincoln cherished, but the battle ended in dismal defeat.

Being too infirm to travel, General Scott languished in Washington, resting in his oversized armchair. Lincoln took a number of puzzling dispatches to Scott's office for interpretation and found the general asleep. Scott glanced at the reports and said McDowell would win. Lincoln returned to the White House, and Scott went back to sleep. After receiving more dispatches heralding victory, Lincoln enjoyed an evening drive, well satisfied with the day's work. While he was away, Seward arrived at the White House in a state of hysteria and reported the battle lost and the army in retreat. He dispatched John Nicolay and John Hay, Lincoln's two secretaries, to find the president and bring him to Scott's office. By then the first civilian spectators from Bull Run began careening into Washington on dust-covered carriages. When a telegram from McDowell confirmed the defeat, Lincoln slumped into a lounge and remained there all night. Sometime during those difficult hours reality struck hard; no summer outing of militia would end the war.[8]

Lincoln did not expect Washington to be attacked, but he questioned his reliance on Scott for competent advice. He suspected both armies had been crippled but were still dangerous, so he made a personal visit to camps of the returning soldiers. He found the troops badly disorganized but morally strong, and he now realized the army, to fight effectively, had to be better organized and properly trained. He needed a military administrator, a person who could pull the army together and perhaps replace Scott, who admitted lapses in his own performance and said, "I deserve removal because I did not stand up, when my army was not in a condition for fighting, and resist it to the last." Lacking a replacement, Lincoln discouraged Scott from resigning. On July 22, together with Scott's recommendation, he summoned McClellan to Washington.[9]

For Little Mac the summons to Washington symbolized a call from Providence, and calls from Providence happened to be the guiding influences in McClellan's life. He rode horseback sixty miles to the nearest railroad station and caught a train to Wheeling, where he met briefly with his pregnant wife before continuing to Washington. While waiting for McClellan's arrival, Lincoln drafted his "Memoranda of Military Policy Suggested by the Bull Run Defeat," which outlined his personal strategy for prosecuting the war. The plan called for strengthening forces in the Washington area, replacing three-month volunteers with three-year men, holding all geographical sectors currently controlled by Federal forces, and rapidly mobilizing. Four days later he added an addendum calling for Manassas to be seized and the Shenandoah Valley occupied by Federal troops. The president's plan would later lead to differences with McClellan over strategy.[10]

In the days before McClellan reached Washington, the *New York Herald* had already extolled the general's military skills, publicizing him as the "Napoleon of the Present War." When the public dubbed him "the Young Napoleon," Little Mac appreciated the tribute. Later, when visiting Matthew Brady's photographic studio, he emulated Napoleon by posing before the camera with his right hand tucked into his uniform coat. In public and on the field he comported himself much like the great Corsican. Major General Carl Schurz noted, "The people fairly yearned for a hero, and were ready to ascribe to the one who appeared now on the scene, all possible attributes of genius and character."[11]

McClellan arrived in Washington on July 26 and, following military protocol, first called on Scott and the following day on Brigadier General Lorenzo Thomas, Scott's adjutant general. Thomas sent McClellan to the White House, where on the following day the president officially put the Young Napoleon in command of the Washington area. Lincoln invited him to return to the White House at 1:00 p.m. to meet the cabinet but excluded Scott from the conference. The lapse in etiquette outraged the ailing general but merely amused McClellan, who informed his wife: "I find myself in a new & strange position here—Presdt, Cabinet, Genl Scott & all deferring to me—by some strange operation of magic I seem to have become *the* power of the land. I almost think that were I to win some small success now I could become Dictator or anything else that might please me—but nothing of that kind would please me." McClellan's reference to becoming a dictator alluded to rescuing the country, not tyrannically ruling it. Whatever the general meant on the first day of formally conferring with the president and the cabinet, he believed he had gained the upper hand. The nation's savior had arrived. Had Lincoln been less deferential, a more assertive posture might have produced a better outcome in the months ahead.[12]

On July 27 the thirty-four-year-old general assumed his official title as commander of the Division of the Potomac, which included Washington and northeastern Virginia. That day he wrote, "There was nothing to prevent the enemy shelling the city from heights within easy range, which could be occupied by a hostile column almost without resistance." McClellan said he "had no army to command—merely a collection of regiments cowering on the banks of the Potomac," but his force consisted of fifty thousand infantry, a thousand cavalry, and six hundred and fifty artillerists—nearly twice the number Beauregard had at Manassas. He also observed streets clogged with deserters and stragglers and blamed it on McDowell's shoddy discipline and poor organization. Perhaps excitement bordering on panic in the city magnified his personal concerns. Conditions were not nearly as perilous as he thought. McClellan, however, did not know the size of the Confederate force at Manassas and needed intelligence, so on July 30 he summoned detective Allan Pinkerton, writing, "Come prepared to stay and bring with you three or four of your best men." Engaging Pinkerton, in whom Little Mac expressed great faith, eventually added to a host of the general's lost opportunities. By relying on Pinkerton for intelligence, McClellan hastened his problems as a field general three days after he took command of a force of troops he officially christened on August 20 the Army of the Potomac.[13]

Relationships between McClellan and Lincoln began congenially, with the general calling the president "Your Excellency" and Lincoln calling Little Mac "George." Lincoln backed the general's requests. "They give me my way in everything, full swing & unbounded confidence," McClellan wrote Ellen. "All tell me that I am responsible for the fate of the Nation & that all its resources will be placed at my disposal. It is an immense task I have on my hands, but I believe I can accomplish it." McClellan did not overly exaggerate when he condemned McDowell's army as "a collection of undisciplined, ill-officered, and uninstructed men, who were, as a rule, much demoralized by defeat and ready to run at the first shot." This assessment also marked the beginning of McClellan's disenchantment with Scott. On July 18 he had written Scott from Beverly, Virginia, "All that I know of war I have learned from you, & in all that I have done I have endeavored to conform to your manner of conducting a campaign." Two weeks later McClellan began complaining of being hampered by the general-in-chief. Old "Fuss & Feathers," a nickname Scott earned by his mania for red tape, could not comprehend the swiftness with which Little Mac conducted his affairs and slowed progress by questioning rather than instantly approving McClellan's many requests.[14]

To conditions in Washington, McClellan applied what he called the hand of the master. The cigar-smoking general, who also enjoyed "the more naked beauties of the quid," set to work furiously. He established a provost marshal department under Colonel Andrew Porter, who with a detachment of regular cavalry rounded up stragglers, returned them to their regiments, and enforced military discipline. Discharged three-month volunteers heading home added to the confusion because they could not be distinguished from new recruits entering the city at more than a thousand a day. McClellan also created review boards to assess the qualifications of officers and dismissed hundreds of them. As fresh troops arrived, he sent them to training camps outside Washington where he had established provisional brigades commanded by friends such as Fitz-John Porter and Ambrose Burnside. He banned alcohol from camps, and by the first week of August the rebuilding of the army had begun. The public recognized McClellan's impact on the army, and it did not go unnoticed by the general. "I saw the crowd gathering around to stare at me," he wrote his wife. "I began to feel how great the task committed to me." Whenever his ego needed positive reinforcement, the public provided it. British correspondent William H. Russell noted, "The people trust him." So did the army. Whenever he reviewed troops, thunderous huzzahs greeted him. He loved military ritual—the flashing colors of the parade with fluttering flags, the beat of drums, and the echo of bugles. His heart beat faster. He loved his soldiers, and the "boys" loved him back. Power nourished his sense of self; salvation of the Union nourished his ambition.[15]

McClellan's second initiative to protect Washington, though the capital was not in danger, consumed his time because he liked engineering projects. Little Mac and chief engineer Major John G. Barnard laid out thirty-three miles of interlocking forts facing Maryland and Virginia. The works consisted of a combination of forty-eight forts, lunettes, redoubts, and batteries mounting three hundred guns. Barnard, who was deaf but extremely competent, designed the forts and supervised the work. McClellan also tried to reinforce Long Bridge, made from earth embankments and half-rotten timbers, so heavy military equipment could be moved across the Potomac to Alexandria. Although the effort failed and a railroad bridge had to be built for military transport, Washington quickly became a fortified capital with a system of defenses so formidable the enemy never launched an assault.[16]

Lincoln marveled at McClellan's energy. He could not have chosen a better man to reorganize McDowell's disillusioned troops and yet attend to the daily arrival of new regiments. Little Mac skillfully accomplished in three months a task that might have killed a man of lesser ability. He never stopped working and seldom slept. He rode about in a plain blue wool uniform without shoulder straps, a good disguise against pestiferous reporters looking to corner the Young Napoleon. His manifest calmness and competence instilled similar traits in those around them. When not at his desk at army headquarters refining the organizational details necessary to assimilate a hundred thousand fresh troops, he rode with his staff through the camps on routine inspections, building morale and observing drill. He added his father-in-law to his staff as inspector general, and whenever the Young Napoleon toured the camps, Colonel Marcy, an old army man of modest ability, joined the entourage but could never keep pace with his son-in-law's rigorous routine. Staff officers tried to avoid riding with McClellan. He wore them out. In August he encountered two mutinies when the Second Maine and the Seventy-ninth New York, regiments that had volunteered for three years, wanted to go home with the three months' men. He sent the ringleaders to the prison on Dry Tortugas Island off the tip of southern Florida to serve out their terms at hard labor.[17]

McClellan still found time to communicate with Lincoln, the cabinet, and General Scott, who, he wrote Ellen, "is fast becoming very slow & old. He cannot long retain command I think—when he retires I am sure to succeed him, unless in the meantime I lose a battle—which I do not expect to do." A problem of overlapping duties between Little Mac and Scott led to temperamental differences over military policy. In early August McClellan set his sights on displacing Scott, and to promote that eventuality, he presented, at Lincoln's request, a lengthy strategy for the president's consideration. Lincoln had already discussed the necessity of replacing Scott, but until McClellan arrived in Washington, there had been no candidates. The president's request for a plan served as a step in determining whether Little Mac could think strategically and to evaluate how well the general's conclusions meshed with his own.[18]

McClellan's Napoleonic memorandum, read before the assembled cabinet on August 3, provided insight into how the general's mind worked. He fashioned the document after European military science and designed grand projects without the resources to implement them. He may have obtained help from the Comte de Paris, pretender to the throne of France, and the Prince de Joinville, both of whom lived in a house in Washington they shared with fellow French officers serving on McClellan's staff. Little Mac did agree with General Scott on the importance of conquering the Mississippi Valley but allocated only 20,000 troops to the effort. He expected to recruit more volunteers from Kentucky and Tennessee, although neither state had offered any troops. He demanded 273,000 men and six hundred guns for himself, including all the army's regulars. He wanted another 100,000 troops for garrisons and a reserve from which to draw reinforcements. Operations elsewhere, he said, took second priority to those in Virginia. Most of his views were supported by his immediate subordinates, who were more concerned about Virginia than Louisiana, Mississippi, Missouri, or Tennessee. They regarded McClellan as the army's tribune, "armed by the people with powers independent of and superior to civil authorities." Another insight into Little Mac's plans surfaced when he mentioned transporting his personal army by water to somewhere on the Virginia coast and striking inland to capture Richmond, which in May had become the Confederate capital. Later he would apply the same tactics against other cities of the South. After suggesting additional expeditions reaching beyond the scope of the president's political and military agenda, McClellan promised to crush the rebellion in one blow if the government gave him 273,000 troops, a figure slightly higher than the one he had proposed in an earlier plan while commanding the Department of the Ohio. He also strongly advocated the protection of southern private property, including slavery. As Margaret Leech observed in her 1941 Pulitzer Prize–winning *Reveille in Washington:* "There was a dramatic quality about him. He had imagination."[19]

What began as a sensible statement on strategy became fundamentally flawed because it concentrated military effort in one theater and neglected others. McClellan also made southern cities rather than rebel armies his objectives and in one grand sweep virtually buried Scott's Anaconda plan. Aside from the impracticality of moving 273,000 men by sea to an undetermined location and keeping them supplied with ammunition and provisions, McClellan also overlooked a prerequisite Lincoln consistently demanded of Scott: to drive the Confederates from Manassas and interpose a strong Union force between Washington and Richmond, thereby safeguarding the capital while advancing through Virginia. After orally presenting his memorandum, McClellan received no comment from the cabinet or confirmation from the president. In a letter to his wife he merely wrote, "I handed the President . . . a carefully considered plan for conducting the war on a large scale . . . I shall carry this thing on '*En grand*' & crush the rebels in one campaign." McClellan's ebullient response to his wife suggests he construed Lincoln's silence as acquiescence, which soon became a major issue the president might have avoided had he not exercised executive patience.[20]

The meeting must have had a catalytic influence on McClellan because he imposed more pressure on himself. Sleeplessness wore on his nerves, increasing his impatience and creating illusory situations bordering at times on paranoia. On August 8 Pinkerton had not yet installed his intelligence operation. He had no hand in deluding the general into believing 100,000 Confederate troops at Manassas were undergoing preparations to strike Washington. McClellan hatched the number without help from his detective, thus tripling the actual size of General Beauregard's army. Having alarmed himself by a self-inflicted fantasy, McClellan scrubbed his grand offensive strategy, now less than a week old, and devoted all his efforts to defending Washington. A mania swept the army to build earthworks. Soldiers tore up orchards and vegetable gardens on both sides of the Potomac, turned them into high mounds and deep trenches and filled them with tents. McClellan's delusions of Confederate strength continued to grow, reaching 170,000 by mid-September. The Confederate general never intended to attack McClellan because his instructions were to remain on the defensive. Fresh regiments continued to flow into Washington and spread about the city and suburbs, but in McClellan's mind those that came were never enough. When he placed his report before Scott, demanding more reinforcements, he also asked that the military departments of Baltimore, Fort Monroe, Pennsylvania, and the Shenandoah be merged into his command.[21]

Scott reacted indignantly. He did not believe Washington in danger, and he did not believe the enemy had 100,000 troops at Manassas. McClellan resented being challenged. Becoming embroiled in disputes with anyone who stood in his way, including superiors, never stopped McClellan, and the scuffle with Fuss and Feathers intensified as each day passed. Although Scott recognized merit in unifying nearby departments under one commander, he disliked the idea of turning them over to McClellan for fear the general might bring all the troops to Washington to build his 273,000-man army. He also fumed upon learning a copy of the request had been surreptitiously sent to Lincoln and refused to dignify McClellan's demands with a reply. The following day Scott sent a statement of his own to Cameron grumbling that, while he had always been open in his communications with his top commander, McClellan had lately become imperious and aloof. Having shared his feelings with the secretary of war, whom he regarded as his superior, the venerable general admitted his infirmities prevented him from fully functioning as general-in-chief and asked to be placed "at the earliest moment . . . on the officers' retired list."

Lincoln did not challenge McClellan's estimates of enemy strength because such matters were supposed to be determined by the general's own people. Little Mac, however, applied his personal knowledge of his one-time southern friends, which included Jefferson Davis, Beauregard, Johnston, and others. McClellan asked himself what he would do if he were them and concluded they would amass a huge force to attack Washington, much like he intended to raise a large force to attack Richmond. Knowing some southern states had been building an army since December 1860, he decided Beauregard must now have at least a hundred thousand troops, perhaps more. If so, Washington would soon be attacked. Having accepted this premise, McClellan believed any movement he made would be challenged by a greater force because it was what he would do if he were fighting himself. Having made up his mind, McClellan adhered to this delusion and challenged anyone who disagreed with him. Scott disputed the strength of Beauregard's force at Manassas and informed Cameron, "I have not the slightest apprehension for the safety of the Government here."[22]

On August 10, learning of dissention between his two top generals, Lincoln entered the conflict. He informed McClellan of Scott's correspondence with Cameron and asked Little Mac to withdraw the letter offending Scott. McClellan condescended and replied, "It is . . . with great pain that I have learned from you this morning that my views do not meet with the approbation of the Lieutenant-General." Lincoln took McClellan's reply to Scott's office and asked the general to withdraw his letter to Cameron. Scott replied to Cameron on August 12, stating he had been slighted and ignored by McClellan, and refused to comply with Lincoln's request. Meanwhile, Scott learned "his ambitious junior" had been colluding with Seward and Chase, rather than with him, on military matters and, after again mentioning his physical infirmities, agreed he would "unavoidably be in the way at headquarters."[23]

During the letter episode McClellan maintained a daily correspondence with his wife, which reveals a great deal about the general's ambitions as well as his state of mind. On August 8 he referred to Scott as "a *dotard* or a traitor" who "*cannot* or *will* not comprehend the condition" of the military situation and "is entirely unequal to the emergency. If he cannot be taken out of my path I will . . . resign & let the [administration] take care of itself." McClellan borrowed the word *dotard* from a recent editorial in Horace Greeley's *New York Tribune*. Although Scott came from Virginia, there was no justification for referring to him as a traitor, especially when hostile southerners were comparing him to Benedict Arnold. On August 9 McClellan continued his rant, writing: "Genl Scott is the great obstacle—he will not comprehend the danger & is either a traitor or an incompetent. I have to fight my way against him & have thrown a bombshell that has created a perfect stampede in the Cabinet—tomorrow the question will probably be decided by giving me absolute control independently of him . . . I have no choice—the people call upon me to save the country—I must save it & cannot respect anything that is in my way." Again alluding to his future, McClellan added, "I will never accept the Presidency—I will cheerfully take the Dictatorship & agree to lay down my life when the country is saved." Postmaster General Montgomery Blair sided with McClellan, writing on August 10 that "old granny Scott" was paralyzing the government and had to be removed.[24]

Rather than living in the field with his army, McClellan remained in the capital to promote his personal and military agenda and await the arrival of his wife and new baby girl. Some people thought it strange, including Brigadier General William T. Sherman, who wrote: "Instead of coming over the river, as we expected, [McClellan] took a house in Washington and only came over from time to time to have a review or inspection. I still hoped he would come to our side of the Potomac, pitch his tent, and prepare for real hard work, but his headquarters remained . . . in Washington City. I then thought, and still think, that was a fatal mistake." For McClellan fatal mistakes were only beginning.[25]

4

"I can do it all"

MCCLELLAN DRIFTED BETWEEN two worlds of his own making. His charismatic image inspired adulation, but he lived with an inner horror of doubting his own capabilities, which he blamed on everyone else. Nicolay and Hay, both very close to Lincoln, observed that the general's "charm of manner, enhanced by his rising fame, made him the idol of Washington drawing-rooms." Little Mac maintained his public image by renting a spacious home on Pennsylvania Avenue owned by Captain Charles Wilkes of the U.S. Navy. Located on the northwest corner of Jackson Square, two blocks from the War Department, McClellan's mansion also housed part of his staff. After breakfast he met with this group before riding through the camps. His conspicuousness in the capital resulted from his need to keep "one eye open at night," as if General Scott and the Confederates were together conspiring against him. He also informed his wife he could trust no one, making it necessary for him to "see as much as I can every day." He made no effort to eliminate the Confederate threat but decided "Genl Scott is the most dangerous antagonist I have—either he or I must leave here." Hence, he never lived among his troops and was always observed galloping to and from the camps.[1]

Lincoln clearly understood Scott's willingness to retire, and even without the insight of having read McClellan's private correspondence, the president observed the young general's abundant ambition coupled with emerging signs of emotional instability. He could not accept Scott's resignation as long as McClellan manifested fantasies and delusions. Nicolay and Hay, having observed many of Lincoln's meetings, noticed how after a few weeks in Washington McClellan's pleasing comportment was "succeeded by a strange and permanent hallucination upon two points: one was that the enemy, whose numbers were about one-third his own, vastly exceeded his army in strength; and the other, that the Government—which was doing everything in its power to support him—was hostile to him and desired his destruction."[2]

From McClellan's perspective his fears were vivid and therefore valid. When Pinkerton's first reports began appearing at headquarters, they corroborated McClellan's fantasies. Little Mac expected the Army of the Potomac to be overrun by Confederates and sought to make Scott the scapegoat. Before coming to Washington, he smothered the old warrior with genuine praise. Three weeks later he did everything in his power to undermine him. When Lincoln refused to accept Scott's resignation, the general-in-chief stayed on because he respected the president and wanted to help him. What Lincoln needed was time for McClellan to reorganize, train, and prime the army for fighting, which despite the general's theatrics and quarrelsome nature, he accomplished with great efficiency. When Lincoln showed support for Scott, McClellan suspended his campaign against the general, but only temporarily. Despite rapid progress in mobilizing the army, McClellan still manifested delusions about the size of the Confederate force at Manassas. Writing Ellen on August 16, he lamented, "I am here in a terrible place—the enemy have from 3 to 4 times my force—the Presdt is an idiot, the old General in his dotage—they cannot or will not see the true state of affairs." Three days later he added, "Beauregard probably has 150,000 men—I cannot count more than 55,000 [of my own]." The following day in another letter he wrote, "If Beauregard does not attack this week he is foolish." The absence of any movement on the part of the Confederates should have resulted in a closer examination of the actual strength of the enemy, but McClellan continued to rely on Pinkerton's spies, who seemed incapable of counting.[3]

McClellan believed some good came from his imbroglio with the general-in-chief. On August 17, with the president's approval, Scott expanded McClellan's Department of the Potomac to include Delaware, Maryland, and the Shenandoah Valley, which McClellan rolled into Army of the Potomac. Being an organization man, he also stated his intentions to form the army into divisions. Little Mac had now achieved another step in the acquisition of personal power, much of which he owed to Scott.[4]

On September 4 McClellan appointed Colonel Randolph Marcy chief of staff. In addition to being Little Mac's father-in-law, Marcy was also part of New York's Democratic political machine, and he had been using all his influence to advance his son-in-law's future prospects. Two days later Marcy reported a rumor from an unknown informant warning of an imminent attack on Washington from Manassas. McClellan reacted without further investigation and warned Cameron, with whom relations were amicable. The secretary conferred with Lincoln and on the following day wrote McClellan: "It is evident we are on the eve of a great battle—one that may decide the fate of the country. Its success must depend on you, and the means that may be placed at your disposal. Impressed with this belief and anxious to aid you with all the powers of my Department, I will be glad if you will inform me how I can do so."[5]

McClellan used the invitation to reinforce his views with Cameron. On September 8 he admitted Washington could be held but still believed he commanded the weaker force. He reported having 85,000 troops spread around Washington but claimed no more than 70,000 and perhaps as few as 60,000 were ready for field operations. He still believed Beauregard, actually Johnston, had at least "130,000 under arms" to counter any offensive movement made by the Army of the Potomac and another 100,000 to strike Baltimore and isolate Washington from the North. McClellan had been avoiding the general-in-chief and welcomed the opportunity to submit his report to Cameron, whom he regarded as more pliable than Scott. Because the president wished to avoid another altercation between Scott and McClellan, he used the incident to ask Cameron what McClellan intended to do with the army because two months of good fighting weather lie ahead. McClellan replied with a litany of reasons why campaigning should be delayed. By claiming a lack of cavalry and artillery and not having the entire regular army united under his command, the general revealed an early aptitude for creating roadblocks against fighting. His objectives were not unclear. He still had visions of commanding a 273,000-man army, which he soon rounded up to 300,000, because Lincoln never vetoed the request. "United in one body," he told Cameron, "they will insure the success of this army."[6]

Lincoln observed unwillingness on McClellan's part to commence active operations unless attacked. Had the president seen one of Little Mac's recent letters home, he might have understood the general's preference to fight defensively. Referring to Johnston's force at Manassas, McClellan wrote, "I have made every possible preparation & feel ready for them." His reaction came from Pinkerton's spies, who warned that Confederates were striking tents at Manassas for a possible attack. A day passed, and nothing happened. "Do not expect Beauregard to attack," McClellan informed his wife, "will not be ready to advance (ourselves) before November." Such information would have been more helpful to the president, who might have been amenable to a November rather than an immediate offensive.[7]

Twenty days later, on September 27, Lincoln grew impatient and called a meeting to discuss military plans with Scott and McClellan, neither of whom had been in open communication since mid-August. Scott had been attending to operations in the West, while McClellan concentrated on operations in the East, and neither had kept the other informed. Lincoln had a plan in mind, but the conference in Scott's office became tense when the general-in-chief, addressing McClellan, said: "You were called here by my advice. The times require vigilance and activity. I am not active and shall never be again. When I proposed that you should come to aid, not supersede me, you had my friendship and confidence. You still have my confidence." McClellan checked his temper, bowed, and claimed to have shaken the general's hand on departing.[8]

Returning from a cabinet meeting three days later, Attorney General Bates penned in his diary: "The public spirit is beginning to quail under the depressing influence of our prolonged inaction. I care not how cautious our commanders may be in securing certain important points (such as this city) . . . but some gallant enterprises are necessary to establish the prestige of the army." Bates portrayed the views of much of the country, summarized discussions held during cabinet meetings, thought McClellan should be ordered to fight, and looked to the president for action. Little Mac, however, made himself clear in an earlier report when he wrote, "Time is a necessary element in the creation of armies," without saying how long it should take.[9]

Frustrated by Scott's behavior and McClellan's stalling, Lincoln tried to move the war along on October 1 by issuing a "Memorandum for a Plan of Campaign." The president waded into military strategy, mainly because Scott and McClellan avoided the task. He suggested Union forces in Kentucky move and secure a railroad junction near the Cumberland Gap between Tennessee and Virginia, thus opening the way for future operations into East Tennessee, where Union sentiment remained strong. He also urged an amphibious expedition be sent to occupy Port Royal off the coast of South Carolina. Both movements would create problems for the South, enabling McClellan in the East and Frémont in the West to "avail themselves of any advantages the diversions may present."[10]

Lincoln's memorandum struck McClellan as an effort to obstruct his own plans by shifting forces to other theaters. He also regarded Frémont, another handsome and magnetic man, as a potential competitor whose command drained forces from the East. A day after receiving the president's memorandum, Little Mac complained to his reliably sympathetic wife: "I am becoming daily more disgusted with this administration—perfectly sick of it. If I could with honor resign I would quit the whole concern tomorrow." Part of McClellan's mood swings could be attributed to a long separation from his wife, whose pregnancy had denied him her company. On October 12 Ellen gave birth to Mary, whom they called May, but several weeks would pass before she grew strong enough to make the trip from Cincinnati to Washington. His other emotional conflict stemmed from facing Beauregard or Johnston in battle, both of whom he respected as competent officers from the old army and former friends. He believed Confederate officers were better than Union officers, and he did not want the Army of the Potomac exposed to battle until superior in strength. This delusion persisted in the months ahead.[11]

Nobody played on McClellan's apprehensions more than the general's chief of intelligence, Allen Pinkerton, who ran a successful detective agency but knew nothing about military espionage. He came to Washington using the name Major E. J. Allen and set up the Secret Service. His detectives collected information by interrogating deserters, illiterate runaway slaves, prisoners, and refugees. He also sent spies behind enemy lines to gather intelligence on enemy fortifications, count regimental flags, and report on conditions in the Confederate army. Pinkerton collected reams of information without mastering the art of massaging raw data into short, accurate reports. His calculations of enemy strength, usually presented in great detail, were gross exaggerations caused by double or triple counting the same information from different sources and making

wild extrapolations. On political and civilian matters his reports were usually more accurate, but McClellan's concerns always tilted toward the size
and capabilities of the enemy's army. Pinkerton's spies never successfully
infiltrated the Confederate army. They spent time in Richmond and became as deluded as the city's inhabitants regarding conditions in the field.

McClellan's reports reflected Pinkerton's estimates of Confederate
strength. The enemy's numbers baffled Lincoln and the War Department. Whether Pinkerton inflated his numbers to confirm McClellan's
own conclusions on enemy strength remains suspect. At a time when Mc-
Clellan claimed 180,000 to 200,000 Confederates at Manassas, Johnston
reported having 44,131 present.[12]

Pinkerton also performed other duties for the general. When the president learned the Maryland legislature intended to meet on September
17 to consider passing an act of secession, he authorized McClellan to
arrest the ringleaders. Instead of sending the provost marshal, Cameron
put Pinkerton in charge of the operation. In the end Pinkerton's detectives located the legislative secessionists, and troops from General Banks's
command made the arrests. Had McClellan confined Pinkerton to this line
of work, rather than military espionage, the final battle of the war might
have been fought during the fall of 1861.[13]

The president knew no more about McClellan's inner thoughts than
chief of staff Marcy or the general's two closest division commanders, Fitz-
John Porter and William Franklin. Mrs. McClellan became the only person having insight into her husband's aspirations and misgivings. About
the only strategy McClellan fully implemented was fortifying Washington,
which he did to shelter his army from the Confederates. "My flanks are
. . . safe," he advised his wife, "or soon will be. Then I shall take my own
time to make an army that will be sure of success. I will advance & force
the rebels to a battle on a field of my own selection. A long time must yet
elapse before I can do this, & I expect all the newspapers to abuse me for
delay—but I will not mind that." Lincoln sensed McClellan had no plan,
and the press complained loudly about the general's dithering.[14]

To Lincoln's expression of impatience during a cabinet meeting on October 10, McClellan replied: "I think we shall have our arrangements made
for a strong reconnaissance about Monday [October 14] to feel the strength
of the enemy. I intend to be careful and do as well as possible. Don't let

them hurry me, is all I ask." The president took Little Mac at his word and replied, "You shall have your own way in the matter, I assure you."[15]

Despite reassurances of confidence from the president, McClellan, a staunch Democrat, resented being grilled by Republicans. In a late-night letter to his wife he complained of being forced to attend a boring cabinet meeting at 8:00 p.m., adding: "There are some of the greatest geese in the Cabinet I have ever seen—enough to tax the patience of Job." Still annoyed the following day, he lashed out against "these wretched politicians —they are a most despicable set of men & I think Seward is the meanest of them all—a meddling, officious, incompetent little puppy—he has done more than any other one man to bring all this misery upon the country & is one of the least competent to get us out of the scrape. The Presdt is nothing more than a well meaning baboon." McClellan continued his tirade, referring to Welles as "the most garrulous old woman" but pegging Bates as "a good inoffensive old man" because he asked no questions. In another letter he grumbled about Lincoln's unannounced visits to army headquarters for no ostensible purpose other than to tell stories.[16]

On the evening of October 12, while visiting at Seward's home, Lincoln received a dispatch from McClellan warning the enemy was in motion and would likely strike at daybreak. "If they attack," McClellan added, "I shall beat them." Lincoln spent a restless night, only to learn in the morning the enemy had not attacked, nor had McClellan.[17]

McClellan explained his unaggressiveness to his wife, accusing General Scott of being "for inaction & the defensive" and endeavoring "to cripple [him] in every way." "I am firmly determined to force the issue," he confided to Ellen, asserting, "A very few days will determine whether his policy or mine will prevail." Lincoln would have been interested in knowing the general's policy, but McClellan said nothing.[18]

In a later conversation Lincoln spoke with McClellan after being confronted by three senators who visited the White House to worry the administration into battle. The president explained that, while he supported McClellan's "deliberateness," the general must give some thought to fighting.

"I have everything at stake," Little Mac declared. "If I fail, I will not see you again or anybody."

"I have a notion to go out with you and stand or fall with the battle," Lincoln replied.

The symbolic gesture horrified McClellan. He later spoke with the three senators, blaming his military inactivity on Scott, and they agreed to make a concerted effort to retire the general.[19]

On October 18 McClellan learned a decision had been reached during a cabinet meeting to accept Scott's resignation. He expected to be named general-in-chief but later learned Scott had recommended Major General Henry W. Halleck as his successor. On October 20, perhaps to display more aggressiveness, McClellan authorized Brigadier General Charles P. Stone, whose division was near Poolesville, Maryland, to make "a slight demonstration" and drive Brigadier General Nathan G. Evan's small Confederate force out of the area.[20]

Stone did not understand what McClellan meant by "a slight demonstration" and sent a detachment from his division across the Potomac River at Harrison's Island. When the Federals ran into resistance from Evans's brigade, Stone notified McClellan, who replied: "Call on Banks for whatever aid you need. Take Leesburg." McClellan expected Banks to reinforce Stone with Brigadier General George A. McCall's brigade but forgot he had ordered the brigade back to Washington, which led to missteps and disaster.[21]

In response to McClellan's order Stone instructed Colonel Edward D. Baker's brigade to cross the river with the option of pushing the rebels out of Leesburg or withdraw the small detachment already operating in Virginia until McCall's brigade arrived. Baker, still technically a U.S. senator from Oregon, also shared a close friendship with the president. By deciding to assault the enemy without first scouting the position or obtaining enough boats, Baker brought on the Battle of Ball's Bluff and lost his life attempting to scale the seventy-foot bank rimming the river. When McClellan remembered late night on October 21 having ordered McCall's brigade back to Washington, he frantically telegraphed Banks to send two brigades to Stone and told Stone to hold Ball's Bluff.[22]

The orders arrived too late. Baker's ill-conceived assault ended disastrously, and his death brought tears from the president. Being in a consoling mood, McClellan spoke to Lincoln: "There is many a good fellow that wears shoulder-straps going under the sod before this thing is over. There is no loss too great to be repaired. If I should get knocked on the head, Mr. President, you will put another man immediately into my shoes."

Lincoln nodded and said, "I want you to take care of yourself." The Ball's Bluff affair led McClellan to believe his army would not be ready to fight before spring.[23]

Although McClellan blamed the disaster on Baker, Congress demanded a living scapegoat. Without justification, the Provost marshal arrested Brigadier General Stone on February 9, 1862. Because no charges were filed, the War Department released Stone from prison on August 16, 1862, and returned him to the army.[24]

McClellan accepted no responsibility for the blunder. "The whole thing took place some 40 miles from here without my orders or knowledge," he confided to Ellen, "it was entirely unauthorized by me & I am in no manner responsible for it." Explanations to his wife became McClellan's way of absolving himself from fault. Radicals, however, suspected Little Mac of intentionally wasting the fall by refusing to launch a serious attack on the enemy because they suspected the general, like many Democrats, sympathized with slavery and plotted to restore southern control of the government.[25]

Although far from being a major engagement, Ball's Bluff brought hopefulness to the South and spread gloom in the North. McClellan feared the setback would delay Scott's retirement, and it did, but only for a few days. Little Mac took no chances, however, of being passed up by Halleck. He befriended Edwin M. Stanton, a prominent lawyer and Democrat who had served as President Buchanan's attorney general. Stanton prepared a carefully composed paper paying tribute to McClellan's record for organizing the Army of the Potomac, and on October 31 Little Mac signed and submitted the ghostwritten report to Cameron in an effort to improve his prospects for replacing Scott. Stanton doubted the move would work because of McClellan's close affiliation with Democrats, who were already fraternizing with the general at headquarters. "What can he [McClellan] accomplish?" Stanton asked. "Will not Scott's jealousy, Cabinet intrigues, and Republican interference thwart him at every step?"[26]

The special effort proved unnecessary. McClellan had convinced both Congress and influential senators such as Chandler, Trumbull, and Wade that Scott's presence provided the principal barrier to launching an offensive. Cameron said Scott would retire the following day and orders would be issued making Little Mac general-in-chief. Before handing his report to Cameron, nobody had seen McClellan throughout the day because he had been closeted with Stanton "to dodge all enemies in shape of browsing Presdt etc." Even McClellan's wife must have known better when he claimed, "I have one great comfort in all this—that is I did not seek this position." He did admit "a sense of relief at the prospect of having [his] own way untrammeled" and denied having any symptoms "of gratified vanity or ambition."[27]

On the morning of November 1, 1861, a messenger from the White House delivered the president's order promoting McClellan to general-in-chief. When the news broke, McClellan jumped on his horse and galloped through the camps to the huzzahs of his troops and the deafening roar of artillery. As he rode back to Washington, carriages filled with politicians, sightseers, aides, orderlies, and generals trailed behind him. After the celebration ended, Lincoln held a discussion with his new general-in-chief. He made no special demands aside from asking McClellan to confer with him "so far as necessary," which was the president's way of saying, "Keep me informed." Later that evening Lincoln called at McClellan's headquarters for a chat because he worried the thirty-four-year-old general might not comprehend the enormous responsibilities imposed on a general-in-chief.

Now free from Scott, McClellan replied, "I feel as if several tons were taken from my shoulders to-day. I am now in contact with you and the Secretary. I am not embarrassed by intervention."

"Very well," said the president, "draw on me for all the sense and information I have. In addition to your present command, the supreme command of the army will entail a vast labor upon you."

Without hesitating, and without realizing he had prepared the way for his own destruction, McClellan replied, "I can do it all." McClellan would have to "do it all" because he trusted no one, not the politicians who lobbied for his promotion and certainly not a Republican president prone to giving advice.[28]

5

"All quiet on the Potomac"

FTER CONSPIRING FOR MONTHS to replace General Scott, McClellan gathered his staff at 4:00 a.m. on November 3 to escort the venerable old warrior to the depot. Rain poured from pitch-black skies as a squadron of cavalry wearing equally black hooded slickers conducted the general's carriage through Washington's deserted streets. No guns roared a parting salute. Any antipathy between the two men had moderated after McClellan paid a remarkably eloquent though contrived tribute to the retiring general-in-chief, "the hero who in his youth raised high the reputation of his country." Later, to his wife, Little Mac referred to the letter as Scott's "military obituary . . . I wrote it *at* him—for a particular market."

As Scott boarded the train, he graciously wished the Young Napoleon, who had made his last months of service as upsetting as possible, swift success in ending the war but privately admitted "his sensations were very peculiar in leaving Washington and active life." The parting made McClellan reflective, confessing to his wife: "It may be that on some distant day I too shall totter away from Washington, a worn out old soldier, with naught to do but make my peace with God. The sight of this morning was a lesson to me which I hope not soon to forget. I saw there the end of a long, active and ambitious life, the end of the career of the first soldier of his nation, and it was a feeble old man scarce able to walk; hardly anyone there to see him off but his successor." In closing, McClellan recovered from his reflections, writing: "At last I am the 'major-general commanding the army.' I do not feel the least elated, for I do feel the responsibility of the position. And I feel the need for some support. I trust God will aid me."[1]

If God would not aid McClellan, at least Lincoln tried. During the first weeks of November the president conferred with the general daily, usually at the White House or the War Department and sometimes at McClellan's home. Lincoln never considered it odd for him, the chief executive, to go to the general instead of having the general come to him. He usually spent more time in other people's offices than his own, often dropping into headquarters and asking, "Is George in?" It was his way of gathering information and learning more about the character and capabilities of the people on whom the country depended. His visits to McClellan were often exploratory missions to render support but also to assess the general's fitness for supreme command. Little Mac disliked being questioned. He preferred subordinates who agreed with him and uncritical admirers. He avoided discussions on military plans, and sometimes he and Lincoln just talked. Although the general grumbled about the president's impromptu intrusions, he admitted Lincoln's anecdotes, although annoying, "were always to the point."[2]

On one occasion General Samuel Heintzelman entered headquarters and found Lincoln and McClellan studying a map of Virginia. Little Mac listened impatiently to the president's suggestions, seldom commenting. On Heintzelman's arrival the conversation ended, and McClellan accompanied the president to the outer door. Little Mac returned to his office, cast an exasperated look at Heintzelman, and, referring to the president said, "Isn't he a rare bird?"[3]

Nightly visits by the president continued until November 13, when an incident brought them to an end. Early that evening John Hay walked with the president to Secretary of State Seward's home, where they decided to visit the general at his home on Jackson Square. The porter answering the door said the general had gone to a wedding but would soon return. Lincoln, Seward, and Hay settled in the drawing room and waited. McClellan returned an hour later and, ignoring the servant's announcement of the president's presence, went upstairs. A half-hour passed, and thinking the porter had not announced his name, Lincoln sent him to get the general. The servant returned and said the general had gone to bed. Lincoln appeared to attach no special importance to the snub and never asked for an explanation. Perhaps he believed the general, whose overt relations had always been courteous and respectful, had overindulged at the wedding. On returning to the White House, Hay mentioned the incident, but Lincoln merely replied "it was better at this time not to be making points of etiquette & personal dignity." Future conferences were conducted at the White House. Historian T. Harry Williams made an observation, writing, "Lincoln had made a bad mistake of being humble with a super-egoist. The egoist mistook humility for weakness." McClellan thought only in linear terms. He never sought advice and made a serious mistake by not recognizing Lincoln's ability to adapt to situations by examining them multidimensionally and from all sides, thus revealing pitfalls in any argument posed by self-proclaimed experts.[4]

After taking control of the army, McClellan made a quick assessment of overall operations and found his far-flung forces stagnating in idleness. Politicians and the northern press ignored the quiet western theater and relentlessly attacked McClellan for the Army of the Potomac's inactivity, which appeared to be guarding Washington from an equally inactive force at Manassas. McClellan suggested as much in a November 8 letter to his friend and fellow Democrat Samuel L. M. Barlow, writing: "The strength of the Army of the Potomac has been vastly overrated in the public opinion. It is now strong enough & well disciplined enough to hold Washington against *any* attack." To other inquiries questioning his inaction, he explained that "time was required to fortify Washington in such a manner that no large force would be required for its protection."[5]

Little Mac ignored the pressure, letting it fall on Lincoln. He occupied his time writing long dispatches to Major General Henry Halleck in Missouri, Brigadier General Don Carlos Buell in Kentucky, Brigadier General Thomas W. Sherman at Port Royal, and General Benjamin Butler at Fort Monroe. Lincoln remained patient because McClellan appeared to be organizing a strategy for striking the South from all sides. At least McClellan thought so when he wrote, "It was my intention . . . that the various parts [of the army] should be carried out simultaneously, or nearly so, and in co-operation with the whole line." He later explained, "Even if the Army of the Potomac had been in condition to undertake a campaign in the autumn of 1861, the backward state of affairs in the West would have made it unwise to do so; for on no sound military principle could it be regarded as proper to operate on one line while all was quiescent on the others, as such a course would have enabled the enemy to concentrate everything on

one active army." The logic made sense had McClellan followed his own
advice.[6]

IN EARLY AUGUST, while McClellan organized the Army of the Potomac,
Lincoln informed the cabinet about a plan hatched by the navy and approved by General Scott for the capture of Hatteras, North Carolina,
and Port Royal, South Carolina. Scott sent Brigadier General Thomas W.
Sherman to New England to raise twelve thousand troops, while the navy
gathered a fleet of ships at Hampton Roads, Virginia. On August 28–29 a
joint operation under Flag Officer Silas H. Stringham and General Butler
captured forts Hatteras and Clark. On November 7 Flag Officer Samuel F.
Du Pont used seventeen ships to convoy General Sherman's expedition to
Port Royal Sound. Together they captured forts Beauregard and Walker,
thus establishing permanent Union bases in the Carolinas. The two joint
operations can be attributed directly to the planning of General Scott and
the navy, and their success added to McClellan's notion that a campaign
against Richmond would succeed faster if conducted on Virginia's peninsula instead of through Manassas. Sherman reinforced this impression
when he stated: "We had no idea when preparing the expedition of such
immense success. Such a panic was created among the enemy by the fall
of Port Royal that they deserted the whole coast."[7]

The navy had begun to upstage the army on strategic expeditions and
on November 15 upped the ante when Secretary of the Navy Welles and
Commander David D. Porter proposed a scheme to capture New Orleans.
Lincoln liked the idea and, with Welles and Porter, met with McClellan.
The president went to a map and outlined the importance of securing
the Mississippi River. After New Orleans, Lincoln said the next objective
should be Vicksburg, adding, "The war can never be brought to a close
until that key is in our pocket." At first McClellan balked, thinking the
expedition would require fifty thousand troops. After Welles suggested
twelve thousand, Little Mac agreed to the program, knowing nothing
would happen for several months, but he resented the president's meddling in army affairs. He later vented his annoyance in a letter to his wife,
writing: "I went to the White House shortly after tea where I found 'the
original gorilla,' about as intelligent as ever. What a specimen to be at the
head of our affairs now!"[8]

Part of McClellan's resistance to the New Orleans expedition emanated from military plans he had recently consummated with western generals. On November 7 he instructed General Buell, commanding the Department of the Ohio, to concentrate east of the Cumberland River in Kentucky with the object of liberating the Unionist element in East Tennessee. He told Buell to "remain on the defensive from Louisville to Nashville, while you throw the mass of your forces by rapid marches . . . on Knoxville." In addition to Ohio, Buell's department included eastern Kentucky, Indiana, Michigan, and Tennessee, with headquarters in Louisville. McClellan expressed enormous confidence in Buell and predicted the Ohioan would become one of the war's great generals. But he misjudged Buell, who decided not to capture East Tennessee by invading it from the north because of logistical problems and instead concocted an idealistic plan to capture all of Tennessee. The decision would later change McClellan's opinion of Buell.[9]

On November 11 McClellan put General Halleck in charge of the Department of the Missouri, which included Arkansas, Illinois, Iowa, Minnesota, western Kentucky, and Wisconsin. Knowing Halleck had once been his rival for supreme command, McClellan gave him a large department far from Washington and the difficult task of cleaning up disorder in Missouri created during Major General John C. Frémont's administration. He ordered Halleck to subdue guerrilla fighting in the state and prepare for operations on or near the Mississippi.[10]

Both policies obliged the wishes of the president, who for political reasons wanted East Tennessee protected from Confederate oppression and enemy activity in the troubled border state of Missouri suppressed. There were few military benefits to be gained by capturing eastern Tennessee, but Lincoln made a case for seizing Knoxville and controlling the East Tennessee & Georgia Railroad, which supplied Confederate troops in Kentucky and Virginia. During evening conversations at the War Department with McClellan, Lincoln consistently placed emphasis on the restoration of the Union and not the abolition of slavery. Little Mac felt the same way and, though he deplored "the condition of those poor blacks," made clear he would "not fight for the abolitionists." In another letter he added: "Help me to dodge the nigger—we want nothing to do with him. I am fighting to preserve the integrity of the Union & the power of Govt—on no other issue."[11]

McClellan never lost sight of local issues. He wanted to keep the enemy engaged in the West and their railroads and river commerce disrupted, making it more difficult for the Confederacy to transfer troops to Virginia. The capture of Hatteras and Port Royal Sound, the proposed expeditions against New Orleans and East Tennessee, and the blockade of southern ports made strategic sense. Earlier in the war Lincoln and McClellan had rejected Scott's Anaconda plan, which they were now implementing to forestall European intervention and which could only be abated by Union victories in the field—especially in Virginia.

On October 31, a day before his appointment to supreme command, McClellan addressed a letter to Simon Cameron stating the importance of "crushing . . . the rebel army at Manassas." He said the campaign "should not be postponed beyond the twenty-fifth of November." On October 31 McClellan still believed he was competing with Halleck for the top job. Eight days later he informed a friend of being unable "to fight with reasonable chances of success" because of the superior strength of the enemy. So, in raw weather on November 20, instead of marching on Manassas, McClellan staged a grand review of the Army of the Potomac at nearby Munson's Hill.[12]

He invited Lincoln to the ceremony, where some fifty thousand soldiers stood in line on a wide, undulating plain at Bailey's Cross Roads in Virginia. Early that morning the people of Washington began gathering on the parade grounds. McClellan arrived with his usual entourage, including cavalry. According to Nicolay and Hay, who also attended the review, the general "displayed [the troops] to the best advantage, and a finer army had rarely been seen." Lincoln rode with McClellan and McDowell, followed by a colorful cavalcade of a hundred general and staff officers, all prancing up and down the entire length of an extended line four miles long. Many young men enjoyed their first glimpse of the president and, for some of them, their last. Never had Lincoln received such hearty cheers, but he took them in stride. Little Mac led the president to an acclivity near the center of the field and together with his officers stood proudly as regiments passed in review. From the direction of Fairfax irregular firing could be faintly heard. The enemy, always aware of McClellan's plans, tried to create a commotion to upset the ceremony. Lincoln also heard the firing and expected McClellan to lead his men against the enemy in the morning. As twilight fell, the president returned to the White House convinced he had witnessed a great army ready to fight. When nothing happened,

Lincoln resumed fretting. November 25 came and went without a battle.

In the days following the grand review Lincoln arranged for a meeting at the White House between Brigadier General Ormsby M. Mitchel, Governor William Dennison of Ohio, and McClellan. After waiting at length for the general-in-chief, who never came, the two visitors became quizzical. "Never mind," Lincoln said calmly. "I will hold McClellan's horse if he will only bring us success."[13]

McClellan postponed the advance on Manassas because of Allan Pinkerton's reports. The detective's first exaggerated estimate of the enemy's strength arrived on McClellan's desk on October 4. Every week or two he updated his reports. Although Little Mac reported having 133,000 present for duty on October 15, he claimed having only 60,000 available for operations against Manassas. Pinkerton reported 90,000 Confederates at Manassas at a time when General Johnston's returns showed 41,000. As the Army of the Potomac steadily increased in strength, Pinkerton upped the number of Confederates at Manassas. Pinkerton's operation quickly became the most inept intelligence service ever employed by a general. When on December 1 McClellan admitted having 76,852 troops available for active operations, Pinkerton reported the force at Manassas at 100,000. Although McClellan might have questioned Pinkerton's calculations, he used them to quash Lincoln's demands for action. Secretary of State Seward, who seldom commented on military affairs, doubted McClellan's claims and said there were probably as many Confederate troops at Manassas as there were soldiers in New York, an estimate closer to the truth.[14]

With the approach of winter, McClellan found valid reasons for delay. On November 25 a snowstorm struck Washington, and the weather turned cold. Rain fell, churning the roads to mud. The army could not have taken the field, and everyone knew it. Buell had not budged from eastern Kentucky, but Little Mac approved the delay because it served his purpose, writing, "Inform me some little time before you are ready to move, so that we may move simultaneously." McClellan also began accusing the government of withholding resources and hatching schemes to place the blame for any failure on him. "If it is so," he wrote, "the fault will not be mine." General Johnston, witnessing McClellan's antics from Manassas, predicted the general would never attack. The national press, looking for war news to print, settled for "All quiet on the Potomac."[15]

After estimating the Manassas force facing him at double its actual strength, McClellan also massaged his returns to minimize his own effective strength. He applied this rule only to the enemy in his immediate vicinity and showed little regard for distant commanders requesting reinforcements. When Rosecrans replaced him in western Virginia and asked for reinforcements, McClellan declared the request "unreasonable." When Brigadier General William T. Sherman wanted two hundred thousand men for operations in the West, McClellan handed the letter to Lincoln and said, "The man is crazy." Little Mac, the supreme commander, regarded every man sent to any other department as robbing from the Army of the Potomac.[16]

AFTER A FOUR-MONTH ADJOURNMENT Congress convened on December 2, 1861, with many questions. Roscoe Conkling in the House and Zachariah Chandler in the Senate sponsored resolutions for separate committees to investigate the disaster at Ball's Bluff. Senator James W. Grimes of Iowa thought the resolutions did not go far enough and proposed a permanent joint committee of three senators and four representatives to inquire into the conduct of the war. On December 20 the Joint Committee on the Conduct of the War was established with Chandler, Andrew Johnson, and Benjamin F. Wade, from the Senate and John Covode, Daniel W. Gooch, George W. Julian, and Moses F. O'Dell from the House. As the majority of the members were radical Republicans—an extremist faction advocating immediate emancipation and a punitive policy toward the South —they became increasingly critical of Lincoln's war plans and openly hostile toward McClellan, who for five months had built the greatest military force on the continent but failed to use it.

Even before forming the committee, Chandler and Wade had repeatedly pressed Lincoln to deploy the Army of the Potomac aggressively. They now felt entrusted by a mandate from the people to become more persistent. Nicolay and Hay later described the committee as "a stern and zealous censor of both the army and the Government; it called soldiers and statesmen before it, and questioned them like refractory schoolboys. It was often hasty and unjust in its judgments, but always earnest, patriotic, and honest; it was assailed with furious denunciation and defended with headlong and indiscriminating eulogy; and on the whole must be said to have merited more praise than blame." The majority of the public supported the committee because no meaningful campaigning had occurred since the disaster at Bull Run, but inflation and the nation's debt had surged with no end in sight.

Lincoln, the cabinet, and McClellan began to feel the committee's impact. The president, who understood the nature of the public, knew he must deal dexterously with this new powerful legislative appendage, and though he consistently defended McClellan's exhaustive preparations, he also regularly reminded the general that time should not be squandered preparing a forward movement. Instead of relieving congressional pressure on the president, McClellan and his immediate subordinates treated the committee with guarded contempt. McClellan seldom spoke to anyone remotely connected with politics. Stephen Sears wrote of a meeting between Lincoln and McClellan attended by historian George Bancroft. Afterward Bancroft wrote his wife: "Of all silent, uncommunicative, reserved men whom I ever met, the general stands among the first. He is one, who if he thinks deeply, keeps his thoughts to himself."[17]

Pressed by Congress for action, the president asked for patience, privately admitting to friends, "If something were not soon done, the bottom would be out of the whole affair." Regardless of the weather or any other factor real or imagined by McClellan, on December 1 Lincoln attempted to be helpful by venturing again into military planning. He suggested a turning movement using the Occoquan River, which was within easy marching distance from Washington. The thrust would threaten Johnston's communications and force the rebels out of Manassas. While half of the Federal army participated in the flanking movement, the other half could strike Manassas. Lincoln asked McClellan how long this sensible plan would take. Having damaged his own popularity by allowing McClellan to avoid marching, Lincoln now wanted something done.[18]

Lincoln also wanted to tell Congress something encouraging beyond what he had prepared for his annual address. McClellan waited ten days before responding and argued that striking the rebels with part of his force while using the other part to destroy the enemy's communications would violate a military maxim by dividing his army in the face of a superior force. McClellan said he would need 154,000 troops to implement

Lincoln's plan, twice the number he claimed to have. After rejecting the president's suggestions, the general wrote, "I have now my mind actively turned towards another plan of campaign that I do not think at all anticipated by the enemy, nor by any of our own people." Lincoln did not ask for details, nor did he ask why his memorandum had been so curtly dismissed. Ten days later the Young Napoleon fell ill with typhoid fever, and the army twiddled its thumbs for another three weeks. McClellan later claimed his mind was never addled, but he required a great amount of sleep. He also left the administration of the Army of the Potomac to his subordinates without allowing them to make decisions or putting anyone in charge. All work came to a standstill while the general sought a cure by calling in a homeopathic doctor.[19]

Lincoln visited regularly but was often turned away because the general was asleep. At times he feared McClellan would die, and because of the general's patent secrecy, Lincoln worried about operations in the West. Were Halleck and Buell on the offensive, as McClellan had promised, or were they waiting for instructions? The president had been promised a coordinated campaign.[20]

On December 31 Lincoln opened communications with Buell and Halleck, writing, "General McClellan is sick," and asked whether the two generals were moving in concert. Buell replied, "There is no arrangement between General Halleck and myself." Halleck replied: "I have never received a word from General Buell. Have written fully on this subject to Major-General McClellan." Lincoln replied, "Delay is ruining us, and it is indispensible for me to have something definite."[21]

Puzzled by the president's question, Halleck advised Buell, "I have had no instructions respecting co-operation." All this was contrary to what McClellan had told the president. Lincoln also learned that Buell intended to strike Nashville, not Knoxville, and that Halleck intended to sit out the winter awaiting reinforcements McClellan never sent. Lincoln suffered another shock when he discovered the armies under Buell and Halleck were much smaller than McClellan had reported, and many of the regiments raised in the West for service in the West had been attached to the Army of the Potomac. On January 6 Lincoln brought the matter to McClellan's attention, and Little Mac then advised Buell that as long as East Tennessee remained in Confederate hands, the Army of the Potomac could not move, which, of course, made no sense. Lincoln concluded after a weeklong exchange of correspondence that neither Buell nor Halleck intended to act. Nor had McClellan instructed them to act. "It is exceedingly discouraging," Lincoln informed Halleck, "as everywhere else, nothing can be done." Attorney General Bates spoke for the cabinet when he noted in his diary, "McClellan is still sick, and nobody knows his plans, if he have any (which with me is very doubtful)."[22]

As General Johnston observed, the Young Napoleon never intended to move against Manassas. McClellan had certainly considered it, having given Cameron and Lincoln assurances as far back as October 31, but he cringed at the prospect of mounting a showdown battle. He wanted to find a way to capture Richmond without having to fight a big bloody battle and succeeded in pressing this unlikely scheme on some of his generals. He failed to see that capturing Richmond without defeating the Confederate army would be a hollow victory. He shared none of these thoughts with the president, but in late November he found General Barnard, chief of engineers, alone at army headquarters. Using Barnard as a sounding board, McClellan said he had a plan to capture Richmond by transporting the army down the Potomac River to Chesapeake Bay and then up the Rappahannock River to Urbanna, which was located about forty miles east of Richmond. From there he would bypass the small Confederate force at Yorktown and lead the Army of the Potomac by forced marches to Richmond, where he would take the city before Confederates at Manassas could respond. Barnard thought Little Mac's "Urbanna Plan" would fail but did not say so at the time.[23]

Before falling ill, McClellan also took Chase into his confidence. Chase had problems raising money and expected to exhaust his cash by mid-February because of huge army expenditures and no military progress. McClellan put Chase at ease by promising to be in Richmond by then. According to Little Mac, Chase praised the plan as "a most brilliant conception" and promised not to say a word. A month later Chase said he never had faith in the scheme. Although McClellan appeared to have set his mind on the Urbanna movement and expected to begin preparations immediately, confiding it to Barnard and Chase without first discussing it with the president suggests flagrant impropriety. Had Lincoln pried, and he should have when McClellan mentioned another plan, he might have hastened the conclusion of the war by a veto, but the president again exercised executive patience, and McClellan avoided confrontation by falling ill.[24]

On January 10, after calling at McClellan's home and finding the general had posted orders not to be disturbed, Lincoln walked to army headquarters to speak with Quartermaster General Montgomery C. Meigs, whose opinion he trusted. After plodding through chilly streets, Lincoln took a seat next to a blazing grate in Meigs's office and glumly asked: "What shall I do? The people are impatient; Chase has no money and he tells me he can raise no more; the general of the Army has typhoid fever. The bottom is out of the tub." Meigs suggested calling an immediate meeting with generals McDowell and Franklin and the cabinet.[25]

Over time Lincoln had expanded his knowledge of military matters. Accustomed to years of self-education and with an intellect already fine-tuned to analyzing issues from different perspectives, the president entered the second year of war with increasing expertise as commander-in-chief. While McClellan dithered during the autumn of 1861, Lincoln borrowed books on tactics and strategy, including Halleck's *Elements of Military Art and Science,* and studied reports from the field. With his knowledge of operations and strategy beginning to percolate, he even spoke of taking the field himself, knowing the hint would find its way back to McClellan. On Meigs's suggestion he decided to test his self-imposed education and summoned McDowell and Franklin to the White House for the first of four emergency meetings with Seward, Chase, and others. Lincoln opened the meeting, saying, "If General McClellan did not want to use the army he [the president] would like to borrow it, provided he could see how it could be made to do something." McDowell thought a swift movement on the flanks of the enemy at Manassas would force the rebels from their works and compel them to fight on an open field. Franklin favored a direct attack on Richmond, by which he meant the Urbanna plan Lincoln knew nothing about. McClellan had evidently spoken to Franklin, with whom he had close friendship, but not McDowell, who had either disagreed with Little Mac's plan or never knew about it. When Lincoln raised the question of transportation to Virginia's peninsula, neither general had an answer, so the president asked them to study the matter and decide what to do.

Franklin and McDowell returned to the White House the following evening with a joint memorandum agreeing to the Manassas plan, which now contained characteristics of the president's Occoquan plan. Lincoln told them to work on it and come back for a third meeting with more details. Seward and Chase attended the third session and also agreed with the plan, the only opposition coming from Postmaster General Blair. Meigs also favored the plan, citing immense difficulties transporting troops and supplies by water to some remote base on Virginia's peninsula. When asked how long it would take to assemble ships for transporting the army, Meigs said six weeks. Knowing the president would dislike the delay, Franklin and Meigs reaffirmed the Manassas plan. After the conference adjourned, Chase tried to protect McClellan from administrative mischief and warned the general a fourth meeting had been called.[26]

On January 13 McClellan miraculously recovered and joined the gathering at the White House. Now furious over the president's meddling in military affairs and fearing the possibility of removal, Little Mac said he had developed his own plan. At Lincoln's request, however, and for Little Mac's benefit, McDowell reiterated what he and Franklin had resolved under the president's orders. McClellan merely said, "coldly, if not curtly," to McDowell, "You are entitled to have any opinion you please," and made no further comment. Little Mac decided McDowell had instigated the plot, "hoping to succeed [him] in command," and Franklin had been coerced and "simply acted under orders." Lincoln tried to discuss the Occoquan (Manassas) plan, but no one would talk, all deferring to McClellan. Little Mac listened for a while and finally said that "the case was so clear a blind man could see it" then lapsed into a discussion of the inadequacy of his forces. Having expressed his thoughts, McClellan assured everyone his health had been restored and the responsibility for planning was back in his hands. Although he retained supremacy over his generals, he wasted an opportunity to unify them by not dealing openly on a matter of great concern to everyone.

Secretary Chase asked McClellan point-blank what he intended to do with the army and when he intended to do it. The general replied impertinently and told Chase that he reported to the president and the secretary of war and not to the secretary of the Treasury. His reticence was justified but not his arrogant silence. As Meigs recalled, McClellan believed any comment made to Lincoln regarding plans would be shared with Tad and reported the next morning in the *New York Herald*. Visitors to the White House often spoke with Tad while waiting to see the president, and Little's

Mac's remarks may have been valid. After remarking that Buell must move first, McClellan refused to answer any more questions. Knowing McClellan's paranoia for not making statements to people he distrusted, Lincoln asked whether the general had any particular time fixed for a movement without actually asking the date. McClellan said he did but refused to comment further without orders from the president. Seward rose, buttoned his coat, and said, "I don't see that we are likely to make much out of General McClellan." Lincoln took the hint and, though visibly dissatisfied, adjourned the meeting. The president had begun to have grave doubts about his supreme commander, but he still wanted to believe in him. Meetings in the future, however, would be held in private. Thoroughly disgusted, Chase lost all faith in McClellan, grumbling privately to Mc-Dowell and Franklin, "Well, if that is Mac's decision, he is a ruined man."[27]

Although McClellan refused to see Lincoln during his illness, he did conduct business with his generals during his confinement. Historian Joseph T. Glatthaar wrote that McClellan "used his illness as a device to reinforce his value to the nation, to make others appreciate him and feel his absence." Although the gimmick worked with the public, McClellan lost a great deal of support among the cabinet. It also marked a change in the way Lincoln would deal with McClellan and military matters. For Little Mac pressure would build.[28]

The January 13 conference acted as a turning point for Lincoln's grasp of military strategy. After discussing the eastern theater without settling on an expedition and discouraged by McClellan's outright rejection of the Occoquan plan, Lincoln addressed a letter to Halleck and Buell expressing his strategic views: "I state my general idea of this war to be that we have *greater* numbers, and the enemy has *greater* facility of concentrating forces upon points of collision; that we must fail unless we can find some way of making *our* advantage an over-match for *his;* and that this can only be done by menacing him with superior forces at *different* points, at the *same* time; so that we can safely attack, one, or both, if he makes no change; and if he *weakens* one to *strengthen* the other, forbear to attack the strengthened one, but seize and hold the weakened one, gaining so much." One might wonder to what extent Lincoln emphasized this strategy when discussing with McClellan the Occoquan plan, which the general obstinately rejected as an enhancement to the Manassas plan.

He still objected to dividing his force in the face of 170,000 imaginary Confederates defending Manassas. Although McClellan generally agreed with Lincoln's strategy, he did not want to initiate a campaign certain to draw more reinforcements into Virginia. Many of the general's personal views remain unknown during this period because Mrs. McClellan had moved to Washington, thereby precluding Little Mac's correspondence to his wife.[29]

MCCLELLAN'S FIRST INKLING of a possible conspiracy against him occurred during his illness, when Stanton entered the general's sickroom to warn, "They are counting on your death, and are already dividing among themselves your military goods and chattels." The general's relationship with Stanton began early in the war, when they met through mutual acquaintances among Ohio's Democrats. A sharp lawyer, Stanton had held minor public offices before becoming President Buchanan's attorney general. Stanton despised slavery but upheld slaveholders' constitutional rights, a view he shared with McClellan.[30]

When Stanton set his eyes on becoming secretary of war, he began playing both ends against the middle. On one hand he angled for support from the radicals by condemning McClellan's inertia while presenting himself to the general as a true and devoted ally. He believed the president lacked executive ability and in October 1861 began worming his way into McClellan's life by assisting in writing the general's status report to Cameron. "From that moment," McClellan wrote, "he did his best to ingratiate himself with me, and professed the warmest friendship and devotion to me . . . His purpose was to endeavor to climb upon my shoulders and then throw me down." Like McClellan, Stanton also held a low opinion of the cabinet and agreed that the war should be fought solely for unification of the nation and not as a way to abolish slavery. Lincoln also shared this view at the time because he understood that any assault on slavery would upset the administration's fragile relationship with border states.[31]

McClellan believed he and Stanton thought alike, that rebel armies should be targeted and not the southern people; injury to the property of noncombatants should be avoided; masters should not be deprived of their slaves; and reconciliation, not subjugation, should be the objective of the administration. He continued to use Stanton on points of law and believed the former attorney general would be more helpful than Cameron as secretary of war. Stanton consulted with McClellan frequently enough to sense the general's loathing of Cameron. He once had a brief, disagreeable relationship with Lincoln during litigation of the McCormick Reaper patent case in 1855 and expected no favors, but the power of being secretary of war appealed to him.[32]

After General Scott resigned, many in government thought Cameron should go too, before corruption and inefficiency in the War Department became worse. McClellan had also heard rumors of Lincoln's consideration of Stanton, who during that time canceled a lucrative partnership with wealthy New York lawyer Samuel L. M. Barlow, a prominent Democrat and the general's personal friend. After weeks passed and nothing happened, Stanton became increasingly critical of the administration, thereby reinforcing McClellan's views. He remained in close contact with the general and during the autumn urged McClellan to arrest Colonel John Cochrane for suggesting free blacks be armed for military service and rebuked Cameron for sanctioning and repeating the statement. Stanton also communicated with McClellan during the *Trent* Affair, which threatened to bring Great Britain into the war on the side of the Confederacy. He objected to Lincoln's negotiated settlement, which resulted in an apology to Great Britain, and told McClellan the government had erred by setting a regrettable precedent.[33]

During Lincoln's war council at the White House with McDowell and Franklin, Stanton warned McClellan of the meetings. The news acted like a tonic, and the general quickly recovered. While McClellan hurriedly dressed for the January 13 meeting at the White House, Colonel Thomas M. Key, a staff aide, hurried to the general's home to report Cameron's resignation and Stanton as successor. Minutes later Stanton arrived at the door and said he would not accept the position unless the general approved. Stanton pledged his support, and McClellan urged him to accept the appointment. Lincoln called the following day to apologize for not having conferred with McClellan on the appointment but, believing Stanton and the general were on friendly terms, expected there would be no disagreement. McClellan shared his euphoria with Barlow, writing, "Stanton's appointment was a most unexpected piece of good fortune," and felt it would produce a positive effect on the North. It did, and naming Cameron minister to Russia also helped. Speaking for the radicals, George W. Julian praised Stanton's selection, expected him to press for an early forward movement, and wrote, "We are delighted with him." McClellan completely misread Stanton's motives. Although the new secretary was energetic, impatient, and entirely ignorant of military affairs, he would bring pressure on McClellan for an immediate advance, winning quick approbation from the Republican radicals running the Committee on the Conduct of the War.[34]

At Stanton's request McClellan met with Malcolm Ives from James Gordon Bennett's *New York Herald.* Stanton arranged the meeting because he wanted the backing of America's largest newspaper. In exchange Bennett wanted the *New York Herald* to be the first to receive military news. With this understanding Stanton departed and left Ives with McClellan. After refusing to discuss his plans during the president's recent conference by arguing that anything said might end up in the *Herald,* McClellan spent three hours with Ives perpetrating one of the greatest military leaks of the Civil War. "What I declined communicating to them," McClellan confided to Ives, "I am now going to convey through you to Mr. Bennett . . . all the knowledge I possess myself, with no reserve." He brought Ives up to date on planned movements in the West, Burnside's operations in the Carolinas, the forthcoming expedition against New Orleans, and how those movements interacted with his grand design to capture Richmond. He trusted Bennett would use the intelligence judiciously and not reveal its source. In the coming months McClellan continued to brief Ives and at times colluded with him to plant disinformation in the *Herald.* Over time even Stanton began to wonder how the *Herald* had obtained so many military secrets. He never suspected McClellan and kept searching for spies among his own staff.[35]

McClellan made the mistake of misreading Stanton's friendliness. The new secretary moved into Cameron's office on January 20 and wasted no time taking control. A *New York Times* reporter stopped at the War Department and saw Stanton "standing at his desk in an ante-room . . . a very pleasant gentleman . . . scrupulously neat in appearance, with heavy frame and immense black beard, an intelligent eye and business manner . . . At a glance you knew him to be the Secretary of War." Stanton always stood when working at his desk, but he was not always the pleasant gentleman portrayed by the reporter. He was, however, honest with finances, feverishly energetic, and passionately industrious. He could also be arbitrary, excitable, frequently dishonest in his human relationships, and, as McClellan and others soon discovered, a bully when dealing with professional soldiers.[36]

Stanton also met with Charles A. Dana of the *New York Tribune* on January 24 and told him, perhaps referring to leaks within the department, "As soon as I can get the machinery of the office working, the rats cleared out, and the rat holes stopped we shall move. This army has got to fight or run away . . . the champagne and oysters on the Potomac must be stopped." Stanton meant business. All of McClellan's social activities were being scrutinized by resentful Washingtonians. The general took luxurious meals every afternoon at Wormley's exclusive restaurant and usually invited at least twenty guests who were not friends of the administration. McClellan never learned of Stanton's message to Dana. He still believed he could control the secretary when on January 29 he wrote Marcy, who had also been afflicted with typhoid fever, "I am getting on very well— Stanton's appointment has helped me infinitely so far, & will still more in the future." McClellan was wrong. Stanton disliked and distrusted the general and over time became his most relentless enemy.[37]

At times Stanton also tried to bully Lincoln, but the president never bent. On one occasion an Illinois congressman stopped at the White House to report having just come from the War Department and to say the secretary had called the president a "damned fool." Lincoln reflected for a moment and replied, "If Stanton said I was a damned fool, then I must be one, for he is nearly always right, and generally says what he means. I will step over and see him." The anecdote illustrates the character of the two men. Lincoln tolerated the secretary's behavior in order to use his talents. On important issues Stanton always came out second. With the possible exception of Seward, Lincoln spent more time with Stanton than any other member of the cabinet. Because of arrogance and despotism, Stanton attracted few personal and fewer political friends. Alexander McClure, who came to know the secretary well, wrote, "Taken all in all, Edwin M. Stanton was capable of the grandest and the meanest actions of any great man I have ever known." This was exactly the type of war minister the president needed and not at all the type of man McClellan wanted as his boss.[38]

6

•———————•

"He doesn't intend to do anything"

OR TWO WEEKS, while Lincoln waited for McClellan to reveal his plans, the general did nothing to ease the president's anxiety. Lincoln walked every day from the White House to the War Department to speak with Stanton, read military and Western Union telegrams, and look for any clues providing insight into McClellan's plans. Located on Pennsylvania Avenue at Seventeenth Street, the War Department stood about two blocks from the White House. If battles were being fought, the president sometimes remained at the telegraph office overnight. It also provided a refuge away from the White House where he could sit and think.[1]

The problem during late January continued to be the absence of military activity, and McClellan began absorbing increased pressure from Lincoln and Stanton. Little Mac urged Buell and Halleck to show more fight in the West but received in return a litany of excuses like those he used to justify delay. Frustrated by McClellan's ineffectiveness in getting the western armies in motion, Lincoln wrote directly to Buell on January 13, with a copy to Halleck, and suggested a joint strike. While Halleck menaced Columbus, Kentucky, Buell could threaten Bowling Green and move into East Tennessee. If the enemy concentrated at Bowling Green, Lincoln suggested leaving a blocking force behind to worry the rebels and for Buell to use the bulk of the army to seize Columbus and East Tennessee, adding, "One or both." Because Lincoln framed the letter as a suggestion instead of an order, neither general responded, perhaps waiting for McClellan's endorsement. Two weeks later Lincoln read incoming dispatches and found one message addressed to McClellan from Halleck mentioning plans to send a joint force under General Ulysses Grant and

Flag Officer Andrew Foote against Fort Henry on the Tennessee River, but Buell's messages contained nothing of substance other than being addressed to McClellan informally as "My Dear Friend."[2]

Despite McClellan's assurances to the contrary, the president felt that Halleck and Buell were not cooperating with each other. His observations were correct. Halleck made the decision to send an expedition against Fort Henry without informing Buell until afterward. When Buell asked whether Halleck needed support, Halleck said no, but later, after he had expanded the campaign, Halleck asked Buell to come and serve under him. Sensing Halleck intended to advance his military fortunes, Buell refused. When Buell finally did move, he marched toward Nashville and away from Halleck. McClellan made several efforts to get the two generals to work together but never succeeded. Stressed by the same stunt he had been playing on the president, McClellan wrote Buell, grumbling, "I repeat, both Halleck and yourself keep me too much in the dark."[3]

Disconcerted by McClellan's silence and inactivity in the West, Lincoln yielded to pleas from Stanton and Welles and on January 27, without consulting anybody, read General War Order № 1 to the cabinet—not for their approval but for their information. He directed a general movement of land and naval forces against the enemy on February 22 without saying whether he had intentionally chosen that date, Washington's birthday, for symbolic effect. The order called for launching six simultaneous offenses without stating specific objectives and held Stanton and Welles, along with the general-in-chief, responsible for defining and executing the missions. Welles already had the navy under way for operations on the upper and lower Mississippi and only needed a commitment from the army. Knowing McClellan would find a reason to resist the order, Lincoln issued Special War Order № 1 on January 31to make clear that he expected the Army of the Potomac to implement the Occoquan plan with the immediate objective of seizing Manassas. He also ordered an adequate force be provided to safeguard Washington. Although little different from previous discussions held with McClellan, this time Lincoln put his wishes in the form of a command.[4]

Both orders have been criticized by historians as blatant intrusions into military operations rather than serving to explain the purpose behind them. The January 27 order was political rather than military, intended to protect the administration from accusations of inaction and not to initiate a series of impulsive battles. The order sounded amateurish because it was, and Lincoln would have to find better ways to deflect pressure from Congress and the public. He deserved and received ridicule for selecting a national holiday for an all-out offensive without taking into account weather conditions and military movements already under way, but the order had a purpose. It provided the underlying basis for issuing Special War Order № 1, which forced McClellan to come clean with his undisclosed plan. The two orders stunned McClellan, who immediately protested and asked permission to submit written objections to the president's orders and reasons for supporting his own proposal. Lincoln never expected an all-points attack to begin on February 22, but he got McClellan's full attention and agreed to listen. He also got the attention of McClellan's generals, who whispered among themselves that their leader's star was waning and nothing but swift victory could save him.[5]

For more than five months McClellan had let the political pressure fall on the president because he knew he could. He showed Lincoln respect to his face by calling him "your Excellency" but disrespected him in private. He never developed a professional and compatible working relationship with the president because he chose not to. Although he recognized Lincoln as his political superior, the relationship ended there. McClellan could never accept the possibility that the president understood military strategy as well as political strategy. To demonstrate that military strategy was the exclusive domain of the general-in-chief, McClellan always claimed to have a plan superior to any proposal Lincoln suggested. After communications began on McClellan's Urbanna plan, Lincoln rejected it for the same reasons discussed on December 1, when the general first mentioned, without being specific, a movement by water to somewhere in Virginia.

McClellan worked fast to avoid commencing operations against the rebels at Manassas. He dated his response January 31 but did not deliver the document to Stanton until February 3, having received five questions from Lincoln about the general's "somewhere in Virginia" plan.

1st. Does not your plan involve a greatly larger expenditure of *time* and *money* than mine?

2nd. Wherein is a victory *more certain* by your plan than mine?

3rd. Wherein is a victory *more valuable* by your plan than mine?

4th. . . . Would it not be *less* valuable [because] it would break no
great line of the enemy's communications, while mine would?

5th. In case of a disaster, would not a retreat be more difficult by
your plan than mine?[6]

McClellan hoped to capture Richmond without much fighting, and going through Manassas would cause bloodshed. Lincoln could not understand why McClellan wanted to go to Richmond when General Johnston's army was at Manassas, twenty-five miles away. He made the mistake of saying to McClellan, "If you will give me satisfactory answers to the following questions I shall gladly yield my plan to yours."

McClellan delivered a twenty-two-page reply to Stanton, from whom he expected support. Stanton merely asked for a verbal explanation of the letter's contents and instructed McClellan to take it to the president. Because he believed the Army of the Potomac would be outmatched by superior numbers at Manassas, McClellan argued against the Occoquan plan. Lincoln did not know the size or composition of the Confederate force at Manassas but erroneously assumed McClellan did. After praising himself at length for building the Army of the Potomac, Little Mac explained that while success at Manassas might have the "moral effect of a victory," the enemy would merely retreat. Fighting at Manassas would not end the war, he said, but the one decisive battle he proposed would. McClellan was both right and wrong.

McClellan never properly addressed Lincoln's five short questions. Instead, he proposed landing at Urbanna, a tobacco port on the south bank of the lower Rappahannock River, claiming it as the best place on the Virginia peninsula to land troops because it was more than fifty miles south of Manassas and about forty miles from the gates of Richmond. From Urbanna the army would enjoy good roads in any weather over the shortest possible land route to Richmond. McClellan claimed the entire area was so lightly defended that the movement would force the evacuation of Manassas, thereby eliminating threats on Washington. The Urbanna plan had merit if executed swiftly, but McClellan showed no aptitude for doing anything swiftly.

Little Mac deluded himself by believing enemy forces would behave as he predicted. With the Army of the Potomac wedged between Johnston's troops at Manassas and the Confederate capital, McClellan believed he could force a fight on ground favorable to his army, or he could move against Richmond and force the Confederates to attack him. Perhaps it was too early in the war for Lincoln to observe flaws in McClellan's strategy, which on one hand sounded aggressive but on the other hand suggested the employment of defensive tactics when it came to the actual fighting. It was too early in the president's learning curve to see the inconsistency of mounting an aggressive campaign to fight defensively. Little Mac also considered defeat and identified his escape route as being down the peninsula to Fort Monroe on the lower Chesapeake. Although he intimated no intention of retreating, McClellan counted on surprise because he believed his army would be severely outnumbered if Confederates at Manassas reached Richmond first, but he promised to move rapidly, occupy Richmond, cut communications supporting Johnston's army, and in one rapid sweep through Virginia win the war. To ensure success, Buell would press into Tennessee and the Deep South while Halleck moved down the Mississippi.

After making his points for the Urbanna plan and asserting, "My judgment as a general is clearly in favor of this project," McClellan closed the letter with an alternative. He may have anticipated Lincoln's question, "Why Urbanna?" or simply had second thoughts about his own plan when he wrote, "I would prefer the move from Fortress Monroe as a base—as a certain though less brilliant movement from Urbanna—to an attack upon Manassas." After the general expended some four thousand words justifying the Urbanna expedition, Lincoln might have become curious by McClellan's closing allusion to operating from Fort Monroe as an alternative. This might have struck most men of Lincoln's intelligence as hinting at indecisiveness. There is no record of any challenge, although McClellan claimed to have had several conversations with the president afterward.

Lincoln should have known after seven months of waiting for action that McClellan never did anything rapidly or aggressively, but he approved the general's strategy despite having bothersome reservations. He still believed the Occoquan plan—a pincers movement against Manassas—would be more practical, less expensive, and safer, but McClellan resisted using

Washington as a base to advance through Manassas because, he argued, the army would have to wait until mud-sloughed roads dried, while all the roads on Virginia's sandy peninsula would be usable and the army could move without hindrance. McClellan knew nothing about the horrible road conditions in Virginia but claimed he did. After many sessions with the general on the procurement of water transport, Lincoln finally agreed the Urbanna expedition might work if executed with speed and good generalship. McClellan had not been tested in the field against a large army, and if he demonstrated the same ability as a field commander as he did organizing the Army of the Potomac, positive results could be expected. Lincoln still had lingering doubts and three courses of action. He could force McClellan to adopt the Occoquan plan, which the general resisted as fatally flawed; he could remove McClellan but without a successor; or he could concede. On February 14 he reluctantly approved the Urbanna plan and authorized the War Department to make arrangements for acquiring transports. He waited until February 27 before issuing orders to actually obtain the ships. By then Lincoln's Special War Order № 1 had expired without ever being rescinded.[7]

In fashioning his letter justifying the Urbanna plan, McClellan did not do his homework, nor did Lincoln. One moot question remained unanswered and unasked. Could Johnston reach Richmond faster from Manassas than McClellan from Urbanna? By landing at Urbanna and assaulting Richmond, the Army of the Potomac would not have broken Confederate communications with Manassas. Two important railroads served Manassas; the Richmond, Fredericksburg & Potomac and the Orange & Alexandria. Lincoln's proposed Occoquan plan would have severed them both. The other puzzle concerned the size of the Confederate force at Manassas. Pinkerton's latest report pegged Confederate forces at 115,000 men with three hundred field guns and up to thirty siege guns. Johnston's last report to Richmond listed 23,440 present. With only 1,300 officers and men serving in the artillery, there could not have been more than a hundred guns. McClellan accepted Pinkerton's report without performing reconnaissance to confirm it, and Lincoln and Stanton accepted the figures because the general trusted his spymaster. During the next five months McClellan prepared every battle plan assuming the enemy was twice his strength.[8]

Such questions no longer made much difference. McClellan had gotten his way, which reinvigorated the general and made him happy with the "gorilla" again. "You have been a kind true friend to me . . . during the last three months," he wrote. "Your confidence has upheld me when I should otherwise have felt weak." The president continued to have doubts about the Urbanna plan, but he would not force an unwanted plan on his general-in-chief. McClellan had compromised the potential success of the movement by promising months ago never to leave Washington unprotected. Although Little Mac predicted that Johnston would evacuate Manassas as soon as Union forces threatened Richmond and any troops left behind to protect the capital would be wasted, the president refused to relent. If McClellan's numbers were correct, and Johnston had 115,000 troops twenty-five miles away at Manassas, it would be a dangerous gambit to shift the Army of the Potomac to Richmond. There were leaks to the press, partly because of McClellan's secret relationship with Malcolm Ives from James Gordon Bennett's *New York Herald,* and if Johnston pounced on Washington while the army was in transit, the result could be disastrous.[9]

Combined with his concerns about McClellan's dangerous venture, personal grief from a closer source knocked Lincoln off balance. In early February his eleven-year-old son, William Wallace, whom the family called Willie, fell ill with "bilious fever," probably typhoid from Washington's polluted water. During the next two weeks eight-year-old Thomas, known as Tad, became ill but recovered. When Willie died on February 20, Lincoln burst into tears. The funeral took place at the White House, and when the president looked into his son's face, his voice cracked when he said, "He was too good for this earth . . . but then we loved him so." For several days afterward Lincoln would retire to his room to weep, and his wife's grief was even more devastating than his. Beyond sadness, and topping every other concern, was McClellan's problematic Urbanna plan. Stanton tried to console the president because his own youngest son, James, suffered from a reaction to a vaccine and later died at the age of nine months. During those long days neither Lincoln nor Stanton spent much time with McClellan, but the general recognized the deep sadness felt by the president and, in addition to expressing sympathy, wrote, "I beg that you will not allow military affairs to give you one moment's trouble

. . . nothing shall be left undone to [delay] an auspicious commencement of our new campaign." Although McClellan meant the genuine and caring letter to be comforting, the last sentence renewed the president's misgivings about the forthcoming expedition.[10]

McClellan should never have proceeded with the Urbanna plan knowing Lincoln and Stanton still remained doubtful. The Urbanna plan had merit, but so did Lincoln's Occoquan plan. Little Mac should have attacked Manassas, and even if victory eluded him, which was unlikely in view of the actual disparity of numbers, the effort would have strengthened the public's opinion of the administration. Instead, McClellan impertinently proceeded with his own plan and expected to have his way with everything, never suspecting or particularly caring whether his behavior and stubbornness jeopardized relations with his superiors. Lincoln would soon come to realize that his general, through arrogance, obstinacy, or ineptitude, would form hasty judgments and refuse to adjust them to actual conditions.

Lincoln also failed as commander-in-chief. After first disapproving the Urbanna plan for valid reasons, he then approved it. Having taken this step, he questioned his own decision for a month before authorizing the required water transportation. He discussed with the cabinet minor movements to guarantee the safety of the capital. One involved the capture of Winchester and Strasburg, thereby blocking the lower Shenandoah Valley and rebuilding the Baltimore & Ohio bridge destroyed at Harpers Ferry. Doing so would reopen the railroad to the Ohio River and speed the movement of troops and supplies. McClellan approved the plan and ordered General Nathaniel Banks to move his division to Harpers Ferry, protect the bridge workers, and capture and hold Winchester against Confederate raids.

McClellan's promise to leave nothing undone suffered a rude setback in late February, when he joined General Banks to watch Federal engineers throw a pontoon bridge across the Potomac River at Harpers Ferry. Bands played and soldiers cheered as part of Banks's division crossed from Maryland to retake possession of the town. Little Mac telegraphed the good news to Stanton and asked that several officers from the engineer corps be brevetted for their fine work.[11]

McClellan's celebration ended abruptly the following day when the timbers and struts to rebuild the bridge failed to arrive. A flotilla of special boats, designed by the engineers, had been built to transport construction materials over the Chesapeake and Ohio Canal, which ran along the north bank of the Potomac across from Harpers Ferry. The boats carrying the spans had to pass through a lift lock opening into the river. When the first boat jammed, engineers discovered they had designed the craft six inches wider than the lock. McClellan advised Stanton of the difficulty and said he would have to deploy more troops on both sides of the Potomac and find another way to get the bridge-building materials across the river.[12]

Stanton went directly to the White House, closed the door to Lincoln's office, and turned the key. He said Banks's Winchester campaign had been canceled because McClellan's canal boats were too wide to pass through the lock. Because the occupation of Winchester had been designed to hold Stonewall Jackson's Confederates in the valley during the launch of McClellan's Urbanna plan, Lincoln asked, "What does this mean?"

"It means," Stanton replied, "that it is a damned fizzle. It means that he doesn't intend to do anything?"

Devastated by the news, Lincoln collected himself and asked how McClellan could let this happen. The Young Napoleon had promised success, and now this. As Stanton prepared to leave, he asked, "Mr. President, how about those brevets?" Lincoln muttered under his breath, and the secretary departed without waiting for an answer.

McClellan avoided Washington and sent his father-in-law to face the critics. After a sharp discussion Lincoln asked Marcy: "Why . . . couldn't the General have known whether a boat would go through that lock before spending a million dollars getting them there? . . . common sense would teach me to go and measure it. I am almost despairing of these results. Everything seems to fail. The impression is growing that the General intends to do nothing." Marcy said he was certain the general could explain everything. Lincoln expressed doubt and unceremoniously dismissed him. Marcy promptly reported the meeting to his son-in-law and described the president as "in a hell of a rage." When McClellan returned to Washington, Lincoln avoided him for two days. Brigadier General Marsena R. Patrick picked up rumors in the War Department, noting McClellan's influence as dropping to "good for nothing." When asked what happened at Harpers Ferry, Chase tersely replied, "It died of lockjaw." Horace White of the *Chicago Tribune* groaned, "It was Ball's Bluff all over again, minus the slaughter."[13]

McClellan's return to Washington provoked another altercation with the president. The capital buzzed with rumors of McClellan's disloyalty, and Lincoln and Stanton began to wonder if the gossip was true. Radicals in Congress said the general had a secret strategy never to damage the South severely but to restore the Union without emancipation and without centralizing national power. They also accused General Marcy of being in sympathy with the South and influencing his son-in-law into "playing politics, not war." In a November conversation with Assistant Secretary of War Peter W. Watson, McClellan disagreed with the department's view that unrestricted war was necessary to subject the South. He said the North should avoid harshness and show the South no more aggressiveness than necessary. "If I felt as you do," McClellan told Watson, "I would lay down my arms!" A few weeks later Zachariah Chandler told the Senate, "I am informed that a very large number of [McClellan's] generals in command to-day have more sympathy with the enemy than they have with the local cause." Chandler spread the word, claiming McClellan had surrounded himself with pets espousing traitorous intentions. Lincoln picked up on the scuttlebutt, grumbling, "Delay is ruining us."[14]

Horace Greeley of the *New York Tribune* began publishing rumors of McClellan's plan to seek a compromise with the South by driving up the cost of war without fighting, thereby discouraging the North and buying peace from Jefferson Davis without admitting defeat. With the country turning against McClellan, Seward wondered how long the president would sustain him. Stanton wondered too. Having lost all confidence in McClellan, he accused the general of taking credit for Grant's victories at Fort Henry and Fort Donelson while doing nothing in Virginia. Little Mac was actually conferring with his generals to find a way to clear out Confederate batteries on the lower Potomac, which were impeding his movement to Urbanna. The Committee on the Conduct of the War had also been haranguing the general to wipe out "that disgrace to the nation—the blockade of the Potomac and the siege of our capital." McClellan knew it had to be done, but he deeply resented comments from Senator Benjamin Wade, chairman of the committee, who said the army should be put to work whipping the rebels, and if they could not win a victory, "let them come back in their coffins." The committee held a session in the basement of the Capitol, where they badgered and probed at McClellan and his officers with relentless accusations. During McClellan's confrontation with the committee, he received no support from Stanton. "I hope to open the Potomac this week," he confided to Halleck, and move "the whole Army in order to keep 'Manassas' off my back. I have but few friends in Congress," he added. "[The] abolitionists are doing their best to displace me & I shall be content if I can keep my head above water until I am ready to strike the final blow." He would not get much empathy from Halleck, who was conducting successful operations in the West and looked for opportunities if McClellan failed. Members of Congress also asked questions about McClellan's camp equipage, which consisted of six immense four-horse carriages daily drawn up before the general's door, each marked "Headquarters of the Army of the Potomac." One reporter contrasted Little Mac with Grant, who had taken the field with only a spare shirt, a hairbrush, and a toothbrush.[15]

Having reached the limit of his exasperation, Lincoln summoned McClellan to the White House on the morning of March 7 to question his stalling and to revisit the Urbanna plan, which some cabinet members and a host of critics viewed as the general's traitorous scheme to leave Washington defenseless. After explaining what measures he took at Harpers Ferry, McClellan said the president "adverted to the more serious—or ugly—matter" stemming from rumors of disloyalty. Lincoln never believed McClellan disloyal but felt compelled to warn him others did. Bates felt the same way, writing: "I cannot concur in believing McC[lellan] a traitor. With more charity I conclude that he is only a foolish egot." Before the president could explain reasons for the allegations, the general jumped to his feet, hotly demanded a retraction, and said he could permit no one to couple his name with the word *treason*. Lincoln said he only intended to repeat what others had said. According to McClellan, Lincoln apologized several times, which is unlikely, but the general departed from the White House obsessed and repelled by accusations of disloyalty. Other than McClellan's comments, no records were kept of this meeting. According to Orville Browning, McClellan later "shed tears when speaking of the cruel imputations upon his loyalty." Fearing he might lose both his command and his splendid campaign, Little Mac promised to meet with his generals to reevaluate the Urbanna movement strictly on the merits of the strategy and without his personal input, after which the president could decide whether he was a traitor or not. Lincoln decided that if all of McClellan's generals believed in the plan, it must be workable, even if it conflicted with his own personal judgment. Stanton warned against giving McClellan the upper hand, but Lincoln ignored the advice. Any major field operation would take pressure off the president, especially if it succeeded.[16]

McClellan summoned his generals that morning for the Army of the Potomac's first official council of war. As promised, he removed himself from the initial discussions and turned the meeting over to his father-in-law, Chief of Staff Marcy. Twelve brigadier generals spent several hours going over the Urbanna plan, which some conferees learned about for the first time. Marcy then brought McClellan into the conference room with a map of eastern Virginia to explain the details and answer questions. McClelland then left the room to let the generals deliberate and vote in private. Eight division commanders voted for the Urbanna plan, one with conditions, and four favored a direct advance on Manassas. General Heintzelman, who with Barnard, McDowell, and Sumner preferred assaulting Manassas, later recorded in his diary that Marcy took him aside and said that McClellan's future was at stake and strong movements were under way in the War Department "to have him superceded [sic] & that he would be unless we approved his plan."

Satisfied his strategy would be supported by at least eight generals—those being Louis Blenker, William B. Franklin, Erasmus D. Keyes, George A. McCall, Henry M. Neglee, Andrew Porter, Fitz-John Porter, and William F. Smith—McClellan concluded the meeting and in late afternoon sent his twelve division commanders with a thirty-five hundred–word written discursive to the White House. Most of the eight generals owed their present status to McClellan and put loyalty to the commanding general first. Little Mac's recording secretary read the meeting minutes, after which Lincoln discussed the details. Having exhausted his questions, the president admitted not being a military man and agreed to accept the conclusions of the majority. He still had reservations but said nothing except to Stanton: "We can do nothing else but accept their plan and discard all others . . . We can't reject it and adopt another without assuming all the responsibility in the case of the failure of the one we adopt." Had Lincoln evaluated the political antecedents of the twelve generals participating in the discussions, he might have recognized that the four senior officers opposing the Urbanna plan were Republicans, and seven of the eight officers favoring the plan were McClellan's "pets," as Stanton called them. With the exception of Keyes, they were also conservative Democrats who opposed emancipation and spoke disparagingly against radicals.[17]

Using his prosecutorial skills, Stanton tried to kill the plan by furiously cross-examining the eight generals. Lincoln felt he had made a pact with McClellan and, to Stanton's chagrin, reluctantly abided by it. In giving the general his way, Lincoln lost more of his own prestige. McClellan felt he had outmaneuvered the president, marking March 8, 1862, as the official beginning of the Peninsular Campaign. He later wrote, "I heard no more of treason in that connection," at least temporarily ending growing accusations that he would not fight. Historian Joseph T. Glatthaar correctly assessed the underlying conflict between the two men, writing, "McClellan believed that politicians should determine when and where the nation engaged in war, but then turn over all details of war fighting to military professionals." Lincoln, however, understood that the North "held him accountable for the outcome of the war, and that he had a constitutional obligation to oversee all military activities." Lincoln intended to remain watchful and intervene whenever his general crossed the line, and this arrangement led to a deeply troubled relationship in the days ahead.[18]

Much later the four generals favoring the Manassas movement (Occoquan plan) claimed McClellan never mentioned it and only discussed why the army should change its base from Washington to the Virginia Peninsula and what action should be taken to rid the Potomac of enemy batteries. Chief Engineer Barnard called the movement by water impractical and complained the vote was taken without discussing his objections. In the days ahead, while acting as the army's liaison with the navy, Barnard provided McClellan with little help because he doubted the efficacy of the plan and resented having his views ignored. The army's three senior generals—Samuel Heintzelman, Irvin McDowell, and Edwin Sumner—said the only purpose of the meeting was to rubber-stamp the Urbanna plan. Erasmus Keyes, fourth in seniority, played into McClellan's scheme by saying he would only vote for the Urbanna plan if rebel batteries were removed from the Potomac. Sumner and McDowell, though they preferred the Occoquan plan, agreed the Potomac batteries had to be eliminated. General Marcy later admitted the entire meeting had been staged by his son-in-law to end discussion on the Manassas option and to justify delay. Stanton expressed disgust and told John Hay, "We saw ten generals afraid to fight." As Stanton feared, Little Mac used his generals to get his way, and Lincoln obtained another lesson in army politics.[19]

7

"McClellan seems not to value
time especially"

INCOLN STILL CONSIDERED the Urbanna plan unwise, too expensive, and dangerous. Although he had taken the unusual step of not adopting the plan until he sounded out McClellan's generals, he could not shake a feeling of uneasiness. After meeting with McClellan's twelve division commanders, Lincoln began exerting his authority, having developed concerns about the general's unwieldy organization for operations in the field. After discussions with the war secretary, Stanton's allies among the Committee on the Conduct of the War, and military men familiar with Napoleon's campaigns, Lincoln issued General War Order № 2, which divided the Army of the Potomac into four corps. He named McDowell commander of the First Corps, with four divisions; Sumner commander of the Second Corps, with three divisions; Heintzelman commander of the Third Corps, with three divisions; and Keyes commander of the Fourth Corps, with three divisions.

Little Mac disliked presidential intrusions and balked. Although Lincoln took seniority into consideration when making the appointments, McClellan wanted to promote friends, in particular William Franklin and Fitz-John Porter. Lincoln also named Brigadier General James Wadsworth, one of the army's many political generals, to command Washington's defenses, and he elevated Major General Nathaniel Banks, another political general, to command the Department of the Shenandoah. McClellan had already committed the Washington post to Major General John A. Dix, a much better choice, but Little Mac had never made it official when he had the opportunity. Lincoln merely did what he thought necessary, and McClellan had nobody to blame but himself for procrastinating. He later and justifiably complained to Stanton about the appointment of Wadsworth, which had been made for political reasons to placate the radicals, because the general was not "a soldier by training" or "fully posted in all the details of the profession." McClellan had other reasons to complain. Wadsworth was a Republican, an ardent abolitionist, and officially in conversation had criticized Little Mac for not advancing into Virginia through Manassas.[1]

With more than 130,000 troops involved, organizing the army into four corps made military sense, but Lincoln expected McClellan to oppose the order because the designated corps commanders were Republicans and the majority of their subordinates, the division commanders, including Porter and Franklin, were Democrats. True to form, the general objected to the arrangement partly because it came from the president and partly because the corps commanders named by Lincoln were the very Republican generals who had opposed the Urbanna plan. Stanton liked the arrangement because he thought he and the radical alliance on the Committee on the Conduct of the War could more easily control McClellan and his division commanders. McClellan had repeatedly planned to divide his army into corps but kept putting it off. Because Lincoln demanded it be done, McClellan asked Stanton on March 9 to suspend the order temporarily, "until the present movement is over," explaining his generals should be tested in battle to determine their fitness for corps command. He also did not want his decisions hampered by corps commanders who were Republicans, though he never specifically mentioned it to Stanton. The secretary replied, "I think it is the duty of every officer to obey the president's orders, nor can I see any reason why you should not obey them." Stanton liked the order and regarded it as a clever maneuver to weaken McClellan's authority. McClellan eventually relented but, to have his own way, made the promotions retroactive to March 3, five days prior to the president's order. The choice of corps commanders created a problem. None of the four generals trusted McClellan, nor did McClellan trust them.[2]

Members of the Committee on the Conduct of the War watched the convolutions in the White House with impatience. They wanted McClellan dismissed, and so did Stanton, but the committee also wanted a Republican running the army and not a Democrat. Knowing the president could not be bullied into replacing the Young Napoleon, Stanton lost a pledge he had made to his radical friends to try one commander after another until he found one who would win battles. The committee approved of breaking the army into corps but not for the reason Lincoln intended. Stanton liked the idea because he believed it would weaken McClellan's authority and force him to confer with his corps commanders, but in regard to this objective he would be disappointed.[3]

Three incidents on March 8 threatened to frustrate McClellan's Urbanna venture, and the first one concerned Lincoln's reservations about changing the operating base from Washington to Virginia's peninsula. The president issued General War Order № 3, again without conferring with McClellan, and specifically instructed him to leave a sufficient force to safeguard the capital and to send no more than fifty thousand troops to Urbanna until every enemy battery and obstruction had been removed from the Potomac. Because McClellan avoided discussions about timetables, and knowing the general's habit of procrastination, Lincoln set March 18 as the target date for transporting the first troops to Urbanna. He also issued immediate orders for the navy to cooperate with the army. McClellan's partisans severely criticized the order because it demanded the protection of Washington and that everything be done in ten days. Lincoln used poor judgment in demanding this deadline, but his intention was to induce activity. He also feared the movement, which depended on surprise, would be detected by the Confederates if the date were extended. McClellan justifiably complained because obtaining the transportation for the movement had been taken out of his hands by the War Department. Stanton had intentionally given the assignment to Assistant Secretary of War John Tucker because he recalled the unfortunate canal boat episode at Harpers Ferry and wanted to avoid another "fizzle."[4]

A second incident on March 8 threatened to end the Urbanna expedition. While discussions with McClellan and his generals were under way at the White House, the CSS *Virginia* (formerly the USS *Merrimack,* sometimes spelled *Merrimac*) steamed into Hampton Roads at the mouth of the James River, destroyed two Union frigates, the *Congress* and the *Cumberland,* and drove the USS *Minnesota* aground. The news did not reach Washington until later, and Lincoln wondered how this disaster might impact McClellan's plans if the *Virginia* steamed into Chesapeake Bay. The navy had only wooden gunboats to confront the formidable ironclad. On the morning of March 9, after conferring with Captain John A. Dahlgren at the Washington Navy Yard, Lincoln returned to the White House and found Stanton, McClellan, Welles, Seward, Watson, Meigs, and Nicolay waiting. According to Welles, Stanton paced back and forth in great anxiety, going to the window every few minutes to gaze toward the Potomac, pausing briefly to condemn the navy for doing nothing. "The *Merrimac*," he declared, "would destroy every vessel in the service, could lay every city on the coast under contribution, [and] could take Fortress Monroe." After catching his breath, Stanton said the Urbanna plan must be abandoned and expressed concern for the safety of General Ambrose Burnside's force in the Carolinas.

After returning from another trip to the window, Stanton said he expected the ironclad to ascend the Potomac, disperse Congress, and destroy the capital. He stared menacingly at Welles and asked what was being done to check the ironclad's advance on New York and Boston. Welles said the USS *Monitor* would soon reach Hampton Roads and to expect a battle. Having never heard of the *Monitor,* Stanton asked about the ship's armament. When Welles said two guns, Stanton stormed furiously about the room. Lincoln expressed no concern because Welles had told him the *Virginia* would go aground if it tried to ascend the Potomac. The following day McClellan was with the president and Stanton when the message arrived that the two ironclads had fought to a draw and the *Virginia* had retreated. Nicolay and Hay said the general reacted to the news "with incredulity, which at last gave way to stupefaction," thus saving the Urbanna plan. Stanton believed McClellan might yet find some excuse to postpone the expedition and assured him, "Nothing you can ask of me or of this Department will be spared to aid you in every particular."[5]

The third incident on March 8 took McClellan completely by surprise. Confederates began withdrawing from Manassas and took batteries along the Potomac with them. On March 9 the Young Napoleon rode to the old Bull Run battlefield to verify the report. On returning to Washington, he claimed to have anticipated the withdrawal, which, he said, was the reason why he had always resisted attacking Manassas. He also penned a letter to Samuel Barlow, bragging, "My movements gave us Manassas with one loss of life—history will record it as the brightest passage of my life that I accomplished so much at so small a cost." That night he telegraphed

Stanton, again attempting to suspend the president's corps order because he did not want to put his army in motion while reorganizing it. He said any delay in revoking the suspension would force him to call off the advance. Not wanting to hinder the long-awaited offensive and expecting the general to pursue the Confederates immediately, Stanton spoke with the president and agreed to McClellan's proposal. McClellan later proudly admitted the ploy worked because he put Stanton in the untenable position of expressing "unnecessary opposition" to a simple request.[6]

McClellan executed one of the most bewildering movements in military history. He marched his magnificently appointed army with all its impressive might to Manassas and, as reported, found the Confederate position abandoned. In the formidable rebel earthworks he witnessed another embarrassing sight, which resulted in, said Carl Schurz, "a burst of grim laughter all over the country." Wooden Quaker guns painted black, their barrels poking out of dirt thrown up to resemble embrasures, had held McClellan back for months. Historian Stephen W. Sears wrote, "The Quaker guns . . . came as one more public embarrassment to a general who had not blushed at being compared to the great Bonaparte." General Johnston merely moved his army to a better defensive position along the Rappahannock River but not because, as McClellan later claimed, the Confederates had learned of his projected movement to Urbanna. Johnston worried about a Federal flanking movement toward Aquia, much like Lincoln had suggested with the Occoquan plan.

Little Mac propagated the story of maneuvering Johnston out of Manassas and repeated it until others accepted the myth as historical fact. On February 22 Jeff Davis, his cabinet, and General Robert E. Lee knew of McClellan's superiority in numbers and decided Johnston's position at Manassas had become untenable. After removing his outposts from nearby Centreville, Johnston quietly and deliberately began the retrograde movement from Manassas, the last rebel unit retiring twenty-four hours before Union troops arrived. Pinkerton's spies and poor Federal reconnaissance never observed the withdrawal until March 7, when Confederates began destroying winter huts, machine shops, and broken-down locomotives. In a letter to a subordinate Johnston made an astute observation, writing, "McClellan . . . seems not to value time especially."[7]

Congress regarded McClellan's tardy movement to Manassas as simply a stupid promenade, which intensified their disapprobation of the general, and they blamed Lincoln for retaining such a commander. George Julian, speaking for the Committee on the Conduct of the War, euphemistically recalled, "They were certain, at all events, that his [McClellan's] heart was not in the work." Even John Hay expressed concern, writing, "People said a great deal about it and thought a great deal more." Lincoln's allies among the conservatives questioned McClellan's motives, but like the president, they expected the general to pursue the enemy with speed and energy. So did Lincoln, and he anticipated a serious battle before the Confederates dug in along the Rappahannock. Federal cavalry looking for Johnston's army found part of it at Warrenton Junction on the Orange & Alexandria Railroad. Instead of fighting, McClellan recalled the pursuit. Lincoln never learned of the circumstances because McClellan never reported it. Instead, McClellan ordered Banks to entrench at Manassas, which was his way of supposedly defending Washington with troops previously assigned to safeguarding the Shenandoah Valley. This was also Little Mac's way of not diminishing the size of the Army of the Potomac, which he still planned to take to the Virginia Peninsula. McClellan's order created enormous problems for Banks, and it would soon create problems for himself.[8]

McClellan seemed more interested in embarrassing McDowell, who had lost the battle of Bull Run in July 1861. During a grand parade across the old battlefield, McClellan cowed McDowell into stepping before his division and presenting the story of the battle. Little Mac chose a location where skulls and human bones picked by crows and turkey vultures lay scattered on the ground. Tears welled in McDowell's eyes as he spoke with humiliation and regret. McClellan stood by, enjoying McDowell's degradation, and said nothing. Why McClellan insisted on such an unseemly display probably emanated from the recent clash of opinions between him and McDowell over the Urbanna plan.[9]

From Lincoln's perspective Johnston's withdrawal to the south side of the Rappahannock made it impossible for McClellan to carry out the Urbanna plan, which relied on Federal control of the lower river. He expected McClellan to pursue Johnston to Fredericksburg and fight him with tenacity. Believing the Urbanna plan had been scrapped, Lincoln held a cabinet meeting on March 11 to express his relief and to discuss other matters. By then McClellan's friends in the administration also began registering doubts about the general's lack of aggressiveness. Stanton, however, having lost all patience with McClellan, launched into a tirade and blamed the general for causing massive confusion in the War Department. He claimed McClellan could not be trusted because he doctored his reports and concealed his plans. He accused the general of "reckless extravagance" and demanded the armies and the country be relieved of "the Potomac incubus." Bates supported the secretary and said, "I think Stanton believes, as I do, that McC[lellan] has no plans but is fumbling and plunging in confusion and darkness." He later added, "Upon the whole, it seems that our genl. went with his finger in his mouth, on a fool's errand, and that he has won a fool's reward." He urged Lincoln to exercise the power granted by the Constitution and "command the commanders."[10]

Lincoln spent the afternoon in thought and during the evening summoned Chase, Seward, and Stanton to his office. Seward arrived before the others, and the president read War Order № 3, stating that as McClellan had taken the field at the head of the Army of the Potomac, he would now be relieved as general-in-chief and would command only the Department of the Potomac. Halleck would command the Department of the Mississippi, with Buell in Kentucky and Tennessee and David Hunter in Arkansas, Kansas, and Missouri. Lincoln also created the Mountain Department in western Virginia with General John Frémont in command. After reorganizing the entire army, he ordered all department commanders to report directly to Stanton, which created a conundrum of having eight independent Federal military departments in the East with no general-in-chief to command them. Seward agreed with the order and thought the president was doing McClellan "a very great kindness in permitting him to retain command of the Army of the Potomac" and giving him "an opportunity to retrieve his errors." Seward thought the order should go out in Stanton's name to strengthen the public's confidence in the secretary. Stanton arrived at that moment and, though immensely pleased by the directive, argued the order should be issued by the president; otherwise, McClellan's friends would accuse the secretary of having demoted the general because of personal vindictiveness. Lincoln agreed and signed the order. The action partly appeased the radicals, although many in Congress wanted McClellan dismissed. The president no longer had a general-in-chief and, partnering with Stanton, assumed the role himself. Major General Emory Upton of the Army of the Potomac criticized the arrangement because neither Lincoln nor Stanton had demonstrated any knowledge of the art of war. Stanton immediately seized the papers in the War Office, which had been McClellan's headquarters in his capacity as general-in-chief, and Lincoln took Bates's advice to "command the commanders" and never again completely yielded that authority to anyone.[11]

Shackled by having army commanders reporting to him, Stanton wanted the power but not all the responsibility. He insisted on having a military man as an advisor and appointed Major General Ethan Allen Hitchcock, a sixty-three-year-old former Indian fighter in poor health and unfit for field service. Hitchcock never wanted to be a soldier, but his family forced him into West Point to carry on the tradition of his grandfather, the Revolutionary hero whose name he bore. Hitchcock resigned from the army in 1855 to pursue his interest in science, philosophy, and spiritualism. A devout pantheist with a passion for the metaphysical, Hitchcock decided to spend his life in study and began writing thick volumes on alchemy and other abstruse subjects. He expressed astonishment when Stanton once asked if he would be interested in commanding the Army of the Potomac, which would have been a disaster because Hitchcock preferred the comfort of a desk. Had the war minister discussed this proposal with the president, Lincoln would have vetoed it. Even Hitchcock, after speaking with Stanton, noted in his diary: "Now—what is to become of this? I want no command. I want no department . . . On the whole, I am uncomfortable. I am almost afraid that Secretary Stanton hardly knows what he wants, himself." Hitchcock was right. The war chief was already muddling through the dregs of the old army looking for McClellan's replacement.

Later Stanton tried a different approach. He expounded on a litany of examples of McClellan's incompetence, accusing him of being "under the influence of Jeff Davis." He came close to driving the old Indian fighter to tears by declaring that Little Mac would not be willing to do anything "calculated greatly to damage the cause of secession." Stanton took Hitchcock to Lincoln and said he wanted him as an advisor. The president knew he had overloaded Stanton and approved the request. Hitchcock accepted the post. He did neither Stanton nor Lincoln much good as a military advisor but excelled as an interesting conversationalist. Hitchcock eventually found his niche as commissioner for the exchange of prisoners, which he performed with skill. McClellan naturally disagreed with the appointment, with good reason.[12]

Lincoln confided his reasons for demoting the Young Napoleon to Governor William Dennison of Ohio, knowing whatever he said to Dennison would get back to McClellan. It did. Dennison invited McClellan to Washington for an urgent conversation, but the general interpreted the summons as a ploy to force his resignation. General Marcy had remained behind in Washington and late on March 11 received a telegram from McClellan, which read, "I think the less I see of Washington the better." With his ego unhinged by what he discovered at Manassas, he remained in the field another day to avoid the military guillotine. Many years later he criticized the administration for having first leaked news of his demotion to the press and complained because "no one in authority had ever expressed to [him] the slightest disapprobation" of his performance as general-in-chief. As a matter of record, McClellan learned of his demotion through Marcy and not the press. As usual, McClellan suspected a conspiracy led by Stanton and wrote his wife: "I regret that the rascals are after me again. If I can get out of this scrape you will never catch me in the power of such a set again—the idea of persecuting a man behind his back." After meeting with Dennison, his whole composure changed. Soon afterward McClellan thanked the president in a letter of patriotic self-abnegation, expressing "official confidence & kind personal feelings" and pledged "no feeling of self interest or ambition should ever prevent me from devoting myself to your service." Statements like this exposed the better side of Little Mac, although he asked his wife to say nothing about his demotion. He also thanked the president for the opportunity to prove himself as a military commander and promised that "no consideration of self will in any manner interfere with the discharge of my public duties." One might wonder what McClellan meant by "public duties" as opposed to military duties, and the answer to that question began unfolding four months later. Meanwhile, the general expressed renewed confidence in Lincoln, writing, "The President is all right—he is my strongest friend." McClellan needed a strong friend because the radicals, with help from Stanton, persisted with an unrelenting campaign to destroy him.[13]

McClellan did not believe his demotion would be permanent because the removal clause read "until otherwise ordered," which implied that Lincoln intended the demotion to be temporary, making it easier for Mc-Clellan to accept it graciously. Alexander McClure, one of the president's close friends, spoke with Lincoln and received the same impression. Although out of patience with McClellan, Lincoln remained willing to bestow high rewards on generals achieving great victories. The Young Napoleon knew he had to be tested in the field and realized the president had done him a favor by making it possible for him to concentrate his full energies on capturing Richmond. What neither the novice president nor his novice general understood was the possible damage done to spring operations by depriving McClellan of the coordination of planned operations in the West with the upcoming Peninsular Campaign. Stanton could not manage field operations, and neither could Lincoln.[14]

With the army in motion, Lincoln looked anxiously to McClellan's first big battle. He yearned to shorten the war but still suffered anxiety from one annoying question—would McClellan fight?

8

"The stride of a giant"

BY RETREATING TO DEFENSIVE POSITIONS on the Rappahannock near Fredericksburg, Virginia, General Johnston defeated McClellan's Urbanna plan without firing a shot. Instead
of pursuing Johnston, McClellan returned to Washington with
most of his army. He claimed the purpose of the movement had been
to expose the troops to the rigors of campaigning. Holding Manassas
as a launching platform into Virginia and securing the railroads would
have made more sense, but doing nothing made the general look foolish.
Within days the entire country learned the truth—McClellan had been
afraid to fight thirty thousand rebels.

The Young Napoleon considered his options. Because the Urbanna
plan had died the day Johnston withdrew, should he pursue the Confederates or find another way to capture Richmond without heavy bloodshed?
On March 12, while languishing in an abandoned house at Fairfax Court
House, near Centreville, he wrote Assistant Secretary of the Navy Gustavus
Vasa Fox, asking, "Can I rely on the *Monitor* to keep the *Merrimac* in check,
so I can take Fortress Monroe as a base of operations?" Fox replied, "The
Monitor may, and I think will, destroy the *Merrimac* in the next fight; but
this is hope, not certainty." In a postscript Fox added, "In my opinion the
Merrimac does not intend to pass by Fort Monroe," which Little Mac interpreted to mean the Urbanna plan could be replaced by the Fort Monroe
plan. In a February 3 letter to the president he had mentioned Fort Monroe as an alternative base where he could operate "with complete security,
although with less celerity."[1]

Anyone probing McClellan's thoughts as he churned up reasons to
transport the army to Fort Monroe might find a general anxious to pro-

long the time before he had to fight. The movement would take the army to a peninsula seven to fifteen miles wide and fifty miles long between the York and James rivers. From Yorktown, McClellan believed a good road led through low, flat country to Williamsburg and then to Richmond. Flanking the road were marshy and heavily wooded sections unknown to the general. Fort Monroe lay at the tip of the Peninsula where the James River, passing through Hampton Roads, emptied into Chesapeake Bay. The formidable fort offered a secure location for establishing a line of communications but certainly not as secure or as convenient as Washington. Expecting Lincoln to challenge the Fort Monroe plan and demand a second council of war, McClellan attempted to avoid another annoying episode with the administration and ordered his generals to meet with him at Fairfax Court House. The captive audience of Heintzelman, Keyes, McDowell, and Sumner, the four corps commanders, and Barnard, the army's chief engineer, approved the Fort Monroe plan but with conditions: the navy must suppress the CSS *Virginia* (*Merrimack*) and destroy rebel batteries on the York River, and the War Department must provide water transportation. Fox addressed the issue of the *Virginia* without addressing the destruction of rebel batteries on the York River because McClellan had never mentioned it in his earlier telegram. In regard to the president's March 8 edict demanding the protection of Washington, the generals agreed without agreeing on the size of the force. General Sumner suggested forty thousand troops for Washington, and Heintzelman, Keyes, and McDowell recommended another twenty-five thousand for the protection of northern Virginia.[2]

McClellan had what he wanted, and the strategy had potential if executed swiftly. Little Mac adjourned the council and sent McDowell—whose relations with Stanton were better than his own—to Washington with a copy of the Fort Monroe plan. Stanton, still wanting McClellan dismissed, wondered why the general had made McDowell, who had always supported the Manassas plan, the messenger. With mounting suspicion Stanton wrote Little Mac, asking if the "purported plan . . . is your plan." McClellan replied it was and said if the administration approved the strategy he would initiate operations immediately. Stanton took the proposal to the White House, and Lincoln, already frustrated and not wanting to impede McClellan's progress, approved the movement with three stipulations:

Manassas must be occupied, Washington safeguarded, and the rest of the army placed in immediate pursuit of the enemy. Cabinet debates followed, challenging the necessity of maintaining a large force at Manassas, thereby depriving McClellan of troops, but the administration had no insurance against the possibility of the Army of the Potomac becoming bogged down on the Peninsula and unavailable if needed for the defense of the capital.[3]

Although thoroughly frustrated and deeply distressed by McClellan's stalling, Lincoln tried to inspire action by issuing blanket approval for the general to establish a new base at Fort Monroe or "anywhere between here or there; or at all events, [to] move the remainder of the army at once in pursuit of the enemy by some other route." Despite being unenthusiastic about the Fort Monroe plan, especially with the army already in Virginia and twenty-five miles closer to Richmond, Lincoln clearly wanted action without further delay. Stanton informed the general, "Whatever plan has been agreed upon, proceed at once to execute, without losing an hour for any approval." Stanton even tried to be amenable, and on March 22 wrote, "Please signify to me your wishes—I am rejoiced that you are getting along so well." Only later did Lincoln learn that Heintzelman, Keyes, McDowell, and Sumner had approved the plan because it was the only one presented for discussion. Little Mac had never mentioned the option of pursuing the Confederates from Manassas. The general now had a free hand to do whatever he chose as long as he occupied Manassas, protected Washington, and did everything expediently.[4]

Lincoln's approval of the Fort Monroe plan remains puzzling. He never liked the new plan any better than the Urbanna plan and should have ordered McClellan to establish his base at Manassas, take advantage of the available railroads, and pursue the rebels. Lincoln's demand to protect Washington and hold Manassas reeked of personal aggravation compounded by doubts about whether McClellan would fight. Had Lincoln trusted his general's ability to wage war, he might not have been so concerned about the safety of Washington. Insisting the capital be protected deprived McClellan of troops. If McClellan wanted those troops, he would have retained them by advancing from Manassas. The question becomes who committed the greatest error, Lincoln by demanding troops for protecting Washington or McClellan by changing his base to Fort Monroe. Lincoln worried too much about being blamed by the public if McClellan lost a battle forced upon him by the administration. He might have done better by replacing McClellan, but Little Mac still had the confidence of what he called "my army." The imbroglio over Washington's security might have been avoided had McClellan met with the president and resolved the issue beforehand. Instead, he sent General Marcy to General Hitchcock with a list of units detached for the protection of Washington. Hitchcock merely glanced at the list, asked no probing questions, and said, "Nothing more would be required." Hence, McClellan started for Virginia believing he had complied with Lincoln's orders regarding the protection of Washington.[5]

The chaos of moving the Army of the Potomac to the Peninsula eclipsed anything previously experienced in American history. The expedition required 389 steamers, sailing ships, and barges from rivers, lakes, and the sea. After arriving at the old brick Virginia town of Alexandria, now filled with sightseers and souvenir collectors, the steamers were to embark and transport 121,500 men and tow 14,592 animals, 1,150 wagons, 44 batteries, 74 ambulances, numerous pontoon bridges, and thousands of tons of supplies and impedimenta two hundred miles to the Peninsula. The success of the expedition depended largely on the cooperation of Stanton. He shared serious misgivings about the movement with Lincoln and Welles, whose gunboats were to silence Yorktown's batteries, although the navy had not yet been informed. Stanton believed the expedition would never get under way if managed by McClellan and grudgingly assigned the task of assembling the flotilla to Assistant Secretary of War John Tucker, who performed the work with remarkable swiftness and thoroughness, writing, "For economy and celerity of movement, this expedition is without a parallel on record."[6]

On March 14, three days before the first transports sailed for the Peninsula, the Young Napoleon announced the expedition to his troops. He carried a portable printing press in headquarters baggage for mass communications with his army, and within twenty-four hours every unit had received copies of the address. The oration sounded oddly reminiscent of words the genuine Napoleon might have spoken: "For a long time I have kept you inactive. I have held you back that you might give the death blow to the rebellion." After praising the Army of the Potomac for being the most well-equipped and best-trained army on the continent, McClellan declared: "The period of inaction has passed. I will bring you now face to face with the rebels." One might wonder what McClellan meant when he added: "However strange my actions seem to you, ever bear in mind that my fate is linked with yours . . . I am to watch over you as a parent over his children; and you know that your General loves you from the depths of his heart." He promised the "least possible losses" but warned, "You have brave foes to encounter . . . I shall demand of you great, heroic exertions, rapid and long marches, desperate combats, [and] privations . . . We will share all these together." When historian Stephen Sears analyzed the general's address, he found a passage borrowed from a speech Napoleon had given his army after the Italian campaign: "And when this sad war is over we will all return to our homes, and feel that we can ask no higher honor than the proud consciousness that we belonged to the Army of the Potomac."[7]

The movement of troops to the Peninsula began on March 17, and for twenty days long lines of blue-clad soldiers, accompanied by military bands, stomped through the streets of Alexandria to embark on transports spewing clouds of thick black smoke from soot-stained stacks. Confederate spies watched, wondering where McClellan was taking the army. Every time the column stopped, soldiers bought whiskey from local street hucksters and got drunk. Not driving rain, sleet, snow, or nightfall interrupted the unremitting procession of men, bucking horses, and obstreperous mules from being shoved on board a waiting craft. Officers complained about the arrangements having been poorly planned by McClellan's staff, but one of Little Mac's advisors, a British military observer, praised the commotion, referring to the immense effort as "the stride of a giant."[8]

McClellan promised the administration a rapid movement to the Peninsula without estimating how long it might take. Brigadier General Charles S. Hamilton's Third Division from Heintzelman's Third Corps began embarking on March 17, and five days passed before Porter's First Division, the next in line, shoved off. With ten more divisions to go, the president's anxiety intensified. McClellan's orders were specific. He instructed Heintzelman to select campgrounds, perform reconnaissance, engage guides, and wait. Meanwhile, sailors returning after disembarking troops at the Hampton–Newport News landing site near the mouth of the James River reported soldiers distressed over the lack of rations and shelter and complained about poor staff work by the officers reporting to the Young Napoleon's father-in-law.[9]

McClellan lingered at Alexandria, watching endless files of blue-clad troops waiting on the wharf for embarkation orders. On March 19, while superintending the confusion, the general received a message from Stanton asking for an official statement of campaign plans. McClellan said he intended to operate from Fort Monroe as his first base, after which he would gain command of the York River and establish a second base up-river at West Point. He expected the rebels to concentrate in a twenty-five-mile area between West Point and Richmond, where he said decisive fighting would occur. West Point had not been mentioned before, so the general explained his intention to get there by overrunning a small enemy force at Yorktown. Until March 19 McClellan had not received accurate intelligence of the area and would not have been able to respond to Stanton's request had Lieutenant Colonel Daniel P. Woodbury, a member of Little Mac's staff, not been summoned to Fort Monroe by General Barnard. Major General John Wool, commanding Fort Monroe, had used his staff to collect most of the information, which dealt mainly with the topographical characteristics of the lower Peninsula and less accurately with its defenses.[10]

McClellan formulated two plans for dealing with the problem. He could take Yorktown and nearby Gloucester by siege, which did not sound like overrunning anything, or he could make a combined attack in conjunction with the navy and destroy Yorktown's defensive works. With naval assistance he would be in position to push a corps up the York River to West Point and begin receiving supplies and reinforcements. He wished to avoid a siege and strongly urged that the navy concentrate its most powerful gunboats to reduce Yorktown.

The problem with the general's hypothesis involved his reliance on the navy, which had not been included in McClellan's new arrangements of suddenly shifting operations from Urbanna to Fort Monroe. Stanton became furious when McClellan declared, "For the prompt success of this campaign it is absolutely necessary that the Navy should at once throw its whole available force, its most powerful vessels, against Yorktown." Welles knew nothing about a complicated joint operation involving gunboats. Nor had anyone made a reconnaissance to determine the location of Yorktown's batteries or the extent of the city's defenses. Stanton took the problem to the president, who admitted being mighty perplexed. Lincoln went by carriage to Alexandria to talk with McClellan, while Stanton made inquiries at the Navy Department. Fox said the only request from McClellan concerned preventive efforts to keep the *Virginia* from entering the York River. The navy had a few ships in Hampton Roads watching the *Virginia* but none available for operations against Yorktown. Once again, McClellan failed to do his homework by assuming the navy would instantaneously do whatever he asked. Despite knowing the importance of silencing Yorktown's batteries, McClellan began moving his army to the Peninsula without first holding discussions with the navy.[11]

A new problem emerged during Lincoln's meeting with the general at Alexandria. After John C. Frémont had been removed from command in the West, his radical supporters descended on the White House asking for something to be done for their favorite general. Lincoln relented, created the Mountain Department, and put Frémont in charge. Frémont wanted more troops and, because of his preference for Germans, asked for Brigadier General Louis Blenker's division, which was en route from Warrenton Junction as part of Sumner's Second Corps. Frémont requested the division because of Stonewall Jackson's activity in the Shenandoah Valley and the battle at Kernstown on March 23. Lincoln also expected Frémont to initiate operations in East Tennessee and wanted to give the Mountain Department more troops. Thus, on March 31, after telling McClellan of his reluctance to deprive the Army of the Potomac of Blenker's force, Lincoln transferred the ten thousand–man division to Frémont. While the creation of the Mountain Department assuaged a political problem for Lincoln, it created a military problem for McClellan. Feeling he owed Little Mac an explanation, the president wrote: "I did so with great pain, understanding you would wish it otherwise. If you could know the full pressure of the case, I am confident you would justify it, even beyond a mere acknowledgement that the commander-in-chief may order what he pleases." McClellan replied, "I fully appreciate . . . the circumstances . . . and hasten to assure you that I cheerfully acquiesce in your decision without any mental reservation." Later he groused about the order, claiming: "The commander-in-chief has no right to order what he pleases; he can only order what he is convinced is right. And the president already assured me that he knew this thing to be wrong." Lincoln made the decision after discussions with Stanton and Hitchcock. While lacking military savvy, Hitchcock understood the nature of politics, which he had spent a lifetime avoiding. He agreed with Stanton that Lincoln could not risk losing the support of the radicals. With McClellan preparing to strike the key blow of the war, the president should not have stripped away Blenker's division, which had just reached Alexandria after a forced march from Warrenton Junction. The rest of Sumner's corps sailed for the Peninsula.[12]

McClellan remained at Alexandria to expedite the movement of troops and on April 1 planned to shove off for Fort Monroe in his floating headquarters, the transport *Commodore*. By then five divisions of infantry, one of artillery, and three regiments of cavalry had reached the Peninsula, giving Little Mac fifty-eight thousand men and a hundred guns to begin his offensive. McClellan had also received valuable information from Fitz-John Porter, who had made a reconnaissance on March 27 and reported only fifteen thousand rebels along the lower Peninsula. The report, though slightly inflated, was the most accurate McClellan would receive during the entire campaign and gave him nearly a four-to-one advantage in manpower. He only needed to issue orders to General Heintzelman, the senior officer on the Peninsula, to attack.[13]

Before the *Commodore* got under way, McClellan learned Lincoln was on the way from Washington. The discussion must have been short. The president expressed concern about the number of troops safeguarding Washington and temporarily detained McDowell's division. McDowell rode back to Washington with the president, and the Young Napoleon sailed for the Peninsula. "I did not feel safe until I could see Alexandria fairly behind us," he informed his wife. "I feared if I had remained at Alexandria I would be annoyed very much & perhaps be sent for from Washington. Officially speaking, I feel very glad to get away from that sink of iniquity."[14]

Lincoln intended to forward McDowell's corps to the Peninsula immediately after the departure of Sumner's divisions, but during an evening discussion with Senator Orville Browning, he admitted having reservations. He spoke of McClellan as having a great talent for preparation but felt he lacked aggressiveness, lost his nerve, and became oppressed as the time to fight approached. The president told Browning he had given McClellan unconditional orders to move swiftly and hoped the general would take the advice.[15]

Meanwhile, General Wadsworth, who commanded the District of Washington, informed Stanton that only nineteen thousand troops had been designated for the defense of the city and that McClellan had left orders to detach seven thousand of them for service elsewhere, which would have reduced the local force to twelve thousand. In December 1861 Chief Engineer Barnard had suggested a minimum of twenty thousand men to garrison Washington's forts, but that was before McClellan decided to take the army to the Peninsula. After venomously castigating McClellan for foul play, Stanton took the report to Lincoln. The president doubted the figures because he trusted McClellan to keep his word but asked Stanton to verify the report. Stanton detailed General Hitchcock and Adjutant General Lorenzo Thomas to investigate Wadsworth's calculations and determine, in their collective opinion, the force necessary to safeguard Washington. The two generals returned to the White House that night, confirmed Wadsworth's report, and said thirty thousand troops were required to man and occupy the forts, which, with a covering force of twenty-five thousand, would make fifty-five thousand for the proper defense of the city. Thus, they concluded, "the requirement of the President, that the city should be left entirely secure, had not been fully complied with." Nicolay and Hay witnessed the discussions and decided that McClellan never feared an attack on Washington unless he happened to be there himself.[16]

Thomas had received a copy of McClellan's report on the distribution of left-behind forces, which had been written on April 1 but not analyzed until Stanton ordered it. Whether Little Mac, who sometimes backdated correspondence, wrote the document before or after Lincoln's visit to the *Commodore* on April 1 cannot be determined, but he likely intended to issue no report until departing from Alexandria.

The devil lay in the details. According to McClellan's calculations, forces protecting Washington totaled 73,500 men. A wiser and less arrogant man would have anticipated the consequences and not resorted to such a clumsy subterfuge. He reported 7,780 at Warrenton, 10,859 at Manassas, 35,467 in the Shenandoah Valley, 1,350 on the lower Potomac, and more than 18,000 in Washington, with four new regiments totaling 3,000 men on the way from New York. Most of the troops at Washington were recent arrivals. He counted the 18,639 troops at Warrenton

and Manassas as the covering force he had promised for the defense of
Manassas. He had intended this force to be larger but had sent some of
the troops to General Banks because of threats from Stonewall Jackson's Shenandoah Valley army. To bring Manassas up to strength, Little
Mac had already detached 4,000 troops from Washington and actually
planned to detach 6,000 more. The report looked like either a sloppy
manipulation of numbers or outright dishonesty. At the time Manassas
had almost no troops. At least four of the eight regiments scheduled for
detachment from Washington and intended for Manassas were double
counted. The 7,780 men at Warrenton were also counted twice, once as
part of the Manassas force and again as part of Banks's force. McClellan
also counted Blenker's division, which had been transferred to Frémont,
as part of Banks's command. After making arithmetic adjustments to Mc-
Clellan's numbers, Hitchcock and Thomas reported the troops actually
available for the defense of Washington included 19,000 in the capital
and 23,000 under Banks, whose corps in the Shenandoah Valley lay too
far from Washington to protect the capital. McClellan later claimed the
men posted at Manassas and Warrenton, though overstated at 18,000,
were part of the defensive force for the capital. Stanton condemned Mc-
Clellan for disregarding the president's orders, and Lincoln forever after
remained suspicious of the general's personal statements regarding troop
strength.[17]

It would not be the first time McClellan manipulated numbers nor the
last. For the Young Napoleon war became a numbers game. On April 7 he
tried to leverage Stanton by complaining of having only 85,000 men for
the Peninsular Campaign. In a fit of temper Stanton took the message to
the White House. Two days later, following another investigation, Lincoln
replied to McClellan, "Your own returns [reported] 108,000 then with you
and *en route* to you," noting there were more on the way. "How can the
discrepancy of 25,000 be accounted for?" McClellan never responded, but
on April 11 he sought empathy from Winfield Scott, who, after having been
deposed by the Young Napoleon, had retired comfortably to West Point,
New York. McClellan complained of the administration depriving him of
50,000 troops but two days later furnished returns to the War Department showing 117,721 troops on the Peninsula. Reinforcements continued
to arrive almost daily, but McClellan had not yet engaged the enemy.[18]

Although Lincoln and Stanton sharply questioned McClellan's motives, the men in the ranks revered their general. Lincoln would have been justified in recalling McClellan for flagrant disobedience to orders, but the long-awaited campaign seemed to be under way. Lincoln did what he thought necessary and retained McDowell's corps for the defense of the capital. The Young Napoleon created his own problem by flagrantly overestimating the size of Johnston's army, which Lincoln now knew. If McClellan got bogged down on the Peninsula and refused to fight, there would be nothing to stop Johnston's so-called 115,000-man army from attacking Washington.

9

"But you must act"

O UT OF THIS CONUNDRUM came one of the great controversies of the war. Partisans of the general then and ever since have contended that, because Washington could not be seriously attacked without exposing Richmond to capture, Lincoln and Stanton erred by attaching undue importance to safeguarding the capital. General Robert E. Lee referred to the strategy as "swapping queens," enabling Johnston to overrun the North while McClellan took Richmond and raided and overran the South. Lincoln could not afford an exchange, nor could Jeff Davis. Seizure of Washington would have been a fatal blow to the Union and likely would have led to recognition of the Confederacy by England and France. Davis could always return the Confederate government to Montgomery, Alabama, where it had started. Lincoln had another concern. Johnston's ability to fight had been tested; McClellan's had not. Little Mac had a cavalier habit of saying, "If the rebel army should take Washington while he was at Richmond they could never get back." The administration held a much different view and believed "the general who would permit Washington to be taken could not be relied on to prevent the enemy from doing what they liked afterwards." Regardless of what McClellan thought, his generals unanimously insisted on the protection of Washington during the council of war held on March 13.[1]

Knowing McClellan had grossly overstated the size of the Confederate force at Manassas, Lincoln decided to place McDowell's corps between Richmond and Washington, thus accomplishing the dual purpose of defending the capital while threatening Johnston's force along the Rappahannock. To McClellan's chagrin Lincoln gave McDowell thirty-five thousand men. If Johnston moved northward, McDowell would be on his flank. If Johnston headed south to defend Richmond, McDowell could follow and join forces with McClellan. Lincoln's decision to retain McDowell's corps as the Army of the Rappahannock can be justified by McClellan's disobedience; whether it was wise depended on other factors unappreciated at the time.[2]

McClellan expected to take the largest army possible to the Peninsula. He did not share Lincoln's fears about protecting the capital, believing his attack on Richmond would ensure the safety of Washington by drawing every Confederate unit to the defense of the rebel capital. Little Mac's generals had been vague about the number of men required to safeguard Washington but generally agreed on forty thousand. Lincoln and Stanton believed the generals attributed the allotment exclusively to Washington proper. While McClellan might be accused of disobedience for providing less than half that number, either intentionally or unintentionally, the president can also be faulted for having been unclear about his requirements.

If McClellan succeeded on the Peninsula, Washington should have been secure. With Richmond under attack, the only possible threat to Washington would have come from Jackson's small army in the Shenandoah Valley, which, without help, Banks and Frémont should have been able to defeat or contain. McClellan never explained such simple details to Lincoln or Stanton because he resented being questioned, and to prevent misunderstanding and eliminate suspicion, he should not have tried to slip away from Alexandria without first having a thorough conversation with Lincoln and Stanton. All Lincoln wanted was adequate protection for Washington. McClellan muffed the opportunity to come clean on April 1, when the president, rather than calling the general to Washington, took a carriage to Alexandria to meet with McClellan on the *Commodore.* Whatever the general said failed to convince the president, so he detained McDowell's corps. McClellan did send data on the disposition of troops safeguarding Washington to General Hitchcock, who never analyzed the details until he was asked to. McClellan probably assumed he had fulfilled his duty of notifying the War Department when the report should have gone directly to Stanton, if not to Lincoln, who on the date of the report asked McClellan for details. Until this moment Lincoln had no indication McClellan intended to do less than what he had promised to do. Lincoln might not have detained McDowell's corps had McClellan been forthcoming, or he might have retained one division and released the others.[3]

Stanton exacerbated the situation by recruiting radicals to join him in accusing McClellan of disloyalty for leaving Washington defenseless, which was not entirely true. The secretary held many surreptitious meetings with radicals that the president knew nothing about. He also coached and employed help from Hitchcock and Thomas, who accused the general of misrepresenting the size of the protective force, which was true. Lincoln did not know what to believe and took the conservative approach because he still questioned whether McClellan would fight. In a private conversation with Senator Orville Browning regarding Stanton's accusations of McClellan's disloyalty, and though equally distressed by the general's antics, Lincoln said "he still had confidence in McClelland's [*sic*] fidelity . . . and that he had never had any reason to doubt it." Knowing a decision must be made, however, Lincoln went to the War Department on April 3, discussed options with Stanton's Army Board, and directed the secretary to detain either McDowell's or Sumner's corps for service in the capital and send the other corps "as speedily as possible" to McClellan. Stanton retained McDowell's corps, the largest in the Army of the Potomac, with 35,000 troops, and sent Sumner's corps, the smallest in the army, with 19,000 troops. This move reduced McClellan's aggregate force to 118,000 on April 13, which included more than 16,000 absentees, as opposed to the 150,000 troops the general claimed he needed. The entire problem could have been avoided had the president simply vetoed the Fort Monroe plan, and despite the debate over the disposition of McDowell's corps, the reduced force had little to do with McClellan's self-imposed delay at Yorktown.[4]

Several years after the war Major General William B. Franklin, who later commanded McClellan's Sixth Corps, wrote an article titled "The First Great Crime of the War." In addition to being one of McClellan's West Point chums, Franklin had always supported the Urbanna plan or any other movement promoted by the Young Napoleon. He called Lincoln's detachment of McDowell's corps for the defense of Washington a crime. He also supported McClellan's demand for more troops at Yorktown, which, he said, would have been avoided had McClellan received McDowell's corps. Little Mac did have difficulties at Yorktown, many of them self-inflicted, but Franklin stretched facts by blaming everything that went wrong on the administration. McClellan also rejected blame for tactical blunders occurring over the next three months, writing, "To say that the force I left behind me was, under the circumstances of the case, insufficient is an untruth which proves either complete ignorance or willful malevolence." McClellan also stretched a point when he said, "The administration actually retained about 134,000 troops for the defense of Washington, leaving me but 85,000 for operations." Lincoln and McClellan both made mistakes, as novices often do, but for the Peninsular Campaign the Young Napoleon had originally asked for 130,000 troops. He eventually received more than 120,000 and later had access to 8,000 more from Burnside's command. Nevertheless, Lincoln suffered a certain amount of deserved criticism for retaining McDowell's corps. Doing so gave McClellan an illusionary excuse to fail at the very beginning of the Peninsular Campaign and magnified the distrust growing between the general, Lincoln and in particular Stanton. General Heintzelman, who never approved of McClellan's methods, nevertheless condemned the retention of McDowell's corps as "a great outrage." Welles thought the whole matter a ruse to force McClellan's resignation in favor of a Republican general. The radicals hoped so too, but McClellan disappointed them all. He held on, a beaten man, defeated by a failure to communicate.[5]

The Young Napoleon arrived at Fort Monroe during a rainstorm on April 2 and, according to his own report, prepared to advance with fifty-eight thousand troops and a hundred guns on a route he had predetermined without first making a thorough reconnaissance. The force consisted of veterans who had fought at Bull Run, including Brigadier General George Sykes's "Regulars" and Colonel Henry J. Hunt's artillery. More troops were in transit, enough to double the size of the Union force on the Peninsula. McClellan seemed to appreciate the importance for prompt and decisive action and with only a single day's delay issued orders to advance.[6]

From Hampton, where McClellan's troops camped, roads led through Little Bethel and Big Bethel to Yorktown, about twenty miles away. There the Peninsula was about nine air miles wide, with the York River on one side and the James River on the other. The first obstacle McClellan expected to meet was Major General John Bankhead Magruder's small division at Yorktown. McClellan estimated the Confederate force at 15,000 to 20,000 men, although Magruder had only 11,500 troops at the time. Half of them manned Yorktown's fortifications, and the other half defended some thirteen miles of defenses along the Warwick River, which flowed diagonally across the Peninsula and emptied into the James. As soon as McClellan moved toward Big Bethel, Magruder telegraphed Richmond for reinforcements and received instructions to delay McClellan's advance. Yorktown had redoubts with heavy artillery and rifle pits that united with defenses strung along the Warwick River, which was actually a sluggish and boggy stream angling through dense woods fringed with swamps. Magruder had dammed the river at five places to make the fords impassable and protected each dam with artillery emplaced in earthworks.[7]

Nothing on the lower Peninsula resembled the open, pristine, and well-drained road to Richmond as stated by McClellan. To most observers the roads were the worst they had ever seen, especially after a rainfall. Cavalry had not made a full reconnaissance, and McClellan knew nothing about conditions along the Warwick River, despite earlier warnings from General Wool's command at Fort Monroe. He knew something about the location of Magruder's outposts, which he assumed would fall back, but he knew nothing about the location and extent of the enemy's defensive works. He counted on the navy to disable the guns in Yorktown's redoubts without knowing where those emplacements were located. To his wife he wrote: "I hope to get possession of Yorktown day after tomorrow [April 5]. I see my way very clearly and . . . will move rapidly." He also wrote Flag Officer Goldsborough, commanding the naval squadron at Hampton Roads, of his intention to invest Yorktown on April 5 and asked for the naval barrage to begin.[8]

At this late date Lincoln had not yet made a decision to detain forces for Washington's protection, so on April 4 McClellan wrote McDowell asking him to land at least one division on the Severn River to capture Gloucester, which lay directly across from Yorktown, and to bring the rest of the corps around to Big Bethel. Little Mac envisioned his plan coming together neatly and that night wrote his wife, "Everything has worked well—I have gained some strong positions without fighting and shall try some more maneuvering tomorrow . . . and may have a fight." McClellan had already stopped his advance and decided on April 4 on a siege, this call occurring one day before he learned that McDowell's corps had been withheld for Washington's defense. An astute observer of

McClellan's behavior at this point in the campaign might conclude that the general intended to maneuver Magruder out of Yorktown by partially surrounding him rather than by fighting him. In an effort to change the president's mind, he promptly warned that a large enemy force, heavily fortified and augmented by reinforcements from Richmond, was blocking his way. "Under these circumstances," he wrote, "I beg that you will reconsider the order detaching the First Corps from my command."[9]

Lincoln anticipated the Young Napoleon's next round of demands and on April 6 replied: "You now have over one hundred thousand troops . . . I think you better break the enemies' line from Yorktown to Warwick River, at once. They will probably use *time,* as advantageously as you can." McClellan had already lost interest in moving rapidly, grumbling that the president had "removed nearly 60,000 men from my command" "To me," he lamented, "the blow was most discouraging. It frustrated all my plans for future operations. It fell when I was too deeply committed to withdraw. It left me incapable of continuing operations which had been begun. It made rapid and brilliant operations impossible. It was a fatal error." McClellan also concocted the notion that Stanton had suspended all recruiting, which was untrue, and thought the president was intentionally depriving him of reinforcements while the enemy daily increased forces on the Peninsula. John Hay watched the frustration grow inside the White House, writing: "Gen. McC. is in danger. Not in front but in rear. The President is making up his mind to give him a peremptory order to march. It is disgraceful to think how the little squad at Yorktown keeps him at bay."[10]

THE ONE GREAT FLAW IN MCCLELLAN's triumphant advance on the Confederate capital during April 1862 was stalling the advance of the Army of the Potomac at Yorktown. McClellan's Peninsular Campaign officially began on the fourth, when he divided his force into two columns: Heintzelman's corps took the right flank with instructions to march directly on Yorktown, and Keyes's corps took the lower road on the left, which connected with the Williamsburg road at Lee's Mills. While Heintzelman assaulted Yorktown, Keyes was to occupy Half Way House north of Yorktown, which should have forced Magruder to withdraw or surrender. Having only ten miles to march, McClellan expected Keyes to cross the

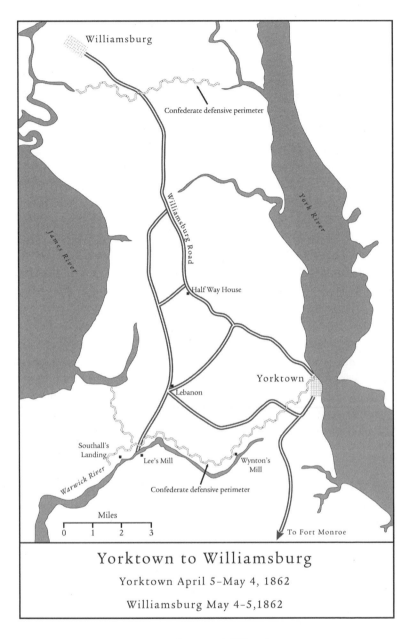

MAP 1. Yorktown to Williamsburg

Warwick River at Lee's Mills and reach the flank and rear of Yorktown the same day.

McClellan suffered a severe shock when he discovered that Magruder's forces were in different positions than he had anticipated. Heintzelman met little opposition until reaching Yorktown, and Magruder's fortifications at Lee's Mills stopped Keyes at the Warwick River. Keyes sent a messenger to McClellan explaining the problem and asked for instructions. At the time McClellan seemed to be more focused on his perceived enemies in Washington than those in his front. Heavy rain had fallen throughout the day, flooding the river to a depth of seven feet and churning roads into mud, making it difficult for supplies and reinforcements to be brought forward from Fort Monroe. McClellan instructed Keyes to hold the ground and take defensive measures. Keyes had 33,000 men facing a small Confederate force of 1,000 troops hunkered down in an earthwork flanked by rifle pits. Heintzelman's 34,000-man corps also came to a standstill outside Yorktown. McClellan had another 33,000 troops in reserve doing nothing. Although Magruder had only 11,500 troops, a few reinforcements began arriving late that day. Without McDowell's corps McClellan seemed to lose his enthusiasm for fighting, but the advance had already stalled, and reinforcements were unlikely to improve Little Mac's indecisiveness. McClellan had pontoons, and had the Young Napoleon promptly ordered Keyes to push forward to Half Way House, there may have been some sharp fighting and some casualties, but the campaign for Yorktown would have ended. Most of Magruder's command would have been surrounded. McClellan's campaign strategy had been exceptionally well designed, but he lost the initiative and his confidence and then attempted to blame his failure on the administration. Alexander Webb, a Potomac artillery officer who wrote the first history of the Peninsular Campaign, pointed to McClellan's habitual mistake of going into battle without knowing the enemy's position.[11]

For two days neither Keyes nor Heintzelman moved, while inexperienced Union cavalry trotted up and down the Warwick River performing imperfect reconnaissance. Magruder's troops staged a theatrical show on the opposite side of the river by tirelessly moving about to convey the illusion of a greater army. The daily demonstrations stymied Little Mac for a month, leaving Magruder to grow gradually stronger.

Instead of attacking the Confederates, McClellan attacked the administration for depriving him of troops and the navy for not silencing the batteries at Yorktown and Gloucester. The general assumed that, by asking the navy to destroy Yorktown's batteries, no more would be required. Flag Officer Goldsborough obliged by sending a small squadron of wooden gunboats into the York River under Commander John S. Missroon with instructions to begin shelling at noon, April 15, at long range. Missroon relied on an old chart showing where Yorktown's batteries were supposed to be located. At daylight, after the mist lifted, he obtained his first clear view of Yorktown's defenses. Missroon reported vast additions to the fortifications and said his gunboats would be destroyed in twenty minutes. McClellan's cavalry had not located the batteries, many of which were masked along both sides of the river. Magruder had strung other batteries above the town, higher than naval guns could be elevated. Missroon said he could provide better support if McClellan would send troops to capture the water batteries. Instead of assaulting the water batteries, which were near Heintzelman's corps, McClellan asked the navy for more gunboats. Goldsborough had no ships to spare because at the general's request they had been detailed to defend against possible attacks by the *Virginia*. According to McClellan, if the navy had done its job and if McDowell's corps had not been detained, he would be at the doorstep of Richmond instead of being bogged down among the swamps along the Warwick River. This may have been true had the proper staff work and communications been made. Instead, deflection of blame to justify his own lack of aggressiveness became standard practice for as long as McClellan remained in command. His siege of Yorktown gave the Confederacy four weeks to move forces onto the Peninsula in defense of Richmond.[12]

Had Lincoln read McClellan's private correspondence, he would have obtained a better impression of what the general was doing—or, rather, not doing. On April 6 Little Mac wrote his wife, Mary Ellen, citing those generals who were personal friends as "doing splendidly." At the time, and at McClellan's orders, none of the generals were doing anything. How hard they were fighting can be measured by their light casualties, about five killed in each division. "Tomorrow night I can tell you exactly what I intend on doing," he informed his wife, but the following night passed without a clue. Instead, he badgered Lincoln and Stanton for more troops, more transportation, and more ammunition. On April 7 he informed Stanton that General Joseph Johnston had joined Magruder at Yorktown and would soon have more than 100,000 men, all in consequence of the president denying him McDowell's corps and Blenker's division. Stanton went to the White House, grumbling, "If [McClellan] had a million men, he would swear the enemy had two millions, and then he would sit down in the mud and yell for three." Magruder did get reinforcements, but his division never exceeded 19,000 effectives and fifty-two guns. McClellan also wrote Lincoln, complaining of having only 80,000 men when his own returns showed 108,000.[13]

McClellan's behavior mystified the president. After hearing from Stanton about the general's many grievances, Lincoln composed a carefully written letter in an effort to get the Young Napoleon to face reality: "Your dispatches complaining that you are not properly sustained, while they do not offend me, do pain me very much." After rehashing all the reasons that led to the retention of McDowell's corps, he asked, "Do you really think I should permit the line from Richmond, via Manassas Junction, to this city to be entirely open, except for twenty thousand unorganized troops?" Lincoln never expected a reply, but on April 11 he walked to the War Department to talk with Stanton and Hitchcock's Army Board regarding McClellan's complaints. He wanted to find a way to reinforce McClellan without endangering Washington. When the Army Board suggested releasing William Franklin's eleven thousand–man division, Lincoln wrote the order immediately. On April 14 McClellan thanked Lincoln profusely and wrote, "The tranquility of Yorktown is nearly at an end."[14]

In the same letter Lincoln asked McClellan to explain inconsistencies in the returns, wherein the general stated having only 85,000 men, when on April 13 his assistant adjutant general, Seth Williams, reported 108,000. "How can the discrepancy of 23,000 be accounted for?" Lincoln asked. The president never received an answer, but on the following day McClellan confessed to his wife that he had "a little over 100,000 effective men." Because his complaints resulted in the release of Franklin's division, four days later McClellan sent another letter to the president asking for Brigadier General George A. McCall's division, adding, "I would prefer that Genl McDowell should not again be assigned duty with me." This statement emanated from McClellan's conspiratorial belief that McDowell had not only plotted with Lincoln and Stanton to be named commander of the new Army of the Rappahannock but was also plotting to take command of the Army of the Potomac. Little Mac also complained to Stanton of being short five divisions and said if the government had not weakened his army, he would be facing Richmond and not Yorktown: "Give me McCall's division and I will undertake a movement . . . which will shake them out of Yorktown."[15]

Lincoln tried to motivate the general with logic. Alluding to the huge Union force on the Peninsula, he wrote, "I think it is the precise time to strike a blow." Although Lincoln knew the most propitious time for an attack had been wasted, he still wanted to give the general reasons to press ahead and wrote:

> By delay the enemy will relatively gain upon you—that is, he will gain faster, by *fortifications* and *reinforcements,* than you can by reinforcements alone. And, once more let me tell you, it is indispensible to *you* that you strike a blow. *I* am powerless to help this. You will do me the justice to remember I always insisted, that going down the Bay in search of a field, instead of fighting at or near Manassas, was only shifting, and not surmounting a difficulty—that we would find the same enemy, and the same, or equal, entrenchments, at either place. The country will not fail to note—is now noting—that the present hesitation to move upon an entrenched enemy, is but the story of Manassas repeated.
>
> I beg to assure you that I have never written you, or spoken to you, in greater kindness of feeling than now, nor with a fuller purpose to sustain you, so far as in my most anxious judgment, I consistently can. *But you must act.*[16]

Three more weeks passed before McClellan developed plans to assault Yorktown and break across the Warwick River. While Little Mac continued to hallucinate over superior forces in his front, on April 22 General Johnston advised General Lee, "No one but McClellan could have hesitated to attack," adding that the Union defensive line was much stronger than his own. Four days later McClellan, still not satisfied with his defensive arrangement, went around Stanton and asked Brigadier General James W.

Ripley of the Ordnance Department to remove from Washington's fortifications a number of twenty- and thirty-pounder Parrott guns and ten-inch mortars and hurry them forward. On hearing of the request, on May 1 the president retorted: "Your call for Parrott guns from Washington alarms me—chiefly because it argues indefinite procrastination. Is anything to be done?" McClellan replied: "My object was to hasten, not procrastinate. All is being done that human labor can accomplish." On the night of May 3, three days before Little Mac's promised assault, Johnston surprised McClellan again, withdrawing Magruder's force to Williamsburg and placing it in a temporary and hastily built defensive line.[17]

At least three generals from the Army of the Potomac scoffed at McClellan's delays. Artillerist Alexander Webb wrote, "The Warwick line could have been readily broken within a week." General Heintzelman testified, "If I had been permitted, when I first arrived on the Peninsula, to advance, I could have isolated the troops at Yorktown, and the place would have fallen in a few days, but my orders were very stringent not to make any demonstrations." William F. Barry, McClellan's artillery chief, complained because the general would not let him fire on Yorktown until all the heavy guns had been hauled across the Peninsula and emplaced, and had he been permitted to fire when the first guns arrived, the enemy would have been compelled to "surrender or abandon his works in less than twelve hours." On May 3, when all the guns finally opened at once, the Confederates stole away in the smoke. Even General Johnston, who arrived in early April to evaluate Magruder's defenses, said the Confederate line could not be defended, but he used the time McClellan gave him to improve defensive works at Williamsburg and Richmond. Nicolay and Hay described the debacle in their biography of Lincoln: "Everyone seemed to see it except General McClellan."[18] After capturing another abandoned works reminiscent of Manassas, McClellan now had nearly 130,000 men on the Peninsula.

10

"I shall aid you all I can"

NEVER WAS THERE AN HOUR during General McClellan's command of the Army of the Potomac when he did not have more troops than he knew what to do with, yet barely a day passed without dispatches arriving at the War Department demanding heavier siege guns, more men, and more implements for digging massive earthworks for defensive purposes. It is difficult to say how long McClellan would have remained behind the vast works built during the Yorktown siege if John Magruder had not withdrawn from Yorktown on May 3. McClellan liked siege warfare, with its deliberateness, engineering problems, and light casualties. He seemed not to appreciate that by capturing the enemy's works, he might not capture the enemy's troops or artillery. On April 20, when writing Lincoln in reference to siege tactics, he said: "I am confident of success, not only of success but of brilliant success. I think that a defeat here [meaning Yorktown] substantially breaks up the rebel cause." The statement demonstrates how little McClellan understood his enemy, and this defect should have prepared Lincoln for the general's disappointing performance as the Army of the Potomac moved up the Peninsula. Had McClellan mentioned siege at any time during his conversations with Lincoln when the success of the operation clearly required speed, the president may have asserted his authority as commander-in-chief and vetoed the campaign.[1]

After Magruder abandoned Yorktown, Lincoln wondered how long it would take McClellan to advance. On May 5, accompanied by Edwin Stanton and Salmon Chase, he arrived at Fort Monroe to evaluate progress on the Peninsula. Stanton invited McClellan to join the gathering, but the general declined for good reason, claiming to be too busy. Unprepared for

Magruder's withdrawal, the Young Napoleon had sent the army forward in a poorly organized pursuit. The moment had again come for the general to demonstrate his ability as a field commander, and he went forth with an army not as large as he had planned against a Confederate force much smaller than his own but twice what he imagined. Nevertheless, northerners rejoiced that the Army of the Potomac was moving at last, and like Lincoln and his small party, they expected to hear promising news from the general's massive expedition.

Rather than languish at Fort Monroe with nothing to do, Lincoln met with Major General John E. Wool, commanding Fort Monroe, and Flag Officer Louis Goldsborough and on March 7 toured Hampton Roads. With Johnston's forces in retreat, he suspected that Norfolk, on the opposite side of Hampton Roads, might be isolated and vulnerable. He also wanted to witness the reaction if the navy shelled the enemy's batteries at Sewall's Point, where the dreaded *Virginia* docked. Goldsborough's officers opposed the idea but obliged the president by agreeing to do so in the morning. Lincoln then conferred with General Wool and received more objections to a reconnaissance in force against Norfolk. Nevertheless, on the morning of May 8 one naval squadron went up the James River, and another moved across Hampton Roads and began shelling Sewall's Point. Rebel batteries opened, the *Virginia* steamed into Hampton Roads, and, according to Chase, "All the big wooden vessels began to haul off." When the *Monitor* appeared, the *Virginia* turned back to Sewall's Point.[2]

For several months Lincoln had been asking McClellan why Wool had not recaptured Norfolk. According to Little Mac, the seventy-three-year-old general said it could not be done. On the morning of May 9, against the advice of Wool's officers, Lincoln, Stanton, and Chase took the gunboat *Miami* and a tug on a reconnaissance and make soundings near the opposite shore. Lincoln had been studying a chart with the pilot, believed he had found an ideal spot to land troops behind Sewall's Point, and went ashore to inspect the site. Wool remained uneasy about putting infantry on the beach, but Lincoln insisted. Shortly after midnight on May 10 the navy put Chase and six thousand infantry ashore on the beach selected by the president. While Chase and Wool led the troops inland, Lincoln remained behind, hustling the troops ashore. The nocturnal expedition met little resistance, passing over abandoned entrenchments and entering

Norfolk midmorning, and Chase accepted the surrender of the city from the mayor. Lincoln delayed his return to Washington and steamed up the Elizabeth River to visit the town. "So," wrote Chase, "has ended a brilliant week's campaign of the President; for I think quite certain that if he had not come down Norfolk would still have been in possession of the enemy, and the *Merrimac* [which fled up the James River] as grim and defiant and as much a terror as ever. The whole coast is now virtually ours." The episode induced some Washington observers to believe the president had better military skills than his generals, citing McClellan in particular.[3]

WHILE LINCOLN MASTERMINDED a mini-campaign to recapture Norfolk, which gave the Union control of the lower James River, McClellan began moving up the Peninsula. From Little Mac's perspective May 4 and the evacuation of Yorkton marked the beginning of his campaign. He was finally on the road to Richmond. "No time shall be lost," he promised Stanton. "I shall push the enemy to the wall." The only question left unanswered was how McClellan might behave when he reached "the wall." By then General Johnston had concentrated a blocking force at Williamsburg. Generals Samuel Heintzelman, Erasmus Keyes, and Edwin Sumner arrived opposite the town's defenses without any instructions from McClellan. They also arrived in confusion because the roads had been churned to mud by steady rain and beat to a froth by Magruder's withdrawal. Heavy artillery remained behind, stuck fast in the mud. No one assumed overall command. Everyone waited for Little Mac, who had remained behind at Yorktown to welcome the arrival of William Franklin's division. While sending the division by water to West Point and superintending its departure, Little Mac's other ten divisions, some taking separate routes, arrived in front of Williamsburg without a plan.[4]

On May 5 the generals continued to wait. Brigadier General Joseph Hooker from Heintzelman's corps grew impatient and at 7:30 a.m. launched an assault against Johnston's rear guard. The Confederates brought forth reinforcements and repulsed the attack. Hooker bitterly reported being left to fight overwhelming forces "unaided in the presence of more than 30,000 of their comrades with arms in their hands." Later in the afternoon Brigadier General Winfield S. Hancock, in another unsupported attack, completely routed the enemy but stopped because the rest of the corps stood by and watched. Hancock's and Hooker's efforts were bloody, expensive, and wasted. McClellan arrived later and, though greeted by cheers, contributed nothing to the day's effort, but in his autobiography he took credit for managing the day's battle. When reporting casualties in Hancock's and Hooker's divisions, he built quite a tale about two fights he never observed. After referring to Johnston's force as much larger than his own and strongly entrenched, he reported the enemy loss as "heavy" and declared, "Victory is complete." McClellan promised to hold the enemy in check while resuming his original plan of moving onto West Point. As a consequence, no serious fighting occurred on May 6. Johnston withdrew, leaving more empty and abandoned works for McClellan to capture.[5]

What McClellan reported as a complete victory was actually another missed opportunity. Johnston never intended to hold Williamsburg. He orchestrated a rearguard action designed to allow Confederate troops time to fall back to Richmond. Johnston admitted: "Had the enemy beaten us on May fifth, as he [McClellan] claims to have done, the army would have lost its baggage and artillery. We should have been pursued from Williamsburg and intercepted from West Point." If that had happened, he said, his troops would have been turned and overwhelmed. Johnston reported no trouble withdrawing from Williamsburg, but McClellan claimed he could not pursue the enemy because of muddy roads. Johnston halted for five days several miles from Richmond and on May 15, after receiving news of the capture of Norfolk and the destruction of the *Virginia,* ordered the army to cross the Chickahominy River and occupy Richmond's defensive works, which began three miles from the city. By then Federal gunboats and transports were passing up the York River and delivering shiploads of ammunition, forage, and provisions to McClellan's new base at White House Landing on the Pamunkey River.[6]

McClellan used the self-imposed interregnum to pick new fights with the administration. On May 8 he telegraphed the War Department claiming that 80,000 to 120,000 rebels had opposed Franklin's division when it landed at West Point two days earlier. The statement made no sense, but Stanton was at Fort Monroe and did not read the message until later. On the tenth McClellan asked Stanton for more men, claiming the enemy was "collecting especially well-disciplined troops from the South." After urging Lincoln to raise more troops by executive decree, he added, "If I am not reinforced it is probable that I will be obliged to fight nearly double my numbers, strongly intrenched." After Allan Pinkerton's inept and patronizing secret service agents upped the enemy strength to 240,000, McClellan asked for all disposable troops in Washington, even if it meant sending McDowell. After McClellan reported 102,236 men present for duty, Lincoln wondered why the general said no more than 70,000 were available for field operations. Little Mac never explained the inconsistency because doing so would only raise more questions. Despite doubting McClellan's manpower claims, Lincoln continued to find ways to reinforce the Army of the Potomac.[7]

In another delaying tactic McClellan protested the organization of his army and asked permission to break it up or at least be authorized to relieve incompetent generals. He blamed the corps organization, which had been one of Lincoln's demands, for the fumbling at Williamsburg and claimed had he not arrived on the battlefield a half-hour later, all would have been lost. McClellan never reached Williamsburg until after the fighting had ceased. In a more truthful letter to his wife he wrote, "Had I reached the field three hours earlier I could have gained far greater results & have saved 1,000 lives." Nothing stopped the general from being present for the fight but his own deliberateness and his unwillingness to create a workable command structure by appointing a second in command. In asking permission to relieve incompetent generals, he merely wanted to replace them with friends.[8]

The president understood McClellan's game and in a private letter replied, "I ordered the army corps organization not only on the unanimous opinion of the twelve generals whom you had selected . . . but also on the unanimous opinion of every military man [with whom I spoke] and every modern military book." Everybody, Lincoln added, looks upon the request "merely as an effort to pamper one or two pets and to persecute and degrade their supposed rivals." Since the altercation over the Manassas plan, which McClellan opposed and Heintzelman, Keyes, and Sumner favored, the Young Napoleon had ceased consulting with his three top generals. Instead, he conferred with Fitz-John Porter, who commanded the First Division in Heintzelman's corps, and William Franklin, who commanded the recently arrived division detached from McDowell's new Army of the Rappahannock. When Lincoln asked what orders the three generals had disobeyed, McClellan ignored the question because he had not issued any orders. Lincoln offered advice, writing: "Are you strong enough, even with my help—to set your foot upon the necks of Sumner, Heintzelman, and Keyes all at once? This is a practical and very serious question for you." Lincoln told McClellan to organize his army however he wished but to fight. Having gotten his way, on May 12 McClellan redistributed some of his divisions and put Porter in charge of the Fifth Corps and Franklin in charge of the Sixth Corps. Two months earlier he had argued against doing this when at the same time facing a fight.[9]

If Lincoln had been able to read McClellan's letters home, he might have recognized differences between his objectives as president and Little Mac's objectives as general. On the day Johnston's forces retired from Williamsburg, McClellan wrote his wife, "Are you satisfied with my bloodless victories?" McClellan considered Johnston's withdrawal from Manassas, Magruder's withdrawal from Yorktown, and the current withdrawal from Williamsburg all bloodless victories. Yet the Confederates continued to grow stronger while waiting for McClellan to fight, and Little Mac blamed his stalling on "always some little absurd thing being done by those gentry in Washington." McClellan had a valid problem, one he had not fully appreciated when moving to the Peninsula. Before reaching the Chickahominy River, he had to leave sizable garrisons behind at Yorktown, Williamsburg, West Point, and along the Pamunkey River to protect his communications. This became a critical concern because infantry and supply units were thinly spread over forty miles.[10]

After promoting Porter and Franklin to corps command, McClellan increased his demands for reinforcements. On May 14, as the army approached Richmond, he worried the president over having to lead troops into a fight of "perhaps double my numbers." Little Mac's exaggeration of Confederate strength can be attributed to Pinkerton's spies, who had still not learned how to count and never would. He urged Lincoln to send him "by water"—for reasons unexplained—every man in McDowell's Army of the Rappahannock, which was camped about fifty miles away, near Fredericksburg. He wanted McDowell's divisions to become part of Porter's and Franklin's corps and told Lincoln he did not want McDowell. Lincoln understood the scheme and merely replied, "I am still unwilling to take all our force off the direct line between Richmond and here." On May 18 Lincoln sent a dispatch under Stanton's signature offering to send McDowell's army by land using the shortest route to make a juncture with the right flank of the Army of the Potomac for a joint attack on Richmond. Perhaps because he distrusted how McClellan might use the force, he added, "General McDowell [will] retain command of the Department of the Rappahannock, and of the forces with which he moves forward." A three-day march would bring McDowell to Richmond, while the water route would take a month, but McClellan continued to argue the point instead of fighting.[11]

Little Mac disliked the arrangement and, instead of expressing gratification for a reasonable alternative, demanded that McDowell be placed explicitly under his orders. He used the new dispute as a reason to delay fighting and wrote his wife, "Those hounds in Washington are after me again." Lincoln's strategy made perfect sense to everyone but McClellan. While the Army of the Potomac struck Richmond from the east, Lincoln wanted McDowell's force to strike Richmond from the north, and on May 17 Stanton issued instructions for a joint attack to both generals. Had the strategy been executed promptly in mid-May, it might have succeeded. Because of delays resulting from McClellan's imbroglio over McDowell's reporting status, the plan suffered a setback when Stonewall Jackson's army struck General Banks in the Shenandoah Valley.[12]

McClellan later explained his delays by claiming the order to move McDowell's army by land instead of by water made it "impossible" for him to use the James River as a base, thereby forcing him to establish depots on the Pamunkey River to succor McDowell's corps. The statement made no sense. McClellan already had depots at White House and Cumberland Landing along the Pamunkey, which had been his plan from the beginning. At the time he had not considered the James River route, nor had he finished disembarking his siege guns and needed the Richmond & York River Railroad to bring them forward. As Major General Alexander S. Webb later explained, "The Pamunkey, as a base of supplies, was one of McClellan's own choice, uninfluenced by McDowell's movements." Besides, the James could never have been part of McClellan's original plan because the mouth of the river at that time was still protected by the

Virginia. McClellan had always intended to use the York and Pamunkey rivers as supply routes and by his own decision put his army east of the Chickahominy River.[13]

McClellan wasted ten days bringing his army from Williamsburg to Cumberland Landing on the Pamunkey River. He established a permanent depot upriver at White House and on May 21 brought the army into line along the Chickahominy. Porter's corps occupied the right wing about seven miles from Richmond, with the rest of the army scattered farther to the left. The Chickahominy, which during the rainy season resembled a massive swamp, originated above Richmond, flowed eastward, and then turned south, emptying into the James at Barrett's Ferry. For McClellan two formidable barriers lay ahead: the river, with its tangled woods and swamps; and the rebel army. McClellan attacked the swollen Chickahominy first and, while laying eleven bridges on boggy banks between Mechanicsville and Bottom's Bridge, passed another ten days fretting the president about reinforcements and the disposition of McDowell's force. He finally pushed Heintzelman and Keyes across the river but kept Franklin, Porter, and Sumner on the north side of the river.[14]

The closer McClellan came to Richmond, the more apprehensive he became about the possibility of having to fight. He expected to be overwhelmed by superior forces and aligned the army for defensive operations when he should have been preparing for an offensive, which had been his purpose in bringing the army to the Peninsula. He disillusioned himself by thinking the administration wanted to sacrifice him. On May 21 he pitched a tale of woe and injustice to his friend General Ambrose Burnside, who commanded the Department of North Carolina. He also bragged somewhat incredulously that history would credit his captures of Manassas and Yorktown as "my brightest chaplets," having won those campaigns "by pure military skill" and without having to fight. In his present predicament, with fighting imminent, McClellan grumbled: "The Government [has] deliberately placed me in this position. If I win, the greater the glory. If I lose, they will be damned forever, both by God and men."[15]

McClellan lost a week arguing with the administration over launching a joint operation against Richmond with assistance from McDowell. On Friday May 23, in an effort to get operations in motion, Lincoln traveled to McDowell's headquarters to get the Army of the Rappahannock on the road to Richmond. McDowell did not want to march on a Sunday, so the president said, "I'll tell you what to do; take *a good ready* and start Monday morning." Lincoln returned to Washington on Saturday and learned that Stonewall Jackson had attacked General Nathaniel Banks's corps in the Shenandoah Valley. He assumed correctly that the Confederates had anticipated McDowell's intention to cooperate with McClellan and sent Jackson down the Shenandoah Valley to threaten Washington. Lincoln expected Jackson's advance to be checked but later learned Banks had fallen back to Winchester. He informed McClellan of the situation and suspended McDowell's movement against Richmond.[16]

Lincoln became more concerned about the possible destruction of Banks's corps than the safety of Washington. He also wanted to put Jackson out of business and saw an opportunity to do it when Banks's retreat pulled the pursuing Confederates deeper into the lower Shenandoah Valley. By forced marches Lincoln saw an opportunity to move part of McDowell's army into the Valley from the east and General Frémont's army from the west and trap and destroy Jackson while Banks fought the rebels at Winchester. The president expected Jackson to turn back, and everything depended on McDowell reaching the Front Royal / Strasburg area and Frémont reaching Harrisonburg ahead of the rebels. At 4:00 p.m. on May 24 he updated McClellan on conditions in the Valley, writing, "The enemy are making a desperate push upon Harper's Ferry, and we are trying to throw General Frémont's force and part of General McDowell's in their rear." To Frémont, who tended to dally, he gave an extra push, telegraphing: "Put the utmost speed into it. Do not lose a minute."[17]

The crisis in the Shenandoah Valley marked the first time Lincoln interceded as commander-in-chief by directing both strategic and tactical operations instead of accepting McClellan's advice. Having taken the step, he expected McDowell and Frémont to obey orders. He believed McClellan would continue to stall near Richmond and nothing would be risked by diverting part of McDowell's force. He also knew McDowell was prepared to march on Richmond and changing direction should not be a serious impediment. In response McDowell put twenty thousand men under Brigadier General James Shields on the road to Front Royal, protesting they would never get there in time. "This is a crushing blow to us," said McDowell, implying the proper strategy was to attack Richmond. "I shall gain nothing for you there, and shall lose much for you here," he warned. "I feel it throws us all back, and from Richmond north we shall have all our large masses paralyzed, and shall have to repeat what we have just accomplished." Lincoln replied: "The change was as painful to me as it can possibly be to you or to any one. Everything now depends on the celerity and vigor of your movement."[18]

As the situation in the Shenandoah Valley continued to worsen, Lincoln could not decide whether Jackson's assault on Banks served as a diversion to prevent troops from going to McClelland or as an actual strike against Washington. He explained his concerns to McClellan, writing: "I think the movement is a general and concerted one . . . I think the time is near when you must either attack Richmond or give up the job and come to the defence of Washington. Let me hear from you instantly." McClellan replied, "The time is very near when I shall attack Richmond," and he accurately informed the president that Jackson's movement was "probably to prevent reinforcements being sent to me."[19]

Several hours later Lincoln learned Jackson had defeated Banks at Winchester and the Federals were in headlong retreat for the Potomac, chased by fifteen thousand Confederates. The president summarized the situation for McClellan, noting that Jackson might capture Harpers Ferry and invade Maryland. Lincoln also sensed an opportunity. If Jackson could be blocked at Harpers Ferry, he could be trapped and defeated in the lower Valley if Shields and Frémont moved swiftly. Lincoln began to feel more optimistic about crushing Jackson's rampaging army, and he used the situation to make a point with McClellan, writing: "If McDowell's force was now beyond our reach, we should be utterly helpless. Apprehension of something like this, and no unwillingness to sustain you, has always been the reason for withholding McDowell's force from you. Please understand this and do the best you can with the force you have." He also reminded McClellan that every rebel soldier in the Valley was one fewer available to fight at Richmond. McClellan resented the lecture. In a letter to his wife on May 25 he wrote: "I have this moment received a dispatch from the Presdt who is terribly scared about Washington—& talks about the necessity of my returning to save it! Heaven save a country governed by such counsels. I get more sick of them every day." After receiving a second telegram from the president later that night, McClellan appended his letter to his wife, adding: "They are terribly alarmed in Washington. A scare will do them good, and may bring them to their senses." The following day McClellan learned that Banks was safely across the Potomac and nobody in Washington was as alarmed as he thought. Instead, Lincoln seemed cheerfully optimistic about Jackson's army being defeated in the lower Valley. McClellan doubted whether Shields or Frémont was up to the task but expressed relief when Lincoln did not order him back to Washington.[20]

As McClellan predicted and Lincoln feared, Shields arrived too late to block Jackson's escape up the Shenandoah Valley, and Frémont took a route different from the one Lincoln had ordered and wasted eight days marching seventy miles, while Jackson marched fifty miles in two days. Lincoln's efforts to trap Jackson failed not because of defective planning but because of poor execution by Shields and Frémont. When the Confederates slipped through the noose, Lincoln continued to send orders through Stanton—"Do not let the enemy escape you"—but all his urgings came to naught. In the end Jackson defeated Frémont at Cross Keys and Shields at Port Republic because neither Union general had made arrangements to cooperate with the other.[21]

Had Lincoln's efforts to defeat Jackson been successful, military historians would have praised the strategy as one of the most brilliant maneuvers of the war. The movement never had much chance of succeeding because of lackadaisical Union generalship, but it was nevertheless worth trying because of rich dividends accruing to McClellan's campaign. Instead, when the tactics failed, McClellan's defenders criticized Lincoln for halting McDowell's move on Richmond and disrupting McClellan's campaign on the Peninsula. Historians blamed Lincoln for being overly concerned for Washington's safety, but his actions suggest otherwise. Instead of pulling McClellan or McDowell back to defend the capital, he sent twenty thousand of McDowell's troops to the Shenandoah Valley to capture Jackson's army. The act was aggressive, not defensive. He had understandable concerns about the safety of Banks's army, and he did not want Jackson raiding Maryland. He expected a greater effort from Banks and Frémont and believed that adding Shields's division from McDowell's corps would make the plan work. He also told McClellan on May 25 to attack Richmond or return to Washington, not because he needed the Army of the Potomac for Washington's protection but because he saw the spring being wasted on the Peninsula by inexplicable delays, inconsequential maneuvers, and lost opportunities. He also believed if McClellan attacked Richmond, the Confederates would have to bring Jackson from the Valley for the defense of the capital. He also left thirty-eight thousand of McDowell's troops on the Rappahannock to aid McClellan, but contrary to instructions from Stanton, McDowell did nothing. McDowell's stalling may have been at least partially attributed to Lincoln's dispatch to McClellan, which read, "You will have command of McDowell after he joins you, precisely as you intended."[22]

Lincoln still expected McDowell to cooperate with McClellan, and though he suspended the order during the crisis in the Shenandoah Valley, he never revoked it. Instead of attacking Richmond or returning the army to Washington, as Lincoln had ordered, McClellan waited for developments. Little Mac condemned the president's efforts to trap Jackson in the Valley because it deprived him of McDowell's command. Nor did he see the advantage of attacking Richmond, although the capital had been weakened by the detachment of reinforcements to Jackson. Lincoln's maneuver demoralized McClellan, who complained to his wife, "It is perfectly sickening to deal with such people," and threatened to break off all connection with the administration. "Every day brings with it only additional proofs of their hypocrisy, knavery, & folly," he griped. McClellan mentioned nothing about fighting the enemy, only about fighting the administration, adding, "If I should find Washn life as bad after the war as it was when I was there I don't think I could be induced to remain in the army after peace." What McClellan lost in late May was his best, but not his last, opportunity to capture Richmond.[23]

For those who believed McClellan could have captured Richmond with McDowell's help, one important factor requires careful study. Both generals lacked aggressiveness. They had been trained in defensive tactics and preferred to fight from behind well-built earthworks. McClellan, in particular, disliked bloodshed. Neither man fought well on open ground and never would. McClellan also believed the Army of the Potomac was vastly outnumbered because Pinkerton's spies had told him so, making it less likely he would pick a fight even if he said he would. McDowell's generals were substandard, and Shields, a political general like Banks and without West Point training, mismanaged his movements in the Valley. Had Jackson been less of a general, Lincoln may have succeeded when he sent Shields and Frémont into the Valley, but the president had not given enough thought to individual capabilities when he dispatched two uninspired and cautious generals to snare the army of a wily Confederate commander. Lincoln was still somewhere in the middle of the learning curve on military operations when he ordered the hurried joint expedition. He would soon learn more about McClellan's generalship in the coming days as well as McDowell's capabilities as a general with an independent command.[24]

Little Mac squandered his best opportunity to attack Richmond in late May and early June while Shields and Frémont were converging on Jackson in the Shenandoah Valley. Although prodded by Lincoln to act swiftly, McClellan saw no advantage for himself without reinforcements and moved forward by inches. He gradually moved part of his army across the Chickahominy but left Porter's Fifth Corps dangling on the north side to protect communications on the York and Pamunkey rivers. Lincoln disliked the arrangement. If the Chickahominy flooded, for several days the weaker force on the north bank would be separated from the main army on the south bank. Although he was aware of the problem, McClellan could do little about it because McDowell's army, should it move against Richmond, would have to be supplied from the Pamunkey River. Under constant pressure from the administration to fight, McClellan advised the president late on the evening of May 26 of "quietly closing in upon the enemy preparatory to the last struggle." Had McClellan not insinuated his intention to attack, Lincoln might have ordered the Army of the Potomac back to Washington. McClellan, of course, knew this.[25]

The young Napoleon's predicament of having Porter's corps at New Bridge on the extreme right flank and on the north side of the Chickahominy did not go unnoticed by the Confederates. On May 27 Porter's outposts clashed with Brigadier General Lawrence O. Branch's North Carolina brigade near Hanover Court House and drove the Confederates back to Ashland. McClellan hailed the fight as a glorious victory and became annoyed when Lincoln attached little importance to it. McClellan also overlooked the strategic significance of the brief but successful fight. Porter had cut the railroad bridges leading to Richmond, thus temporarily preventing Confederate forces in the Valley and along the Rappahannock from reinforcing Richmond. For several days the Confederate capital lay at the mercy of the Army of the Potomac. The fight ended without a sequel, and at McClellan's direction Porter's corps marched back to camp satisfied with the outcome.[26]

Porter's engagement boosted McClellan's morale, and he used the victory to badger Stanton for more troops. He warned if the government failed to comply with his demands, "irreparable" damage would result because, he claimed, every rebel unit in the eastern theater was coming to Richmond. He again insisted on having all Federal troops in Virginia sent to him by water. Annoyed by McClellan's dictatorial tone, the president replied, "That the whole force of the enemy is concentrating in Richmond, I think can not be certainly known to you or me." Lincoln understood the situation in Virginia better than McClellan, and he knew Jackson's army was still in the Valley and other Confederate units were still watching McDowell along the Rappahannock. "I am painfully impressed with the importance of the struggle before you," Lincoln replied, "and I shall aid you all I can consistently with my view of due regard to all points," but he made it clear that the distribution of troops as well as all strategic decisions would be made by him and such dictates from the general were inappropriate. McClellan might have done something on May 29 had he felt better but spent the day in bed suffering from fever and headaches brought on by malaria and neuralgia.[27]

After observing McClellan's and McDowell's movements combined with repercussions from the Hanover Court House engagement, General Johnston made preparations to strike the Army of the Potomac. On May 31 McClellan had an aggregate of 127,000 officers and men, of whom 98,000 were present for duty. Johnston's force consisted of about 62,000 effectives. At nightfall on May 30, after learning some of McDowell's troops had returned to Fredericksburg, Johnston called his generals together. He canceled the attack on the north side of the Chickahominy and redirected it at the Federals occupying the south bank at Seven Pines. Johnston showed little concern for Union forces on the north side of the river because he assumed, and correctly, that McClellan did not expect to be attacked, so he issued orders to throw twenty-two of twenty-seven brigades from his seven divisions against Heintzelman and Keyes. During the night a savage rainstorm struck the area—one of the worst in memory—and flooded the Chickahominy, thereby threatening to sever communications between McClellan's divided army. Although swollen streams and soggy ground retarded the movement of Confederate troops, the first big battle for Richmond began on the morning of May 31, when Johnston struck Keyes corps at Seven Pines and Franklin's corps at Fair Oaks. In what historian Douglas Southall Freeman termed "a battle of strange errors," both sides committed forty-one thousand troops. Part of Keyes's corps advanced to within four miles of the Confederate capital, so close they could see the spires of the city and hear church bells ringing. McClellan reported five thousand casualties and Johnston six thousand. Johnston suffered a disabling wound, after which Robert E. Lee took command of the Confederate army. On June 1 Lee withdrew his forces to Richmond's defenses after a day of ineffectual maneuvering. The Army of the Potomac might have laid siege to Richmond had Lee not studied McClellan's generalship over the past weeks and believed he could beat him by maneuvering and forcing a fight.[28]

During the battle Lincoln telegraphed McClellan, "Stand well on your guard—hold all your ground, or yield any only inch by inch and in good order." To boost Little Mac's morale, he promised to send reinforcements. Like at Williamsburg, McClellan did not appear on the battlefield until the second day, as the enemy was withdrawing. He made no tactical changes, though he observed the enemy falling back to Richmond in disorder. Having often bragged about how he had captured Manassas, Yorktown, and Williamsburg with little bloodshed, he now came face-to-face with thousands of dead and wounded. The sight horrified him. Instead of taking advantage of Lee's withdrawal, and with the army's morale riding high, McClellan paused to replace washed-out bridges. "It is certain we have gained a glorious victory," he wrote his wife, but mentioned being "tired of the sickening sight of the battlefield, with its mangled corpses and poor suffering wounded." "Victory has no charms for me when purchased at such cost," he confided. McClellan revealed an underlying trait, one that would prevent him from ever becoming a great general, when he added, "Every poor fellow that is killed or wounded haunts me." He loved his men too much to see them harmed—a fatal flaw for a general charged with the responsibility of winning battles. This emotional attachment acted as a bond between McClellan and his men, and Lincoln never came to understand his general's abhorrence of bloodshed.[29]

Aside from spilling blood, the Battle of Seven Pines and Fair Oaks ended inconclusively because McClellan failed to follow up a potentially stunning victory. The Confederate attack failed to destroy either Keyes or Heintzelman and had the effect of bringing a few brigades from Franklin's and Sumner's corps across the river. Most of them never fired a shot or lost a man in action. François Ferdinand d'Orléans, the Prince de Joinville, who served as a volunteer on McClellan's staff, wrote, "The Federals had the defensive battle they desired; had repulsed the enemy; but arrested by natural obstacles that were not insurmountable, they had gained nothing by their success. They had missed an unique opportunity of striking a blow." General John G. Barnard, the chief engineer who had conducted the siege at Yorktown, also complained, later writing: "The repulse of the rebels at Fair Oaks should have been taken advantage of. It was one of those occasions which, if not seized, do not repeat themselves. We now know the state of disorganization and dismay in which the rebel army retreated. We now know that it could have been followed into Richmond. Had it been so, there would have been no resistance to overcome to bring over our right wing [against the Confederate flank]." Although McClellan had molded a great army, a monument to his administrative ability, he squandered its greatness through mismanagement at Seven Pines and Fair Oaks. Little Mac had some justification for delay because many of the temporary bridges had been taken out by the storm, but when he and his troops finally appeared on the field on June 1, he had already decided to let the enemy retire unmolested.[30]

After nothing happened, General Lee used the interregnum to reorganize the Confederate army, restore morale, and, like McClellan had recently predicted, bring all the military units scattered throughout Virginia, including Jackson's Valley Army, to the defense of Richmond.

11

"I almost begin to think we are invincible"

INSTEAD OF PROBING FOR ADVANTAGES after the inconclusive Battle of Seven Pines and Fair Oaks, McClellan yielded the upper hand to General Lee. Little Mac never moved in foul weather, and for much of the week it rained hard. The Chickahominy overflowed its banks, sweeping away bridges, and the ground became foot-deep mud. Men and horses slipped, and wagons and artillery sank to their axles, sticking fast. Cut in two by the swollen river, the army occupied time by digging trenches in the muck. Lee expected no trouble from McClellan and received none.

McClellan continued badgering the administration for reinforcements. The general's hallucination that the rebel army was twice the size of his own had become a permanent fixation daily enhanced by Pinkerton's incompetent spies. Following the Fair Oaks affair, Lincoln detached McCall's division from McDowell's corps and sent it by water to McClellan. He also placed Fort Monroe under McClellan's command, replaced General Wool with Major General John A. Dix, and sent ten veteran regiments up the Peninsula to quench McClellan's insatiable thirst for troops. In total McClellan received twenty thousand reinforcements to replace five thousand casualties lost at Seven Pines and Fair Oaks. "I am glad you are pressing forward reinforcements so vigorously," the Young Napoleon advised Stanton. "I shall be in perfect readiness to move forward and take Richmond the moment McCall reaches here and the ground will admit the passage of artillery."[1]

McCall's division of ten thousand men and five batteries of artillery arrived on June 11, and two days later McClellan assigned the unit to Fitz-

John Porter's Fifth Corps. McClellan then moved with his headquarters staff to the south side of the Chickahominy, leaving Porter's corps dangling on the far right flank and vulnerable to attack, especially if the river reached flood stage again.

Since landing the Army of the Potomac on the Peninsula, McClellan had received 39,441 reinforcements. For apologists denouncing the administration for having withheld McDowell's corps, McClellan now had most of it, including William Franklin's magnificent division, George McCall's division, and sundry other units intended for McDowell but diverted to the Peninsula. Yet a day seldom passed without McClellan clamoring for more. Lincoln once again expressed a willingness to send the remnants of McDowell's corps by land, but McClellan insisted it come by water. Because McDowell, on reaching Richmond, wanted McCall's division returned, McClellan howled, "If I cannot control all of his troops, I want none of them, but would prefer to fight the battle with what I have, and let others be responsible for the results." Once again, McClellan wanted McDowell's troops but not McDowell.[2]

The general's petulant outbursts flabbergasted the president. He did not want McClellan picking a fight with Stanton when he should be picking a fight with Lee. He solved the problem by holding back McDowell, using the bedraggled condition of Shields's division as an excuse. McClellan retained McCall's division, and McDowell remained at Fredericksburg. At this point the weather cleared, the river dropped, roads dried, and McClellan no longer had reasons to delay. Having committed on June 7 to be ready to move as soon as McCall's division arrived, he now hesitated and increased his demands for more reinforcements. With an army of 156,838 men, of which at least 127,000 were present for operations, McClellan wasted most of June in busy and bustling activities equivalent to mere idleness.[3]

On June 18 Stonewall Jackson's sixteen thousand–man army was still in the Shenandoah Valley, reinforced by ten thousand men from Lee's army, which gave McClellan a two-to-one numerical advantage for an assault on Richmond. McClellan knew Lee had weakened Richmond, and so did Lincoln, who wrote: "If this is true, it is as good as a reinforcement to you of equal force. I could dispose of things if I could know about what day you can attack Richmond." Lincoln implied that because Jackson had been reinforced, he might transfer more of McDowell's troops to the Valley if McClellan did not intend to use them. Little Mac replied, "A general engagement may take place at any hour," and then argued that Lee's detachment of units to the Valley merely confirmed the enemy's superior strength and justified his request for more troops. He then closed, adding, "After tomorrow we shall fight the rebel army as soon as Providence will admit." Lincoln disliked the general's allusion to waiting for Providence. McClellan gave the president no clues, but a letter home revealed how he planned to bring forward his artillery, shell the city, and carry it with little loss of life. This approach epitomized McClellan's tactics at Yorktown, where he had failed to damage the enemy. The general adored his men enough never to want them hurt. Gloating to his wife, he said: "If you could see the faces of the troops as I ride among them you would share my confidence. They will do anything I tell them to do." Had Lincoln seen the letter, he would have directed McClellan to tell his troops to take Richmond.[4]

WHILE MCCLELLAN COMPLAINED, procrastinated, and practiced static warfare, Brigadier General James E. B. "Jeb" Stuart, with twelve hundred Confederate cavalry and four guns, set out from Richmond on June 12, crossed to the north side of the Chickahominy, rode completely around the Army of the Potomac, recrossed the river, and on April 15 returned to Richmond with vital intelligence. Stuart's reconnaissance covered some 150 miles, during which he lost one man. It is rare for a general on a mission behind enemy lines to inflict such insult on an opponent without suffering injury. McClellan curbed his embarrassment by congratulating himself that Stuart had done so little physical harm, claiming only two schooners and fourteen wagons had been destroyed. By turning the reconnaissance into a raid, Stuart startled McClellan and knocked him off-balance. This would have been an ideal time for McDowell to join McClellan for a combined attack on Richmond, but Little Mac regarded his communications along the Pamunkey River in jeopardy. He postponed any plans he might have considered for attacking Richmond and turned his attention to changing his base to the James River, thereby giving Lee time to expand his army to eighty thousand effectives.[5]

On June 18 McClellan began rerouting supply ships to the James. Six days later he wrote Commodore John Rodgers asking for gunboats to be moved up the James to Drewry's Bluff to support the base change. He also intimated his intention to press an attack on the Confederate capital and on June 25 advanced his picket line at Seven Pines to within four miles of Richmond. He intended the pseudo-aggressive movement to serve as bait to draw out the enemy and ordered his generals to fall back to their entrenchments on contact so the men could fight defensively.[6]

Pushing Federal pickets forward resulted in the Battle of Oak Grove, also known as Henrico, King's School House, and The Orchards. Although it became the first of the Seven Days' battles, Lee refused the bait. Samuel Heintzelman's Third Corps, still located at Fair Oaks–Seven Pines, drove in Confederate outposts with skirmishers. Joe Hooker's troops edged forward until they butted up against Major General Benjamin Huger's division. Instead of directing the action, McClellan sent General Marcy to stop Hooker's advance. McClellan arrived during the afternoon and spent time in a tree observing the battlefield. After interrupting the fight Hooker had started, he then resumed the attack, this time with Keyes's Fourth Corps in support. The battle ended at Richmond's main fieldworks about four miles from the capital. Lee showed no interest in assaulting McClellan's entrenchments, and though he worried the unexpected attack might be the forerunner to a major offensive, he did not change his plans to attack Porter's Fifth Corps in the morning. McClellan reported the mini-offensive a success, but it failed to lure Lee into a fight and cost McClellan 626 casualties.[7]

McClellan now learned that Jackson's Valley Army had reached the area and became doubly concerned when erroneously informed by Pinkerton that another army under Beauregard had arrived from the West. Anticipating an imminent attack, he telegraphed an urgent message to Stanton: "If I had another good division I could laugh at Jackson." Later, after conferring with Pinkerton, he warned Stanton: "The rebel force is stated at 200,000, including Jackson and Beauregard. I regret my inferiority in numbers, but feel I am in no way responsible for it." After blaming the government for not responding to his requests for reinforcements, he morbidly predicted his death. Pinkerton estimated the size of Lee's army at 180,000, which was actually about 81,000, and McClellan merely rounded it off to 200,000 by grabbing another 20,000 out of thin air. Stanton showed the telegrams to Lincoln, who wrote Little Mac: "Your being overwhelmed by 200,000, and talking of where the responsibility belongs, pains me very much. I give you all I can, and act on the presumption that you will do the best you can with what you have, while you continue, ungenerously I think, to assume that I could give you more if I would."[8]

How much longer McClellan would have dallied, perfecting his preparations, will never be known because Lee took the initiative after deciding the Young Napoleon would likely waste time until forced to fight. Lee's army actually consisted of about 80,762 effectives, compared with McClellan's June 20 report of 156,838 men, which, by eliminating absentees and Dix's force at Fort Monroe, left McClellan with 105,445 effectives. Both armies contained the best men and material their governments could provide, and the Confederate force had nearly doubled in size since Fair Oaks.[9]

Unlike McClellan, who was fixated on changing his base while pleading for reinforcements, Lee made his preparations quickly and energetically after Stuart returned from his reconnaissance. On June 16 Lee ordered Jackson to join him, emphasizing the importance of doing so secretly. To mask the movement, Lee detached two brigades from Richmond and in plain sight put them on the road to the Valley, knowing the demonstration would be observed by McClellan's spies. Although both brigades marched back to Richmond that night, the ruse worked, giving credibility to Pinkerton's overestimate of Lee's strength and McClellan's delusions of being outmatched. McClellan expected Jackson to arrive by June 25 somewhere on the army's right flank and rear but made no use of this knowledge other than to reproach the government for not sending him more men. Jackson actually arrived ahead of his army and on June 23 met with Lee to discuss an attack on Porter's Fifth Corps, which, as Lincoln recently warned, remained exposed on the north side of the Chickahominy while the main army camped on the south side. Jackson agreed to have his army in position by June 26, giving himself, as it would turn out, too little time.[10]

Lee's contempt for McClellan showed in his orders. He prepared to send fifty-seven thousand troops to the north side of the Chickahominy to strike the Federal right wing while leaving only twenty-five thousand troops to safeguard Richmond against McClellan's main force, which was

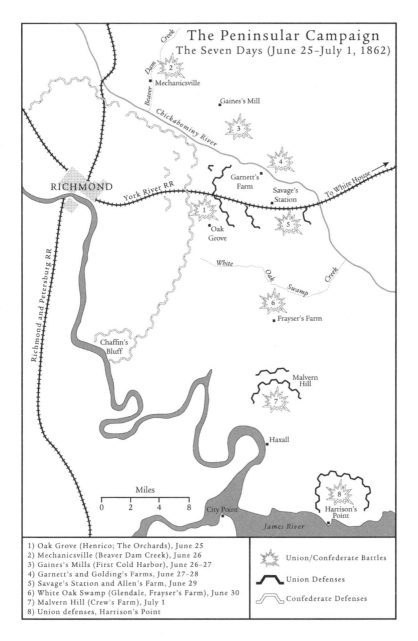

The Peninsular Campaign
The Seven Days (June 25–July 1, 1862)

RICHMOND

Chickahominy River

Dam Creek

Beaver

Mechanicsville

Gaines's Mill

York River RR

Garnett's Farm

Savage's Station

To White House

Oak Grove

Richmond and Petersburg RR

White

Oak

Swamp

Creek

Frayser's Farm

Chaffin's Bluff

Malvern Hill

Haxall

Miles

0   2   4   8

City Point

Harrison's Point

James River

1) Oak Grove (Henrico; The Orchards), June 25
2) Mechanicsville (Beaver Dam Creek), June 26
3) Gaines's Mills (First Cold Harbor), June 26–27
4) Garnett's and Golding's Farms, June 27–28
5) Savage's Station and Allen's Farm, June 29
6) White Oak Swamp (Glendale, Frayser's Farm), June 30
7) Malvern Hill (Crew's Farm), July 1
8) Union defenses, Harrison's Point

Union/Confederate Battles

Union Defenses

Confederate Defenses

MAP 2. The Peninsular Campaign

located on the south side of the river and a few miles from Richmond. Lee intended to drive Porter's corps out of Mechanicsville, thereby forcing McClellan to bring some part of the army back across the river to aid Porter. With Jackson's eighteen thousand men cooperating from the left, Lee hoped to capture the York River Railroad, surround Porter, and sever McClellan's communications. If Union forces unexpectedly attacked Richmond, Lee planned to recross the Chickahominy farther downstream, strike McClellan's rear with infantry and cavalry, and drive the Federals back across the Chickahominy. Either way, Lee expected McClellan to bring the Union army back to the north side of the Chickahominy, where he could drive it off the Peninsula. Jefferson Davis did not like the plan because it exposed Richmond, but he remembered that McClellan was an engineer and would likely behave like one and that he would worry foremost about his line of communications.

Almost every military scholar of the day would have vetoed Lee's plan because once he crossed the Chickahominy, four Federal army corps and part of another could march into Richmond. Historian William Swinton, who followed the Army of the Potomac and knew a great deal about tactics, said McClellan had three choices: he could concentrate the entire army on the north side of the Chickahominy and deliver a general battle; he could concentrate on the south bank and march directly on Richmond; or he could transfer the right wing to the south bank and retreat to the James River. Swinton thought the second option best, being "very bold and brilliant." Most military historians agreed. Swinton also thought retreating to the James was the least inspired of the three alternatives, and it was this option that dominated McClellan's actions on the day Lee struck Porter's Fifth Corps at Mechanicsville. At this hour the fate of Richmond depended entirely on McClellan's generalship. Only nine brigades in two Confederate divisions—John Magruder's and Benjamin Huger's—stood between Richmond and more than eighty-five thousand Federals. While assaulting Porter, Lee detailed Magruder to worry McClellan with demonstrations. Little Mac had his own dilemma. If he captured Richmond, could he hold it and keep his communications open without first destroying Lee's army? He should have asked himself the same question before taking the Army of the Potomac to the Peninsula.[11]

On the afternoon of June 26 the second of the Seven Day's battles opened when five infantry brigades from Major General Ambrose P. Hill's division swept through the village of Mechanicsville and advanced for about a mile before butting up against Porter's well-prepared defenses at Beaver Dam Creek. Jackson, who was supposed to assault Porter's rear, failed to arrive in time. Porter's force consisted of McCall's, Morell's, and Sykes divisions; in all 17,330 infantry, 2,534 artillery, and 671 cavalry. As Hill advanced, Federal artillery and deadly rifle fire from army regulars raked the Confederate line. At sunset Lee made one more attempt to turn the Federal left flank. Porter rushed in reinforcements and opened with devastating artillery fire. Lee's attack miscarried, mainly because Jackson became confused by the terrain and went into camp four hours before the fight ended. Instead of flanking the Federals out of their defenses, Lee attacked frontally and lost 1,484 men; Union casualties were 361. The Battle of Mechanicsville, also known as Beaver Dam Creek, imposed a disturbing defeat on Lee's superior force, and Porter never lost his advantage of position.[12]

McClellan stood by on the other side of the river listening to the sound of artillery. That night, after the battle, he crossed the river to visit his friend and found an exultant and victorious army virtually unscathed by an afternoon of fierce fighting. In the opinion of several authorities, had Porter commanded the army instead of McClellan, Richmond might have fallen the following day. Porter understood the advantage of having Lee on one side of the river and Richmond on the other and told McClellan he would hold the line on Beaver Dam Creek while Little Mac moved the main body against the rebel capital. Instead of accepting Porter's suggestion, McClellan returned to headquarters to decide what to do. Around 3:00 a.m. he ordered Porter to retire to a defensive position four miles downriver and await developments. General James Longstreet, whose division participated in the attack on Porter, said McClellan's foolish decision to abandon a strong position literally "gave up the *morale* of their success, and transferred it to our somewhat disheartened forces." Equally puzzling is McClellan's own statement when he pointed to June 26 as "the day upon which I had decided as the time for our final advance." If he thought it safe to attack Richmond with Lee's army in front of him, why would he not attack Richmond when most of Lee's army was seven to eight miles on the far side of the Chickahominy fighting Porter? The answer reverts to McClellan's delusion that Lee's army contained two hundred thousand troops as well as concern for his own communications. Porter's withdrawal to Gaines's Mill, which soon led to the third of the Seven Days' battles, resulted from McClellan's efforts to fight defensively. His fixation on moving his base to the James trumped any advantages won by Porter on the battlefield. If McClellan wanted to fight defensively, he should not have gone to the Peninsula. Nevertheless, after the Beaver Dam Creek battle he telegraphed the administration at 9:00 p.m. from Porter's headquarters: "Victory today complete & against great odds. I almost begin to think we are invincible." McClellan had not been on the battlefield during the day, and victory was far from complete. Only one of McClellan's five corps had been involved, and instead of childishly claiming victory, he should have given the administration a thorough assessment of the situation. Lincoln wanted to help McClellan in every way possible, and declarations of victory one day and omens of disaster the next gave the president no meaningful intelligence on which to base his actions. From the latest dispatch Lincoln might had believed McClellan needed no help at all.[13]

The oddest inconsistency in McClellan's actions was his total failure to execute his own plan for assaulting Richmond. On June 23, three days before Lee attacked Porter at Mechanicsville, McClellan anticipated the movement. Through Marcy he asked Porter to check the enemy's advance but to hold him there long enough for the Army of the Potomac "to make the decisive movement which will determine the fate of Richmond." Porter's action at Beaver Dam Creek three days later produced the exact conditions McClellan wanted. Little Mac now had the option of either assaulting Richmond or transferring forces to the north side of the river to defeat Lee. Instead, he lost heart and did nothing. Porter believed McClellan's stubborn stand would open the way for the capture of Richmond—an impression reinforced by General Alexander Webb when he arrived from army headquarters to witness Porter's fight. Only his personal relationship with Little Mac prevented Porter from registering disgust when ordered to withdraw.[14]

Lincoln never learned about McClellan's missed opportunities on the Peninsula until 1863 because the general's reports were usually designed to worry the administration. The general even claimed on June 26 of being attacked by Jackson, which never happened. He spread constant gloom over the likelihood of having his communications severed. Demands for reinforcements festooned every complaint. General Barnard, chief of engineers, regarded McClellan's behavior as mystifying. On June 26–27 he offered three recommendations, any of which might have resulted in the capture of Richmond. Instead of probing for advantage on the battlefield, McClellan concentrated every effort on changing his base to the James. He understood so little about Lee's repulse at Beaver Dam Creek that he wrote his wife: "We have again whipped the secesh badly. Stonewall Jackson is the victim this time."[15]

On June 27, with Richmond still vulnerable, Lee pressed toward Gaines's Mill and found Porter in new defensive works. In the third battle of the Seven Days, Porter checked the Confederate advance at Boatswain's Swamp, which broke into flames and stifled the attack. Lee ordered a halt and waited for Jackson to get into position on Porter's flank. Once again, Jackson failed to arrive on the field because of faulty maneuvering. Porter received reinforcements from Franklin's Sixth Corps about the time Jackson arrived on the field, and with 25,000 troops the reinforced Fifth Corps held off 57,000 Confederates. Porter saw an opportunity to break the Confederate line and asked McClellan for another division. Still believing Lee's army contained up to 200,000 troops, McClellan vetoed the request. An hour before dark the Confederates struck simultaneously along Porter's front. Federal lines cracked, and Porter began an orderly withdrawal to the south side of the Chickahominy. The bloody daylong fight at Gaines's Mill cost the Confederates 8,750 and Federal forces 6,837 casualties. Porter's defense gave McClellan time to continue his withdrawal to the James. Throughout the day Magruder demonstrated in front of McClellan's main army and stymied more than 60,000 Federals, while Porter's corps did most of the fighting.[16]

McClellan had missed a third and more favorable opportunity to seize Richmond because Lee was now farther away and too disorganized to come swiftly to the aid of the capital. General Webb, who remained with Porter throughout the day, said "The sacrifice at Gaines's Mill . . . was warranted, if we were to gain Richmond by making it, and the troops engaged in carrying out this plan, conceiving it to be the wish of the general commanding, were successful in holding the rebels on the left bank." Porter performed his task capably, while McClellan failed to take any advantage of an opportunity conceived by his own strategy. When Little Mac pulled Porter's Fifth Corps to the south side of the Chickahominy, William Swinton lamented, "The Army of the Potomac turned its back on the Confederate capital and all the high hopes the advance had inspired."[17]

Webb puzzled over McClellan's inertia and adopted the theory that Little Mac thought the capture of Richmond, with Lee beyond the Chickahominy, would not be a proper military movement because of its distance from his base along the York River. The idea made little sense because the James River base had already been established, and at the time McClellan could have used either one. According to military maxims, Little Mac's thinking would have been unsound had he not believed 150,000 enemy troops were demonstrating in his front instead of 25,000. Neither Webb nor Porter knew that on June 25 McClellan had firmly decided to retreat to the James, where supply ships were already waiting. McClellan's behavior suggests that he was more worried about being attacked by Magruder's small force on the south of the Chickahominy than by Lee's heavy assaults against Porter on the opposite bank.[18]

Thanks to Porter's determined defense, McClellan actually won the first of the Seven Days' battles without knowing it. Instead, he complained to the administration about being forced to retreat: "Had I 20,000 fresh and good troops we would be sure of a splendid victory tomorrow." McClellan never knew what to do with the troops he had, and twenty thousand more would have made no difference. His efforts were not focused on fighting but on retreating to the James with help from the navy. "We have met a severe repulse today," he misinformed Flag Officer Goldsborough, "and I am obliged to fall back . . . I look to you to give me all the support you can in covering my flank." Even Major General Daniel H. Hill, who led one of the Confederate attacks on Porter, said: "During Lee's absence Richmond was at the mercy of McClellan . . . The fortifications around Richmond at the time were very slight. McClellan could have captured the city with very little loss of life. The want of supplies would have forced Lee to attack him as soon as possible, with all the disadvantages of a precipitated movement."[19]

McClellan was also rattled by Magruder's demonstrations late on June 27 and early on June 28, when two Confederate brigades tested the Federal line at Garnett's Farm and Golding's Farm, the fourth of the Seven Days' battles. The Federals quickly checked Magruder's poorly coordinated advances. Had McClellan been conscious of the Confederate missteps, he could have brushed away Magruder's weak thrusts and marched into Richmond. Instead, Little Mac personally retired to Savage's Station in the rear and never came onto the field. "They have outnumbered us everywhere," he informed his wife, "but we have not lost our honor." The army had not lost its honor, and McClellan would still have several opportunities on the Peninsula to redeem his own.[20]

On the far side of the Chickahominy, McClellan never visited the battlefield at Gaines's Mill and during the night of June 27 summoned Porter across the river with instructions to destroy the bridges behind him. He then announced his base-changing plan—an extremely complicated maneuver of transferring more than 100,000 men across a fighting front stretching from one side of the Peninsula to the other. He advised Stanton on June 27 not to expect to hear from him for several days and then shortly after midnight sent a lengthy dispatch filled with inaccuracies emanating from his own fantasies. "I know the full history of the day," he wrote delusively: "On this side of the bank we repulsed several strong attacks"—which were actually Magruder's theatrical demonstrations—and "On the left bank our men [Porter's] did all that men could do," which was accurate. He then referred to his army as sad remnants, although most of the men south of the Chickahominy had not fired a shot or been fired upon. He referred to Porter's regulars as "superb" but never visited the battlefield to observe their valiant defense. He said if he had another "20,000 or even 10,000 fresh troops to use tomorrow" he would take Richmond, which he had no intention of doing under any circumstance. He then promised to cover his retreat and "save the material and *personnel* of the army." "I have lost this battle because my force was too small," he declared, although what McClellan lost was the possibility of winning the war without the horrendous bloodshed that followed in the years ahead. "I again repeat that I am not responsible for this," he added. "You must send me very large reinforcements and send them at once. If I save this army now, I tell you plainly that I owe no thanks to you or to any other person in Washington. You have done your best to sacrifice this army." Colonel Edward S. Sanford, military supervisor of the telegraph, omitted the last two sentences from the copy delivered to Stanton. This fact remained unknown until 1907, when David Homer Bates published it in *Lincoln in the Telegraph Office*.[21]

Stunned by the telegram, and completely baffled by McClellan's unexpected withdrawal, Lincoln authorized Stanton to forward to Richmond twenty-five thousand troops from General Halleck's command in the West "by the nearest and quickest route." The president soon developed second thoughts, but McClellan's message caused instant panic within the War Department. Lincoln might not have reacted at all had he read Little Mac's private correspondence dated June 27, in which the general proudly told his wife: "We have repulsed them everywhere . . . All well & very busy." A day later he added: "The Army has acted magnificently. I thank my friends in Washn for our repulse."[22]

At sunrise June 28 the movement to the James began. McClellan had withdrawn his headquarters to Savage's Station, soon to become the site of the fifth Seven Days' battle. Instead of monitoring the action on the battlefield, he spent the afternoon and evening directing the withdrawal of the army's supplies. Although McClellan never demonstrated speed when advancing, he moved with celerity when retreating and began a swift and orderly withdrawal. General Keyes moved his corps across White Oak Swamp and placed it in position on the far side to cover the passage of other units. Porter followed and took position on roads leading out of Richmond. Franklin withdrew from the extreme right after skirmishing at Golding's Farm. Keyes and Porter continued to lead the withdrawal until arriving at Malvern Hill, thus securing the left flank of the army where the last battle of the Seven Days' would be fought.

McClellan's movement took Lee completely by surprise, as the Confederate general had expected the Federals to return to the north side of the Chickahominy to protect their communications. Lee had continued down the north bank of the river in search of Porter and did not learn until June 29 that McClellan was moving toward the James. Forced to revise his entire battle plan, Lee turned about and sent his troops along parallel roads to intercept the Army of the Potomac near Charles City Crossroads, which lay midway between White Oak Swamp and the James. Lee attempted a complicated convergence on McClellan's flanks from different directions, but he had forgotten lessons learned at Beaver Dam Creek and Gaines's Mills of the dangers when attacking Federals holding prepared defensive positions. Edwin Sumner repulsed Magruder at Allen's Farm, and later, after retiring to Savage's Station, he and Franklin met another fierce onslaught from Magruder and defeated him again.[23]

With the way wide open to Richmond, Sumner insisted on advancing immediately. Franklin reminded him of McClellan's orders to withdraw across White Oak Swamp that night. Sumner shouted back: "No . . . I never leave a victorious field. Why, if I had twenty thousand more men, I would crush this rebellion. McClellan did not know the circumstances when he wrote that note. He did not know that we would fight a battle and gain a victory." While Sumner debated the matter with Franklin, an aide-de-camp arrived from McClellan's headquarters and said the order must be obeyed. Sumner chafed because McClellan, far in the rear, had never come onto the field to assess the situation, and he believed Little Mac had bungled another opportunity. During a later inquiry by the Joint Committee on the Conduct of the War, McClellan was asked whether he had participated in the battle of Savage's Station or directed the movement of troops, to which he replied, "I had given general orders for the movement of the troops, but the fighting was done under direct orders of the corps commanders." In other words, McClellan's previously written orders trumped any victories or opportunities opened on the battlefield as a result of fighting. Those orders had come from a panicked general who believed he was being attacked by two hundred thousand rebels. McClellan did, however, post his troops in excellent defensive positions, which paid dividends during the remainder of the army's retreat.[24]

The sixth of the Seven Days' battles—known variously as White Oak Swamp, Frayser's Farm, Glendale, and other locally familiar names—occurred on June 30. After Franklin crossed White Oak Swamp and destroyed the bridge, he occupied the heights on the far side and prevented Stonewall Jackson from impeding McClellan's retreat. Confederates attacking the flanks failed to breach Federal lines, forcing James Longstreet and A. P. Hill to attack the Union center at Frayser's Farm on nearly equal terms. At 4:30 p.m. the Confederates struck Joseph Hooker's, George McCall's, and Philip Kearny's divisions, which were supported by John Sedgwick's and Henry Slocum's divisions. Because the Federal divisions came from different corps, no one assumed overall command. Nor was McClellan present to direct the battle. A savage and obstinate fight ensued, which for both sides became another crucial point of the campaign. If Lee had pierced the Union center, chaos would have spread throughout the army. Instead, five Federal divisions stopped Lee's assault. If McClellan had come onto the field and concentrated his army at Frayser's Farm,

Lee should have been thrown back and the road opened to Richmond. All honors would have gone to the Young Napoleon for drawing the Confederates from the capital, forcing Lee to extend his lines, checking Jackson at White Oak Swamp, and then destroying the Confederate army. The Prince de Joinville, who had been serving on McClellan's staff but was now preparing to return to France, took General Franklin aside and said: "Advise General McClellan to center his army at this point and fight the battle today. If he does, he will be in Richmond tomorrow." Instead, McClellan had vanished to the rear in search of a defensive position closer to the James, while Jefferson Davis, Lee, and Longstreet were all on the battlefield and under fire from Union guns throughout the afternoon. When darkness ended the fighting, seven Federal division commanders, left to their discretion and without direction, checked Lee's army, moved trains and artillery by Long Bridge Road, and moved onto Malvern Hill.[25]

McClellan never seemed to notice why his army was consistently whipping the Confederates, and it was General Lee's contempt for the Young Napoleon's generalship that drove him to the disastrous assault of Malvern Hill. Brigadier General Andrew A. Humphreys, McClellan's chief topographical engineer, had laid out a defensive position on a hill much like one Porter had used at Gaines's Mill. The hill was flanked by swamps and winding ravines, with the lower end open and partly covered with woods. On the heights Porter posted Federal artillery, arranging it to fire over Heintzelman's and Sumner's brigades occupying the slope and around Keyes's corps on the left flank. Confederates could lay concealed in the woods and organize attacks, but they had to cross open ground before scaling the hill. Union gunboats in the James also covered the flanks, lobbing shells into the ravines and marshes. Lee could not restrain himself from one final thrust to force the surrender of a timorous Union general. Jackson had finally come up, and Lee had his entire army unified for the final push on Malvern Hill.

Although some of Lee's generals expressed concern over the strength of the Union position, Lee and Longstreet believed the Army of the Potomac had been so demoralized by McClellan's tactics that the position could be carried if it were attacked en masse. Lee's hurried and poorly coordinated attack on Malvern Hill began at 1:00 p.m. and lasted until nightfall. He wasted a vast amount of valor and Confederate blood, while on the Union side Porter's Fifth Corps, with George W. Morell's division and Darius N. Couch's division from Keyes's corps, absorbed the brunt of the attack. Together they threw the Confederates back. Magruder's division made the most sensational charge of the day shortly after 4:00 p.m., and his nine brigades melted away under furious discharges from Sykes's artillery and deadly infantry fire. The Confederates hammered away at the Union position until nightfall, when Jackson ordered his men to fall back.[26]

McClellan was not on the battlefield but, instead, at Haxall's Landing under the protection of gunboats on the James River. He came to the field for a short time during the morning, posted several batteries, and for a while remained on the right wing away from the fighting. He said he was anxious about the right wing, which was never threatened. After predicting the left and center would hold, he returned to Haxall's Landing, boarded a gunboat lying offshore "to select the final location for the army and its depots," and listened to the fighting. Had Little Mac remained on the field, he would have witnessed a great victory won by troops under the command of his subordinate generals. In 1886 McClellan said he had twice visited the battlefield and made an "entire circuit of the position" and later "rode along the lines" and "remained in the vicinity," but this version contradicted his testimony before the Committee on the Conduct of the War and those who reported his activities during the battle. It is not difficult in 1886 to say what happened in 1862 when one has, as McClellan had, all the reports of the battle to interpret as he wished. He called the Battle of Malvern Hill a "complete victory" without explaining his reasons for withdrawing after winning.[27]

Lee expected to be assaulted the morning of July 2, and a member of Jackson's staff admitted the army would have been forced to retreat. Although Porter and artillery chief Henry Hunt advised holding the position to organize a counterattack, McClellan withdrew that night to a new base at Harrison's Landing and entrenched. A comparison of losses demonstrates how well the Army of the Potomac fought.

	KILLED	WOUNDED	MISSING	TOTAL
Confederate Army	2,823	13,703	3,223	19,749
Army of the Potomac	1,734	8,062	6,055	15,489

The significant statistic is the killed and wounded, among which the Confederates suffered measurably more than the Federals. In 1886 Mc-Clellan proudly stated what his army had accomplished in 1862 without mentioning what the army might have accomplished had it been competently led. The retreat by McClellan, the invader, made Lee the hero of the hour. As historian John Codman Ropes observed, "The moral and political effect of the whole series of movements and battles was entirely to the advantage of the Confederates."[28]

The most disturbing aspect of the Seven Days' battles came down to McClellan's inability to act aggressively despite having seven opportunities to battle Lee and perhaps capture Richmond. Impressed by the phantasm of facing two hundred thousand enemy troops, McClellan never seriously considered offensive operations. He pulled his men off Malvern Hill and retreated farther down the James to Harrison's Landing in order, he said, to reach a point where his supplies could be delivered safely. By behaving in this manner, McClellan did what no general could afford to do. He admitted defeat when he had not been defeated. After calling the engagement at Oak Grove—the first encounter of the Seven Days' battles—a complete victory, he called the potential victory at Malvern Hill a defeat in order to justify his withdrawal. McClellan clearly could not evaluate battlefield conditions and made little effort to try. Lee followed, but after witnessing the ability with which the Army of the Potomac fought, he stopped attacking—a decision to which both Longstreet and Jackson agreed. On July 8 Lee withdrew most of his army to Richmond, and the Peninsular Campaign came to an end. Winning battles meant taking risks. Historian Thomas J. Rowland summed up McClelland's performance on the Peninsula, writing: "McClellan was not willing to take those risks. In that respect, he was flawed and cannot be considered a great commander. It does not mean that he was irretrievably a dismal one."[29]

On the night of July 2 McClellan wrote his wife from the steamer *Ariel*, his headquarters afloat. Although he had been on Malvern Hill only briefly, he spoke of being attacked "on my own front" and with only seven brigades "held our own at all points after most desperate fighting." From his statements Mrs. McClellan must have envisioned bullets whizzing by her husband's ears, although no one recalled seeing him on the battlefield during the heavy afternoon fighting. Her uncle was killed that day, along with one of her husband's friends, and this added genuine tragedy to her impressions. McClellan soon felt safe, which gave him time to cast blame on the administration for all his failures.[30]

12

———•———

"I have no reinforcements to send you"

B Y MOVING TO HARRISON'S LANDING on the James River, Mc-Clellan took the Army of the Potomac out of the war. He sent his father-in-law, General Marcy, to Washington to worry the president about the possible catastrophic surrender of the entire army. Not knowing the extent of the disaster and deeply troubled by Marcy's allusion to the possibility of "capitulation at once, or within two or three days," Lincoln sent McClellan a dispatch intended to bolster the general's morale: "Save your army at all costs. Will send reinforcements as fast as we can. Please tell me at once the present condition of things."[1]

Marcy's visit, combined with McClellan's dispatch to Stanton on June 28 shifting responsibility for failure to the administration because his "force was too small," deeply troubled the president but in a different way than Little Mac intended. With the Army of the Potomac holding a tenuous defensive position on the James River, Lincoln envisioned thousands of Confederate reinforcements pouring into Richmond from the West and forming a second army to attack Washington. Based on McClellan's alarming reports, Lincoln believed this scenario could happen. If he sent reinforcements to McClellan, they would be useless on the Peninsula and too far away to support Washington. After studying options, Lincoln did what McClellan least expected. Instead of denuding Washington and sending massive reinforcements, he consolidated the forces commanded by Nathaniel Banks, John Frémont, and Irvin McDowell and formed the Army of Virginia under Major General John Pope. This move occurred on the heels of McClellan's June 26 telegram warning of being overwhelmed by two hundred thousand Confederates. The order put Pope in charge of defending the capital and protecting western Virginia. Lincoln did not explain his reasons to McClellan, but he did explain them to Seward, writing, "If we send all the force from here to McClellan, the enemy will, before we can know it, send a force from Richmond and take Washington." Lincoln believed it was possible, especially if Lee's army contained, as McClellan claimed, two hundred thousand troops.[2]

Lincoln originally intended to form the Army of Virginia to support McClellan's operations by placing sixty thousand troops between Washington and Richmond to assist in capturing the Confederate capital. At the same time McClellan closed on Richmond from the east, Pope would approach from the north. Once the armies merged, McClellan would command both. Lincoln expected the two armies to cooperate in a pincers movement on the Confederate capital. He had not known on June 26 that Lee had struck McClellan's right wing or that the army was withdrawing to the James. While arrangements for the offensive were under way in Washington, General Marcy arrived to report McClellan's withdrawal. The news nullified Lincoln's plans for an offensive because McClellan's change of base prevented Pope from being supplied from the York River. By moving to the James without first informing the War Department, McClellan isolated his army and lost the opportunity of being reinforced by Pope.

Lincoln's choice of Pope to command the Army of Virginia also led to consequences unknown to the president at the time. Pope came from Illinois with a notable fighting reputation in the West, which made him an attractive choice for independent army command. Stanton brought him to Washington ostensibly as an advisor but actually as a replacement for McClellan, whom he despised. A solidly built officer, Pope looked magnificent in uniform. He spoke effusively about his own merits and of the importance of fighting aggressively, which impressed the president. He also spoke to the Committee on the Conduct of the War and called the movement to the Peninsula a great mistake, claiming that McClellan should have advanced on Richmond from Washington. He thought McClellan's forces should be brought to Aquia Creek and combined with his own troops. With such an army he would march across the South and take New Orleans. The radicals were delighted, for here was a Republican general who shared their views. They were about to press Lincoln into replacing McClellan with Pope when the newly assigned general, two weeks after assuming command of the Army of Virginia, issued an outlandish letter in circular form that astounded and outraged every soldier under his command. No general ever got off to a worse start with his men. Pope said he came from an army that only saw the backs of its enemies—an army that always attacked and always won. The statement implied that western soldiers were superior to eastern soldiers. The Army of Virginia hated its general, and there is some evidence that Stanton had a hand in composing Pope's infamous letter, which pleased the radicals but no one else. Lincoln now had another situation on his hands because radicals wanted McClellan replaced immediately.[3]

Shortly after the Army of the Potomac reached the James River, Lincoln summoned Pope to a cabinet meeting to discuss ways of supporting McClellan. Pope agreed to assault Richmond but only if McClellan was willing to advance at the same time. He doubted McClellan would cooperate, even if given preemptory orders, and let the Army of Virginia be destroyed. Lincoln awoke to the startling revelation that McClellan and Pope hated each other. McClellan did not want Pope's help, and Pope demonstrated no enthusiasm for helping McClellan.[4]

Having reached this crossroads, Stanton received a telegram from McClellan on July 1, which read: "If none of us escape, we shall at least have done honor to the country. I shall do my best to save the army. Send more gunboats." Stanton received the dispatch on the same day the Army of the Potomac defeated the Confederates at Malvern Hill. McClellan had not learned of the victory because he had sulked off to Haxall's Landing listening to the distant sounds of battle. Later that day another dispatch from McClellan arrived at the War Department: "I need 50,000 more men, and with them I will retrieve our fortunes." A day later McClellan still did not comprehend the shattered condition of Lee's army when he wrote: "I hope that the enemy was so severely handled yesterday as to render him careful of his movements today. I now pray for time." Lincoln called for another 300,000 volunteers, but he also advised McClellan that beyond the Army of the Potomac there were not 75,000 men in the entire eastern theater. He also called the general's request "simply absurd" but promised to strengthen the Army of the Potomac as quickly as possible, providing the general agreed to use it. "If we had a million of men we could not get them to you in time," Lincoln replied. "We have not the men to send. Maintain your ground if you can, but save the army at all events, even if you fall back to Fort Monroe." Meanwhile, Lincoln promised to attempt to draw 11,000 troops from the West, 11,000 from Washington, 10,000 from Burnside's army, and another 10,000 from South Carolina.[5]

General Marcy embarked for Washington to inform the president that his son-in-law, if reinforced, still intended to attack Richmond, which was now twenty-five miles away instead of four. On returning to Harrison's Landing, Marcy then assured McClellan of the president's complete support and friendship, but Little Mac still believed the president did not fully appreciate his efforts to save the army from destruction and was intentionally withholding reinforcements. Although McClellan told Marcy, "I am now ready to fight. I will save this Army & lead it to victory in spite of all the enemies in all directions," he said nothing to Lincoln.[6]

Lincoln had moments when he could not decide whether he was being clearheaded or in a stupor when reading McClellan's messages. After several days of listening to the general's claims of being on the brink of eternity, he received a new telegram proudly stating that the army had lost only one gun and one wagon. Once again, McClellan claimed to have beaten the enemy before falling back, calling his movement unparalleled in the annals of war because he had "preserved our trains, our guns, our material, and above all, our honor." Furthermore, he added, "I have not yielded an inch of ground unnecessarily but have retired to prevent the superior force of the Enemy from cutting me off." McClellan now seemed convinced he had saved the army and, as he implied, placed it securely along the banks of the James River, but he also claimed the army had been reduced to fifty thousand effectives and demanded a hundred thousand fresh troops at once.[7]

Lincoln saw through McClellan's gyrations between panic on one hand and sudden outbursts of confidence on the other hand better than Stanton and the military men they both used as advisors. He never questioned McClellan's ability to fight defensively, only his will to fight offensively. On the night of July 4 Quartermaster General Meigs woke Lincoln up to say the Army of the Potomac must be ordered back to Washington immediately to prevent McClellan's capitulation. He said all supplies would have to be destroyed and animals killed, but the men must be brought to safety. Lincoln sent Meigs away and went back to bed. As long as there was a chance to capture Richmond from the James, no advantage would be gained by returning the army to Washington, especially with Pope's army poised on Lee's flank. Several months later Lincoln mentioned the incident to John Hay and said, "I who am not a specially brave man have had to sustain the sinking courage of these professional fighters in critical times." The president's comment would apply equally so in the coming weeks.[8]

Lincoln doubted McClellan's estimate of the enemy's strength, but to protect Washington he needed a blocking force against the possibility the general was right. McClellan's questionable claims of Lee's two hundred thousand–man army changed Lincoln's mind about bringing reinforcements east to serve on the Peninsula, so he rescinded a previous order to Halleck to forward twenty-five thousand western troops to the James River. On July 4 he gave McClellan discretionary authority to remain on the James or return to Washington, adding, "To reinforce you . . . is impossible." Marcy, however, had been working with the War Department and told McClellan that ten thousand troops would be coming from David Hunter's command in South Carolina, ten thousand from Ambrose Burnside's command in North Carolina, and eleven thousand from Washington. In addition to cheering up McClellan, the information also cheered up Lincoln, who still had visions of the Army of Virginia cooperating with the Army of the Potomac against Richmond. "If you can hold your present position," Lincoln wrote McClellan, "we shall 'hive' the enemy yet." The message served as a short pep talk, and the president hoped it did some good.[9]

Lincoln recalled receiving a June 20 dispatch from McClellan, which read, "I would be glad to have permission to lay before Your Excellency, by letter or telegraph, my views as to the present state of military affairs throughout the whole country." Although curious to know what was on McClellan's mind, the president could not get away from Washington at the time and did not want the general's thoughts conveyed by telegraph or letter. A more recent dispatch, claiming the army had dwindled to fifty thousand effectives, deeply troubled him. Lincoln admitted being more concerned about the morale of the men, how badly the army had been damaged, and whether McClellan still had the confidence of his generals. On July 7 he embarked on the steamer *Ariel* with Assistant Secretary of War Peter H. Watson and that night arrived off Harrison's Landing. Being overly anxious to see the condition of the troops, he reviewed them by moonlight. Meanwhile, diarist George Templeton Strong noted: "We have been outgeneraled. The blame rests, probably on the War Department. What's very bad, we begin to lose faith in Uncle Abe."[10]

On July 8 McClellan came on board to present his "Harrison Bar Letter," a document containing his personal political views on policy on which, he implied, the salvation of the country depended. Lincoln did not come for political advice or to discuss emancipation, which McClellan cautioned against making a war objective to placate congressional radicals. He also said the war should be fought against the Confederate government but not against the southern people, which instantly struck Lincoln as an irresolvable inconsistency. Nor did McClellan want southern property confiscated, including slaves. "A declaration of radical views, especially upon slavery," he wrote, "will rapidly disintegrate our present Armies." Had Lincoln been more vigilant, he might have foreseen Little Mac's objections to emancipation and not whether the armies would fight but whether the general would fight. McClellan also suggested a general be appointed to advise the president on political matters but also to carry them out. "I do not ask for that place myself," McClellan intimated. "I am willing to serve you in such position as you may assign me, and I will do so as faithfully as ever." Lincoln read the letter without comment. He found nothing in it pertaining to military planning, stuffed it in his pocket, and focused the conversation on ways to end a costly and unproductive campaign. Perhaps because Lincoln questioned nothing in the letter, McClellan seemed pleased, writing his wife that if the president followed the guidelines outlined in the message and made those principles his own, the country might yet be saved. He assumed the president had no policy and proceeded to give him one; otherwise, said McClellan, "our cause will be lost." Nicolay and Hay later wrote that the "letter marks the beginning of General McClellan's political career. He had always been more or less in sympathy with the Democratic party, and consequently in an attitude of dormant opposition to the Administration." Not every historian agreed. T. Harry Williams believed "McClellan intended the letter for the private consideration of Lincoln alone," although the same document reappeared in 1864 to promote the general's views when running as the Democrat's presidential nominee. The letter contained political advice far beyond privileges normally granted generals. That McClellan also sent copies home with instructions "to preserve it carefully, as a very important record," demonstrates the political importance he attached to it. Nicolay and Hay probably formed their opinion knowing the general had in late 1861 aligned himself with Democrats who ever afterward never stopped currying his favor as their presidential candidate.[11]

In the early1860s McClellan was no different than any other commanding general when it came to understanding basic civics. Winning generals might be excused for expressing political comments. Although the public still had confidence in McClellan, he had not earned the right to meddle in policy decisions. Chase concluded, "I did not regard Genl. McClellan as loyal to the Administration, although I did not question his general loyalty to the country." Welles believed the general had hastened his own downfall. Reading between the lines, Lincoln thought McClellan wanted to be reinstated to his former job as general-in-chief. Before arriving at Harrison's Landing, he had already considered filling the position, but not with McClellan.[12]

Lincoln was less interested in McClellan's letter than the state of the campaign and the condition of the men, whom he found in excellent spirits. When McClellan insisted the rebels were poised to attack, Lincoln convened the corps commanders and spoke with each one privately. Franklin, Heintzelman, and Sumner, contradicted McClellan and said the enemy had withdrawn; Keyes agreed with Little Mac, warning Lee would advance on Washington and the army should be withdrawn; and Porter said Richmond should be attacked. When Lincoln asked if the army could be withdrawn safely, Franklin and Keyes said it could be. Others wanted to stay and fight. McClellan said little but warned "it would be a delicate & very difficult matter" to withdraw the army at that time. He also objected to Lincoln's questions but saved his complaints for his wife, writing, "I do not know what paltry trick the administration will play next—I did not like the president's manner." Lincoln was not in the mood for tricks. He only wanted to know if the army could be withdrawn without being attacked and whether to keep McClellan's and Pope's armies separate or merge them. Little Mac provided no help. He warned his wife the president intended to do something foolish and accused him of being quite incapable of understanding the magnitude of the crisis. McClellan anticipated being relieved, writing: "I feel that I have already done enough to prove to history that I am a General, & that the causes of my want of success are so apparent that no one . . . can blame me hereafter. My conscience is clear at least to *this* extent . . . that I have honestly done the best *I* could." McClellan actually did the best he could without comprehending what could have been done better.[13]

McClellan did not confine his comments to family but shared them with friendly Democrats. Convinced his head was on the block, the Young Napoleon wrote Samuel Barlow on July 15 condemning the "stupidity & wickedness at Washington which have done their best to sacrifice as noble an Army as ever marched into battle," adding, "I have lost all regard & respect for the majority of the Administration, & doubt the propriety of my brave men's blood being spilled to further the designs of such a set of heartless villains." He instructed Barlow, "Burn this up when you have read it." One might wonder whether McClellan ever understood his role as commander of a field army. His duty involved risking lives to gain victories, whether he liked or disliked the administration. At times he tried to set himself and his army apart from the government, and this self-imposed independence always led to less than acceptable results. McClellan disliked casualties, but he could not win battles without them.[14]

Lincoln returned to Washington perplexed by an unaccountable disappearance of half of McClellan's army, yet during his visit he found the troops in fine shape and in greater numbers than expected. On July 13 he advised the general that 160,000 men had been sent to Virginia and asked McClellan why he had reported only half that number present. Where, asked Lincoln, were the others? "If I am right," he said, "and you had these men with you, you could go into Richmond in the next three days." McClellan first replied to his wife, claiming to "be on the brink of eternity." He then did a recount, admitting he had 88,665 soldiers present for duty, 38,250 absent, and 16,619 sick. McClellan gave no reason for the huge number of absentees, nor did he explain why so many men were on the sick list. He still believed he faced an army of 200,000 Confederates and continued to demand enormous reinforcements and another chance to capture Richmond.[15]

As July wasted away, McClellan's generals lost faith in their commander and believed the army should return to Washington. Lincoln wanted an expert opinion, so to McClellan's chagrin he brought Major General Henry Wager Halleck to Washington as general-in-chief and put

Ulysses S. Grant in charge of operations in Mississippi and Tennessee. Pope informed Chase that Halleck would get rid of McClellan.[16]

Halleck was a logical choice without being a good choice. He had made the mistake of telling McClellan he never wanted to be general-in-chief. Known in the army as "Old Brains," Halleck had graduated third in a class of thirty-one at West Point and in 1846 authored the *Elements of Military Art and Science*. He had been an able administrator in the West without demonstrating any skill as a field commander. Lincoln and Stanton had been running the war machine in Washington ever since demoting Mc-Clellan to field commander, and the responsibilities had become especially harsh for the secretary of war, who was a brilliant lawyer without military experience. Lincoln had been formulating all the strategy and wanted a military man in Washington with whom to discuss decisions he questioned making himself. Right now he needed someone other than Stanton to help him decide what to do with McClellan. Over time Halleck would eventually prove to be another incompetent general, and though he held the title of general-in-chief until March 1864, Lincoln used him as his personal chief clerk when communicating with the army. Halleck showed his reluctance in coming to Washington by finding excuses to linger in the West and delay his departure. Lincoln became unnerved by Halleck's dawdling because of concerns for McClellan's situation on the Peninsula, writing: "I am very anxious—almost impatient—to have you here. When can you reach here?" Lincoln knew little about Halleck, having never discussed military matters with him. Old Brains would soon become another of Lincoln's disappointments. Gideon Welles portrayed him as a bureaucrat who did nothing "but scold and smoke and scratch his elbows." Halleck enjoyed giving counsel but not making decisions. The experiment later led to a chief of staff arrangement unique in military command organizations of the day. Mark M. Boatner III referred to Halleck as "a man completely lacking in attractiveness or charm—pop-eyed, flabby, surly, and crafty—he had the reputation of being the most unpopular man in Washington." Nevertheless, Halleck played a major part in the clerical administration of the war, and Lincoln put him quickly to work on an important errand—to determine whether the Army of the Potomac should be returned to Washington or reinforced on the Peninsula. Lincoln favored withdrawal but wanted an expert opinion.[17]

After McClellan learned of Halleck's appointment, he informed his wife, "I cannot remain as a subordinate in the army I once commanded." He also believed members of the administration wanted Halleck to relieve him rather than doing it themselves, so he wrote letters to Marcy's friends in New York asking for help finding a civilian job. Influential Democrats knew McClellan's value to the party and urged him to keep his command. Barlow said all fault for failure "would be thrown upon Stanton . . . and it is your duty under almost all circumstances to stand by the country." McClellan replied he had never considered Halleck's appointment a reason to resign, writing, "My fate is linked with that of the Army of the Potomac, and so long as I can be useful with it I must remain with it." He continued to be troubled. Rather than blame himself, he blamed the incompetence of Lincoln and the duplicity of Stanton for his bruised ego. He never wanted to resign, but he also wanted to avoid the humiliation of being removed by those he considered inferior. Zachariah Chandler, however, sensed an opportunity to get rid of "the traitor McClellan" and led the charge among the radicals to destroy the general swiftly. "I can hold my tongue no longer," Chandler declared, "and *will not try.*" Over the next few days Lincoln began to feel the sting of Chandler's efforts to remove McClellan. Welles blamed the movement on Stanton and Chase, accusing them of stirring up the radicals "to get rid of McClellan."[18]

Halleck arrived in Washington on July 23, discussed the situation on the Peninsula, and two days later met with McClellan at Harrison's Landing. As his first test as supreme commander, Halleck had to decide whether to relieve McClellan if he thought the general would continue to avoid fighting. Lincoln had preapproved McClellan's removal, pending Halleck's decision, and confided to Senator Orville Browning of Illinois this arrangement with Old Brains. Lincoln soon learned his new supreme commander would always choose the path of least resistance and usually did nothing when faced with a tough decision. Lincoln also told Browning if he sent McClellan a hundred thousand men today, a few days later the general would claim the enemy had four hundred thousand and ask for a hundred thousand more before entertaining a movement.[19]

During July Lincoln gave up on McClellan. Convinced the general would never win a battle, he looked for other ways to minimize radical attacks on the administration. After creating the Army of Virginia, he began drafting the Emancipation Proclamation, with which he hoped to placate the radicals. While working on the document, he told a friend, "[The] pressure . . . is still upon me and increasing." Ten days later he surprised the cabinet with a draft of the proclamation. Later, summing up his action, he said: "It had got to be midsummer, 1862. Things had gone on from bad to worse, until I felt that we had reached the end of our rope on the plan of operations we had been pursuing; that we had about played our last card, and must change our tactics, or lose the game!" Seward talked him out of releasing the proclamation until the Union scored a victory. Lincoln agreed to wait—but not indefinitely—and locked the draft in his desk.[20]

As expected, McClellan did nothing. After Malvern Hill the army remained idle, and on July 8 Lee pulled back to Richmond to reform. McClellan's letters home reveal his state of mind. On July 11 he wrote, "I have commenced receiving letters from the North urging me to march on Washington & assume the Govt!!" Two days later, concerned about his personal status, McClellan wrote, "I have no faith in the administration," and, turning on Stanton, added: "I think he is the most unmitigated scoundrel I ever knew, heard, or read of . . . Enough of the creature—it makes me sick to think of him." On July 20, upon hearing Halleck was being brought to Washington as general-in-chief, McClellan wrote: "I am sick & weary of this business—I am tired of serving fools & knaves—God help this country—he alone can save it. It is grating to have to serve under the orders of a man whom I know by experience to be my inferior. But so let it be." After an exhaustive letter-writing campaign to his wife in which he never failed to condemn the administration, he announced a startling revelation: "*I have proof that the Secy* [Stanton] *reads all my private telegrams.*" If so, McClellan showed no restraint and in the same letter called the secretary "the most depraved hypocrite & villain that I have ever had the bad fortune to meet with." Although Stanton had come to hate McClellan, there is no evidence he was reading the general's private correspondence, but it would not be unlike Stanton to do so. The secretary, however, did want to know what McClellan intended to do with the army, which was the reason he and Lincoln sent Halleck to Harrison's Landing.[21]

Halleck asked the general to explain his plans, and McClellan said he intended to cross the James River, assault Petersburg, and then attack Richmond from the south. Halleck called the plan impractical and said the Army of the Potomac and Pope's Army of Virginia should concentrate at some point where they could cover Washington and operate against Richmond. Halleck added, however, that if McClellan felt strong enough to capture the Confederate capital without Pope's help, reinforcements would be supplied. McClellan jumped at the opportunity to be free of Pope and, after claiming the enemy had two hundred thousand men, said he could take Richmond with thirty thousand fresh troops. He even convinced his generals, including Heintzelman, who wrote, "We were all in favor of an immediate advance, [as] soon as Gen. Burnside's forces arrived." Halleck said the president could promise only twenty thousand men, and if that were not enough, McClellan must withdraw the army to some point where it could be unified with Pope's forces. McClellan said there would be no difficulty withdrawing his army but he preferred to stay on the James, await the arrival of reinforcements, and attack Richmond. Halleck told McClellan to make up his mind and commit to a plan either to join Pope or to attack Richmond. The Young Napoleon consulted with his officers, none of whom liked Pope, and informed Halleck he was "willing to try it," meaning he would attack Richmond. Old Brains thought McClellan sounded like a man of action, so he asked no more questions and departed for Washington to advise the president.

Years later, long after Grant had moved on Petersburg in 1864, McClellan would complain that Lincoln had prevented him from winning the campaign by scotching his Petersburg plan. He also remarked, "Of all men who I have encountered in high position Halleck was the most hopelessly stupid." Had Halleck approved the movement, however, McClellan would have done nothing because he expected General Beauregard to arrive from the West with a second army and pin him between Richmond and Petersburg. According to Heintzelman, McClellan never intended to do anything. Lincoln also decided not to reinforce McClellan and suspended the movement of Burnside's troops, who with others were waiting for orders at Fort Monroe. The action irritated the general, who accused the administration "of withholding all support from me . . . almost ruining my army" by sending him "not a man."[22]

McClellan's delusion that Lee had 200,000 troops also infected Little Mac's generals, some of whom believed the myth. Little Mac told Halleck he had 90,000 effectives. If he really believed the enemy had 200,000 men, it would have been inconsistent for him to attack Lee with only 20,000 reinforcements or for Halleck to accept the plan. The unanswered question will always be whether McClellan truly believed Lee had 200,000 men or merely found it self-serving to say he did. General Meigs, by reading the Richmond newspapers and applying common sense, pegged Lee's army at 105,000, which was about 25 percent too high because he counted 152 regiments and incorrectly assumed they were all at full strength, each with 700 men. McClellan in early August reported his own army at 113,000 present for duty. Halleck returned to Washington and said McClellan would attack Richmond if given 20,000 reinforcements. Lincoln doubted the statement, and Little Mac informed his wife, "Halleck is turning out just like the rest of the herd."[23]

Lincoln wanted Halleck's help in finding someone to replace McClellan and brought General Burnside from North Carolina to Fort Monroe. When Halleck traveled to Harrison's Landing and at Lincoln's request, he picked up Burnside at Fort Monroe as a possible replacement for McClellan. Lincoln did not know Burnside and McClellan were close friends. Because of his loyalty to McClellan and lacking confidence in his own abilities, Burnside rebuffed Halleck's offer. Old Brains took the usual path of least resistance and assured Lincoln that McClellan would fight. Burnside saved McClellan, and Halleck received his first lesson on the befuddling management of the war in the East.[24]

On returning to Washington, Halleck received a flurry of requests from McClellan for reinforcements and arguments why the Army of the Potomac should not be withdrawn from Harrison's Landing. McClellan feared Lincoln might order a withdrawal and wanted Halleck's assurance the army would be reinforced and allowed to stay on the Peninsula. Instead, Halleck gave the general an incentive to put the army in motion, writing, "General Pope again telegraphs that the enemy is reported to be evacuating Richmond and falling back on Danville and Lynchburg." McClellan doubted the intelligence. After several days had passed, Halleck heard rumors that McClellan intended to do nothing and that most of his generals thought the army should return to Washington. Halleck agreed and ordered McClellan to ship the sick northward as quickly as possible. On August 5, without taking any steps to obey Halleck's order, McClellan sent Hooker's division on a reconnaissance in force to Malvern Hill.

Hooker's cavalry drove away a weak Confederate force in a sharp clash, sometimes called the second battle of Malvern Hill. McClellan appeared on the field after the fighting ended. With spirits brightened, he informed Halleck on August 5 that he could march his army to Richmond in five days if he had thirty-five thousand additional troops. Halleck realized he had been duped and replied, "I have no reinforcements to send you." He told McClellan if Pope's army came under attack, reinforcements would have to be drawn from the Army of the Potomac, rendering it too weak to remain on the James. Lincoln had been monitoring the correspondence flowing between Halleck and McClellan and told the general-in-chief to order the Army of the Potomac back to Washington before it wilted in Virginia's climate. On August 3 Halleck sent the order to move the army to Aquia Creek. When McClellan howled, Old Brains said the order had come from the president. "It will not be rescinded," Halleck replied, "and you will be expected to execute it with all possible promptness." Not everyone agreed with the order, including artillerist Emory Upton, who wrote: "The worst that could be said of the Peninsula Campaign was that thus far it had not been successful. To make it a failure was reserved for the agency of General Halleck."[25]

On August 6 McClellan replied to Halleck, "I will obey the order as soon as circumstances permit." After this point Halleck became more peremptory in his orders. McClellan behaved as usual and continued to treat Halleck with the same indifference to orders as he did with Stanton and Lincoln. Later that day Lincoln spoke to a large assembly of discouraged people—mainly politicians, reporters, and "ladies"—grouped below the steps of the east front of the Capitol. Annoyed by McClellan's failure, they wanted answers. Lincoln admitted that the trail of blood, fever, and squandered opportunities marking the Peninsular Campaign had not met his expectations. Among other issues the crowd wanted the widely rumored quarrel between Stanton and McClellan explained. Lincoln delivered a carefully crafted politician's speech, painting a veneer over the discord within the War Department, and said, "Gen. McClellan's attitude is such that, in the very selfishness of his nature, he cannot but wish to be successful, and I hope he will—and the Secretary of War is in precisely the same situation . . . and both of them together no more than I wish it."[26]

Three days later any wishing abruptly ended, when on August 9 Stonewall Jackson fought a furious battle at Cedar Mountain and repulsed General Banks's corps, which was marching in the van of Pope's army. This development immediately intensified demands from Washington for McClellan to expedite the withdrawal of the army. Little Mac replied: "There shall be no unnecessary delay, but I cannot manufacture vessels . . . It is not possible for anyone to place this army where you wish it, ready to move, in less than a month. If Washington is in danger now, this army can scarcely arrive in time to save it. It is in a much better position to do so from here." When Lincoln asked General Meigs why the Army of the Potomac had no transports, the quartermaster reported that McClellan currently controlled every steamship in the country and promised to scavenge any sailing ship not in use. Instead of embarking the army at Harrison's Landing, McClellan marched the men back across the Peninsula and recrossed the Chickahominy. After passing through Williamsburg, the columns split up to embark on waiting ships at Fort Monroe, Newport News, and Yorktown. No stops were made to test the defenses of Richmond. Heintzelman lamented, "This splendid army has to be broken up to get rid of him," meaning McClellan.[27]

On August 24 McClellan stopped at Aquia Creek and telegraphed Halleck, asking, "Where is Pope?" and "Where I can be of most use?" Halleck made his first big blunder as supreme commander by replying, "I do not know either where General Pope is or where the enemy in force is." McClellan sailed for Washington and on August 27 arrived at Alexandria, just as Pope's meanderings reached a critically perilous stage.[28]

Lee's so-called two hundred thousand–man army had also thrown Lincoln off stride. Had he known Lee's force was closer to seventy thousand, he might have kept the Army of the Potomac on the James, changed commanders, and attacked Richmond. With a hundred thousand men in the Army of the Potomac and fifty thousand more in the Army of Virginia, Lincoln had plenty of troops to overwhelm the Army of Northern Virginia in 1862. He only needed a skillful general, and neither McClellan nor Pope met that standard. The Army of the Potomac would not be so close to Richmond again until 1864. Having Halleck in Washington serving as supreme commander never met Lincoln's expectations. Instead of promoting a master of military science, Lincoln had shackled himself to an irascible bureaucrat who evaded responsibility. Old Brains soon proved to be as conservative, cautious, and indecisive as McClellan and prone to accept Little Mac's wild estimates of Confederate strength. His textbook training told him never to leave two smaller armies widely separated with a strong enemy force in between, so on arriving in Washington he sought to unite McClellan and Pope. Lincoln cannot be faulted for bringing Halleck, the army's renowned military theoretician, to Washington for leadership and counsel, but he can be faulted for waiting too long to fill the vacancy and not evaluating the general before making the appointment. Lincoln and Stanton were both desperate for help. Suffering from the illusion of Lee's greater force, they charged McClellan with saving the army, which from the limited perspective of those in Washington he did. After the Harrison Bar meeting on July 8 the president began to suspect the Young Napoleon of bungling the Peninsular Campaign. After Halleck returned from Harrison's Bar in late July, McClellan's removal from command became a frequent topic of discussion in cabinet meetings. Lincoln hesitated because he did not have a replacement. Although McClellan blamed all his troubles on the administration, and though some historians may disagree, no one was more responsible for the army's failure on the Peninsula than the general himself.

13

"He is troubled with the 'slows'"

ECRETARY OF THE TREASURY Salmon Chase agreed with Edwin Stanton on the removal of McClellan, and the sooner the better. Chase had spoken with General Pope, who had warned the president that he could not safely command the Army of Virginia if its success depended on cooperation from McClellan. When Lincoln asked why, Pope said support from McClellan would fail the moment it became the most needed. Pope had also warned the president that if the two armies were to cooperate, McClellan should not change his base to the James. Once on the Peninsula, Pope could only be supplied through West Point on the York River and White House on the Pamunkey River. Lincoln conveyed Pope's concerns to McClellan, which ensured its rejection.[1]

On July 4, 1862, eight days after taking command of the Army of Virginia, Pope wrote McClellan a cordial letter in an effort to establish a cooperative working relationship. McClellan replied three days later, clearly foreshadowing his intention to resist withdrawing from the James. When on August 3 Halleck, with Lincoln's approval, directed McClellan to move his army to Aquia Creek, every repeated order, entreaty, and reproach failed to hasten Little Mac's efforts to comply in less than three weeks. Meanwhile, Pope made a demonstration toward Gordonsville on August 8 to take pressure off McClellan's withdrawal, which on the following day brought on the Battle of Cedar Mountain. The effort did aid McClellan because Lee began moving James Longstreet's corps and Jeb Stuart's cavalry from the Peninsula. McClellan, however, displayed no celerity in aiding Pope, and on August 9 Halleck sent another dispatch: "You must send reinforcements instantly to Aquia Creek. Considering the amount of transportation at your disposal, your delay is not satisfactory." McClellan attempted to postpone detachment of his troops by suggesting a rapid movement toward Richmond to take pressure off Pope. Halleck ignored the request after speaking with Lincoln, and the withdrawal from the Peninsula continued. Brigadier General John F. Reynolds's Third Division, the first troops to reach Aquia Creek, did not arrive until August 23.[2]

Lincoln voiced concern over McClellan's perceived stalling after the Battle of Cedar Mountain. Stanton suspected as much. Sensing an opportunity to rid the administration of a field commander he had come to despise, the secretary sent Adjutant General Lorenzo Thomas to Fort Monroe to spy on McClellan. Thomas spent several days looking for dereliction on the part of Little Mac and found none. "I parted with General McClellan yesterday," Thomas wrote on August 16. "The movement was progressing finely and will be successful. The army is in fine spirits and splendid fighting condition . . . No one could have made the movement more skillfully or in less time." Knowing McClellan's enterprise for organization, Lincoln expressed relief. Gideon Welles, however, remained watchful. He believed Stanton had become too absorbed in his efforts to dispose of McClellan to notice Pope's dangerous situation.[3]

Thus far Pope had made no tactical mistakes. He put his army in good condition on the north bank of the Rappahannock, checked the advance of Jackson's corps at Cedar Mountain, and opened the way for McClellan's unmolested withdrawal. He also repulsed several attempts by the enemy to cross the Rappahannock, believing it would hasten the arrival of McClellan's divisions at Aquia Creek. Pope's position led to Lee's flanking movement, which brought Jackson's corps around the right and rear of the Army of Virginia. On the evening of August 27 Jackson's "foot cavalry" struck the Federal supply depot at Manassas Junction and severed Pope's communications with Washington. By then Fitz-John Porter's Fifth Corps and Samuel Heintzelman's Third Corps had reached Aquia Creek, which potentially expanded Pope's force to seventy-five thousand troops. With McClellan's two corps in between Longstreet's corps (thirty thousand) and Jackson's corps (twenty-four thousand), Pope lost a unique opportunity to block Longstreet's forces, which was twenty miles away, while destroying Jackson's. With Jackson out of the way, Pope could turn back and destroy Longstreet. Because of poor communications and poor scouting,

Pope never knew he had the upper hand. Jackson's sudden appearance at Manassas startled Pope, who lost his head and threw away his best chance for victory.[4]

During this period McClellan became increasingly bitter toward Pope and the administration. He deflected his concerns about being replaced by telling his wife he hoped the Confederates would attack so he could "beat them & follow them up to Richmond." He accused the administration of trying to force him to resign but told Mary Ellen he would resist because he considered it more politically advantageous to be relieved or dismissed. "I am convinced the dolts in Washington are bent on my destruction," Mc-Clellan wrote, adding, "If I succeed in my coup everything will be changed in the country so far as we are concerned & my enemies [in Washington] will be at my feet." He never clarified what he meant by that broad claim. Little Mac wrote this letter on the same day he held a private conversation with Fitz-John Porter, who also on that day wrote editor Manton Marble, a Democrat, "Would that this army was in Washington to rid us of incumbents ruining our country." Porter spoke too freely to others, which eventually led to his court-martial.[5]

McClellan cheered up on August 21 because he received a telegram from Halleck warning that Pope was hard-pressed and asking Little Mac to come to Washington as quickly as possible. At first McClellan balked, convinced that nothing but the administration's fears "will induce them to give me any command of importance or treat me otherwise than with discourtesy." After receiving a steady flow of irritating telegrams from Halleck, McClellan finally received one that caught his attention. Pope was not yet in serious trouble, but Old Brains correctly assumed Lee would want to destroy the Army of Virginia before McClellan arrived to reinforce it. Halleck was becoming increasingly concerned because he believed Mc-Clellan, at Fort Monroe, was proceeding with deliberate slowness. Little Mac was actually progressing at an excellent pace and trying to save his equipment, supplies, and animals while jockeying for water transportation. He arrived at Aquia Creek on the morning of the twenty-fourth and found the entire area unsuitable for landing and supplying a large body of troops. Aside from being asked by Halleck to hasten to Washington, Mc-Clellan had no orders and believed the general-in-chief had lost control of the situation. Sensing another opportunity to save the government, retain his command, and win new laurels, he informed his wife he would take a fast steamer to Washington, writing, "I begin to think I may still be master of the situation."[6]

Halleck became aware of Pope's dangerous situation soon after the Cedar Mountain affair on August 9. Pope had served under Halleck in the West, and Old Brains harbored misgivings about Pope's ability to control a force being rapidly expanded by perverse Army of the Potomac reinforcements. Faced with the likelihood of a major engagement, he preferred having McClellan in charge. As an inducement for merging the two armies quickly, he promised the Young Napoleon command of all Federal forces in Virginia once this was done. At first McClellan regarded Halleck's promise as a ruse to hurry him along, but he also recognized an opportunity to retain command if Pope suffered a military setback. Before departing for Washington, McClellan went to Falmouth, near Fredericksburg, to speak with Ambrose Burnside. He felt better after Burnside confirmed that Halleck intended to unify the two armies as soon as Little Mac reached Washington. Still skeptical, McClellan informed his wife on August 22 that he still expected "to be shelved" upon reaching the capital unless Pope was defeated, and he intended to ask Halleck for clarifying orders before arriving in Washington.[7]

At this juncture, thinking Old Brains had the McClellan-Pope situation under control, Lincoln approached Halleck with questions about the breakdown of operations in Tennessee. General Don Carlos Buell had not liberated East Tennessee, and Lincoln wanted to know why. He accused Buell of being as slow as McClellan and told Halleck to relieve him. Halleck defended Buell and persuaded Lincoln to give him one more chance. The president said Buell must win or go. Lincoln intended to apply the same standard to McClellan and Pope, but on August 27 Old Brains had not heard from Pope. Halleck's ignorance of the situation was about to take a huge toll on his credibility.[8]

Meanwhile, from Aquia Creek McClellan requested orders and asked for Pope's location and needs. He also pressed for clarification of his status, claiming he could not regulate the movements of divisions lent to Pope until he assumed command of both armies, adding, "I cannot decide where to be of most use." Because Halleck had devoted several days to saving Buell, he lost complete track of Pope. Instead of responding to

McClellan's request for command clarification, he dodged the question, fearing his answer would be unacceptable to Lincoln and Stanton. After admitting ignorance of Pope's situation, he urged McClellan to come to Alexandria at once. By then Jackson's corps had crossed the Rappahannock, moved around Pope's rear, and cut the Union general's communications with the War Department. Hearing nothing from Pope, Halleck began to worry. On August 27, hours before Jackson struck the Federal depot at Manassas Junction, McClellan reached Alexandria, made camp in a nearby field, and again asked Halleck for clarification of his status. Old Brains replied, "I have no time for details," adding somewhat vaguely, "You will therefore, as ranking general in the field, direct as you deem best; but at present orders for Pope's army should go through me." Because of the resulting command confusion, most Federal officers believed that Halleck should have taken direct command of both armies, but Old Brains preferred his desk job. This state of affairs left McClellan with no definite information about his status except that he should send troops from his own army to the command of another general he distrusted and with whom, by Halleck's directive, he could not communicate.[9]

Prior to and during Second Bull Run neither Halleck nor Pope anticipated Lee's maneuvers. For four days Lincoln tried unsuccessfully to understand the movements of the armies while watching Halleck crumple under the strain. Heintzelman and Porter were both moving their commands inland from Aquia to Fredericksburg and were able to provide some general information about Pope's whereabouts. When on August 27 McClellan reached Alexandria and reported Franklin's and Sumner's corps were available to assist Pope, Halleck did not know where to send them. How Old Brains expected McClellan to "direct as you deem best" from Alexandria without knowing Pope's location provides an example of how Halleck, the master tactician, responded to crisis. In an effort to extract a decision from Halleck, McClellan wrote: "I am not responsible for the past and cannot be for the future, unless I receive authority to dispose of the available troops according to my judgment. Please inform me at once what my position is. I do not wish to act in the dark." While Halleck vacillated, Stonewall Jackson raided the Federal depot at Manassas Junction.[10]

Feeling vulnerable, McClellan chose to do nothing reckless. Without explaining his reasons to Halleck, he did explain them to his wife, writing:

"Our affairs here are much tangled up, and I opine that in a day or two your old husband will be called upon to unsnarl them. In the meantime, I shall be very patient—do the best of my ability whatever I am called upon to do & wait my time."[11]

Lincoln also tried to pry information from Halleck. Failing in this endeavor, he telegraphed McClellan during the afternoon of August 29, asking, "What news from the direction of Manassas Junction?" Little Mac had been delaying his return to Washington to avoid Lincoln, but he grasped the opportunity to circumvent Halleck and reopen communications with the president. By then Jackson had left Manassas Junction and moved to Groveton. McClellan admitted Jackson had disappeared and suggested two alternatives: to concentrate all available forces to open communications with Pope or to let "Pope get out of his own scrape" and concentrate on making the capital safe. "Tell me what you wish me to do," McClellan replied, "and I will do all in my power to accomplish it. I wish to know what my orders and authority are. I ask for nothing, but will obey whatever orders you give me. I only ask a prompt decision, that I may at once give the necessary orders." Little Mac was no longer irrational as on the Peninsula, leaving Lincoln to wonder whether communications had broken down between Halleck, McClellan, and Pope. He replied immediately, saying all forces should immediately open communications with Pope, but he deferred the methodology for unifying the effort to Halleck. What McClellan meant by suggesting that Pope "get out of his own scrape" left much to interpretation. The phrase obviously upset Lincoln because he ignored the general's request for orders and did not define his authority. McClellan's defenders brushed off the offensive words as having been made in haste during an emergency merely to convey a thought without intending to suggest the destruction of Pope as an alternative.[12]

After Halleck did nothing to resolve the command confusion he helped create, Stanton stepped in and issued orders stating that Burnside at Falmouth was to command his own corps except that part sent to Pope; McClellan was to command the Army of the Potomac except that part sent to Pope; and Pope was to command the Army of Virginia and all troops attached to him—with Halleck in command of all. Although Lincoln clearly wanted Halleck to order McClellan to join Pope and destroy Lee's army, Old Brains listened to Little Mac instead of the president. Going contrary to the president's directive to Halleck, McClellan told the general-in-chief to order the troops back to Washington and requested a meeting in the morning. Halleck agreed and ordered McClellan to take command of Washington's defenses but not Pope's army. The outcome worked to Mc-Clellan's personal advantage but cost Pope dearly and for the second time in less than a month destroyed Halleck's credibility as general-in-chief. From McClellan's correspondence with Halleck over the period from August 27 to September 1, Little Mac's efforts were far less helpful than he later claimed, and his inaction partly led to Pope's defeat. Within hours Lincoln came to realize the war in Virginia was out of control and back in his hands. Meanwhile, McClellan went diligently to work assembling troops for the more compatible task of defending Washington instead of supporting Pope.[13]

JACKSON'S RAID AT MANASSAS JUNCTION stunned Halleck and startled Pope, who marched rapidly north to confront the Confederates. Still confused the following day, Pope did not locate Jackson's corps until late on August 28, when Federal scouts located the enemy near Groveton on the old Bull Run battlefield. Pope fought sporadically, looking for ways to force Jackson into the open, when on August 29 Longstreet's corps arrived. On August 30 Pope hammered away at Jackson's position, unaware of Longstreet's presence on the Federal left flank. During the afternoon he dispatched a glorious message to Halleck claiming he had fought a fierce battle and driven the enemy from the field, which from his perspective appeared to be true. Notified by Halleck, Lincoln went to army headquarters and found Old Brains flush with exuberance, claiming, "The greatest battle of the century was now being fought." Lincoln expressed gratitude but remained circumspect. He stayed until late, waiting for news of final victory, and finally went to bed. Never had his hopes soared higher for the one victory that would break the Confederacy's back.

In the meantime McClellan sent one of his German aides, Major Herbert Hammerstein, to reconnoiter the front. Hammerstein returned before daylight and said the Federals had been defeated. He also told McClellan the soldiers wanted him back. From his experiences on the Peninsula, McClellan could imagine it all—abandoned guns, long lines of defeated soldiers, dead and wounded on the field, and stragglers milling through the countryside in search of safety. On the morning of August 31 he telegraphed Halleck and announced Pope's defeat. Lincoln did not wait for confirmation from Pope. He summoned Hay and said, "Well, John, we are whipped again." Pope contacted Halleck to report the army still intact and requested permission to retire to Washington, although many of his troops had already streamed back to the capital in a driving rainstorm. They blamed Pope for the disaster and were already howling for McClellan's return, the only general they trusted. Pope, however, accused McClellan's officers of demoralizing his troops and refusing to cooperate. Lincoln and Stanton never saw the telegram Halleck sent to McClellan on the night of August 31, which read: "I beg you to assist me in this crisis with your ability and experience. I am entirely tired out." On September 1 Lee struck Pope's flank at Chantilly and drove the rest of the Army of Virginia back to Washington. At the time McClellan had the larger part of three corps in the Washington area. They could have been used to turn Lee back, but as Pope's army retreated, Halleck adopted McClellan's plan and used the troops to buttress the defenses of Washington.[14]

It will always be argued whether McClellan was using Pope's predicament and Halleck's indecisiveness to preserve his own status or whether he still believed Lee's army contained up to 120,000 troops and did the very best he could by advising Halleck to save Washington. Both factors probably drove McClellan's actions, but retreating to Washington would enable him to fight defensively if he must fight at all. When on August 17 he told his wife he intended to become "master of the situation" and would soon be placed in command of both armies, he admitted being disappointed after he reached Alexandria to find his divisions being stripped away. Yet on August 27 he informed Mary Ellen, "I shall do all I can to help him [Halleck] loyally & trouble him as little as possible, but render all the assistance in my power without regard to myself or my own position." During the next five days he did try to help Halleck without going out of his way to help Pope, whom he accused of having "a total absence of brains" in conducting warfare. Little Mac was correct in one respect because Pope never tried to organize lines of retreat. McClellan also impressed Lincoln, without impressing Stanton, with his personal effort to save Washington, which was never in danger, and he did reorganize elements from Pope's army, which were retreating to the capital in dazed disorder. He also obstructed Halleck by retaining Army of the Potomac forces in Washington that could have been sent to the aid of Pope, but he expected the capital to be assaulted by Lee's masses at any hour. Halleck should have taken personal control of all reinforcements and sent them to Pope without deferring to McClellan.[15]

On August 30 McClellan informed Halleck, "You now have every man of the Army of the Potomac who is within my reach," which included Franklin's and Sumner's corps. Neither force moved far from Washington because Halleck had forgotten to arrange for transportation. McClellan stripped the wagon train from his headquarters and sent it with all his available cavalry to his corps commanders. The effort came too late to help Pope, partly because McClellan had for three days held both corps back for the defense of Washington. In a letter to his wife that night the general wrote: "They have taken all my troops from me—I have even sent off my personal escort & camp guard & am here with a few orderlies & aides. I have been listening to the sound of a great battle in the distance— my men engaged in it & I away! I never felt worse in my life."[16]

On August 30 McClellan also received from Halleck the answer to his status, which restricted his command to "that portion of the Army of the Potomac that has not been sent forward to General Pope's command." McClellan demanded clarification and wrote Halleck: "Under the War Department order of yesterday I have no control over anything except my staff, some one hundred men in my camp here &the few remaining near Fort Monroe." Little Mac already knew the answer, having written his wife earlier that morning: "I feel like a fool here—sucking my thumbs & doing nothing but what ought to be done by junior officers. I leave it all in the hands of the Almighty—I will try to do my best in the position that may be assigned to me & be as patient as I can." The Almighty, in this chaotic matter, happened to be the president.[17]

With growing anxiety Lincoln observed Halleck's inability to take charge in a crisis, but during a conversation with John Hay he drew a comparison between Old Brains and McClellan. "Halleck is wholly for the service," the president said. "He does not care who succeeds or who fails so the service is benefitted." Old Brains did not realize until too late that McClellan had a different agenda. Little Mac wanted to retain the remnants of his command without interference from Halleck. Lincoln particularly disliked McClellan's earlier comment suggesting as one plan of action to let "Pope get out of his own scrape." He also complained about McClellan's cowardice for unnecessarily blowing up the Chain Bridge to protect Washington and meddling with the deployment of Franklin's and Sumner's corps when on August 28 Halleck tried to send them to reinforce Pope. McClellan ordered the Chain Bridge partially destroyed because he believed Lee would use it to bring 120,000 Confederates into Washington. At the time Lee had about 49,000 men and Pope 76,000. "Envy, jealousy, and spite are probably a better explanation of his [McClellan's] present conduct," Hay concluded. "He is constantly sending dispatches to the President and Halleck asking what is his real position and command. He acts as chief alarmist and grand marplot of the Army."

On September 1 the president evinced equal displeasure when Pope retired to Centerville and said he would be "able to hold his men." Lincoln groused: "I don't like that expression. I don't like to hear him admit that his men are 'holding.' We must hurt this enemy before it gets away. Pope must fight them." By then hatless and dust-covered spectators from the battlefield had begun filing into Washington with terrifying stories. According to one rumor, General Irvin McDowell had performed acts of treason and had been shot by General Franz Sigel, and William Franklin and Fitz-John Porter had deliberately caused General Pope's defeat. Stanton did not know what to believe. He abhorred the possibility that McClellan might resume control of the army. On September 1, during a small dinner party at the White House, he capitalized on the Franklin-Porter rumor, saying, "Nothing but foul play could lose us this battle . . . it rest[s] with McClellan and his friends."[18]

Early on September 2 Lincoln took a carriage to Halleck's home to inspire more aggressiveness. On the way he passed countless wet and threadbare stragglers plodding into the capital, many of them drunk and without weapons. The president made a mental note to have General Wadsworth close down the city's saloons. When Old Brains said McClellan's officers refused to cooperate with Pope, Lincoln escorted Halleck to the general's home. McClellan denied the accusation but said he would rectify the problem, if it were true. Lincoln read several dispatches in Halleck's possession and concluded that while McClellan could have done more to aid Pope, he at least made an effort to be helpful. Among Porter's correspondence, however, he observed a general contempt for Pope. During the meeting McClellan sent a dispatch ordering Porter to give Pope full cooperation. Little Mac sensed from Lincoln's distressed reaction that the order should have been issued several days earlier. When he spoke with Pope later, the president obtained the other side of the story. Pope blamed McClellan, Porter, and other Army of the Potomac officers for his defeat at Bull Run, claiming they had disobeyed his orders. After reading Pope's report, Lincoln told the cabinet that Porter and two other officers, but not McClellan, would be brought before a court of inquiry. He also removed Pope from command, partly because the general could never serve under McClellan. When Pope wrote Halleck asking his status, Old Brains replied that McClellan would temporarily command all troops returning to Washington without directly answering Pope's question. On September 5, as instructed by Lincoln, Halleck finally relieved Pope of command "to reconcile differences which exist in the two armies." Pope returned to the West and held minor commands for the balance of the war.[19]

Months later Porter stood trial on charges of refusing to obey Pope's orders. Forty-five days later the court found Porter guilty and on January 21, 1863, dismissed him from the service. In 1878 a military tribunal reheard the case and decided that Porter had acted properly at Bull Run. It had been Porter's disdain of Pope, expressed in his letters to Burnside, McClellan, and others that had led to his dismissal and not his performance on the battlefield. Confederate generals credited Porter with being one of the best commanders in the Army of the Potomac. The problem of properly supporting Pope had more to do with McClellan, who delayed the release of troops, ammunition, and supplies because of his concerns for the safety of Washington. Little Mac did not try to hasten Pope's defeat. He simply could not act decisively in a crisis and thus had acted normally, especially when confronted with illusions of 120,000 imaginary rebels.[20]

What annoyed the president most concerned Halleck's ineffectiveness in refusing to take a more assertive role in funneling reinforcements to Pope. Had Halleck on August 29 directly ordered Franklin's and Sumner's corps (twenty-five thousand men) to aid Pope and had McClellan not interfered and forestalled those movements, the outcome at Second Bull Run could have been reversed. Yet Pope had caused much of the problem by not understanding the battlefield and by issuing orders, as he had with Porter, that could not have been obeyed. Sumner later blamed McClellan for keeping him out of the fight by claiming his corps needed rest, which Sumner testified was blatantly untrue. Evidence later surfaced showing that McClellan had forthrightly disobeyed Halleck's orders to deploy Franklin's corps in support of Pope by throwing up roadblocks to obstruct the movement. It is difficult to know whether McClellan believed those troops would be needed to keep Lee's grossly inflated army out of Washington or whether he simply wanted to retain control over the last remnants of what had once been his army.

Either way, Halleck should never have given McClellan discretionary authority to "dispose of all troops as you deem best," thereby deferring his authority as general-in-chief and allowing Little Mac to control or impede the movements of reinforcements to Pope. McClellan's expressed preference on August 29 "to leave Pope to get out of his own scrape & at once use all our means to make the Capital perfectly safe" was the direction he took despite knowing the president wanted the two armies combined to defeat Lee. More facts began emerging months later. On August 27, for example, General Herman Haupt went to McClellan for permission to forward a train of supplies and ammunition to Pope, who desperately needed everything. McClellan vetoed the request and offered no alternative. But on the morning of September 2 such facts were still unclear when Lincoln verbally directed Little Mac to take command of Pope's forces as they returned to the city.[21]

Lincoln's reinstatement of McClellan drew sharp criticism from the cabinet. Chase and Stanton had been busy colluding on ways to force McClellan out of the military service, including a manifesto signed by the cabinet demanding the general's dismissal. Stanton went farther, insisting McClellan be court-martialed. Welles refused to sign the petition, and so did Bates. Stanton disclaimed any responsibility for Lincoln's decision to put McClellan in charge of the capital and condemned the general as being incapable of conducting offensive warfare. Lincoln called the order temporary and limited to the reorganization of the army. Chase thought "McClellan ought to be shot" for having created a "national calamity" by impeding Pope's battle. During a cabinet meeting Stanton suggested McClellan be retained in rank but left "without anything to do, with no men or orders

. . . to gnaw on a file." Lincoln listened but responded that Little Mac would be useful in Washington: "McClellan knows this whole ground; his specialty is to defend; he is a good engineer, there is no better organizer. [He] can be trusted to act on the defensive, but he is troubled with the 'slows.'"

Knowing he could not change Lincoln's mind, Stanton worried that McClellan's temporary reinstatement could become permanent and returned to the War Department morbidly depressed. Lincoln fought melancholy because his hopes for a successful summer campaign had ended in another gloomy disaster. As the nation's capital began filling with freight cars bearing the wounded, Lincoln faced a new reality. He could not leave the war in the hands of Halleck, who crumbled under pressure and became indecisive. Although barely a month had passed since Halleck arrived in Washington as supreme commander, Lincoln, by necessity, resumed command of the war. Stanton did not like the arrangement, arguing that McClellan would shirk all responsibility by shielding himself under Halleck while Old Brains shielded himself under the president. After Chase suggested replacing McClellan with Burnside, Hooker, or Sumner, the meeting adjourned without further action.[22]

During the crisis on the morning of September 2, Lincoln never considered Washington threatened, but McClellan did. In his autobiography written twenty years later, Little Mac claimed both Lincoln and Halleck had asserted that "it was impossible to save the city." He also stated that Stanton might have thought so too because, according to McClellan, the secretary was preparing to send the Washington arsenal by ship to New York and had a fast steamer waiting to take the president, the cabinet, and Halleck to safety before the rebels penetrated Washington's defenses. According to Nicolay and Hay, the president and Halleck never considered the capital in danger and referred to McClellan's statements as fanciful delusions hatched by a man during his last years of life. The general refuted this claim in his own correspondence when on September 2 he told his wife that Lincoln had reinstated him to command Washington's defenses. It was McClellan, not Lincoln, who feared for the safety of the capital. Still believing the Confederate army was more than twice its actual size, McClellan wrote to Mary Ellen: "I do not regard Washington as safe against the rebels. If I can quietly slip over there [from Alexandria] I will send your silver off."[23]

By September 5 Lincoln had gathered enough information, including Pope's report, to have a clearer impression of what had happened at Bull Run. Hay overheard many of the conversations in Lincoln's office and in private warned the president of the public's mounting feelings, expressed in the daily mail, against McClellan. "Unquestionably," Lincoln replied. "[McClellan] has acted badly towards Pope! He wanted him to fail. That is unpardonable, but he is too useful just now to sacrifice." Later he added, "If he can't fight himself, he excels in making others ready to fight." In Lincoln's opinion McClellan had never learned how to act decisively and was merely behaving normally. Although the cabinet remained opposed to the general, Lincoln asserted: "We must use the tools we have. There is no man in the Army who can man these fortifications and lick these troops of ours into shape half as well as he." Nicolay and Hay observed, "It may . . . be said that McClellan, so far from suffering at the President's hands for his unbecoming conduct . . . gained a position of advantage by it." Few better examples exist of Lincoln's uncanny genius of being able to put aside personal differences in order to produce a better military and political outcome over all the objections of his advisors. Democrats were aware of the growing breach between the president and his general, and this boosted Little Mac's standing as the party's leader. Lincoln did not want to take action against McClellan dictated by personal jealousy or pique, and as Pope reported, the Army of the Potomac was still devoted to Little Mac. This sentiment became manifest later in the day when McClellan rode into the night and met Fitz-John Porter's corps returning from Chantilly. Hundreds of cheering, shouting, crying soldiers surrounded him, begging him to lead them to victory. So Lincoln made an intellectual decision instead of an emotional one and reinstated McClellan to local command. The general never appreciated the magnanimity with which he had been treated and attributed it to his own indispensability.[24]

On the evening of September 4 Jackson's corps passed through Leesburg, Virginia, and fifty-five thousand rebels began wading across the upper Potomac singing, "Maryland, My Maryland." Welles said Lincoln had anticipated the movement and, paraphrasing a statement by the president, wrote, "They [the rebels] may venture to cross the upper Potomac, but they will not venture to come here." The invasion upset Lincoln's intention of confining McClellan's role to reorganizing the Army of the Potomac. The situation demanded immediate action to check the enemy's advance. The president sent for General Burnside and for the second time in a month offered him command of the Army of the Potomac. Burnside declined and said McClellan should lead the army. Without consulting either Stanton or Halleck, Lincoln merged the Army of Virginia into the Army of the Potomac and reluctantly restored McClellan to field command. The decision instantly revitalized army morale. Stanton grumbled but fell in line, admitting, "The best defense . . . is to strengthen the force now marching against the enemy under General McClellan." The radicals did not agree. They threatened a popular uprising, some demanding the president's resignation on the charge of being "fickle, careless, and totally unqualified."[25]

McClellan received a marvelous opportunity to redeem himself. On September 5 he wrote his wife: "Again I have been called upon to save the country . . . Truly God is trying me in the fire." There was a very tall man in the White House also trying him, and this time he wanted results.[26]

14

"If I cannot whip Bobbie Lee . . ."

HAVING MADE HIS DECISION to reinstate the Young Napoleon, Lincoln watched as the general responded with new bursts of energy. "McClellan," said Lincoln on September 5, "is working like a beaver. He seems to be aroused to doing something by the sort of snubbing he got last week." McClellan was back to doing what he did best, congenial staff work, and he performed it rapidly and efficiently. Army of Virginia troops were not in the exaggerated state of demoralization Pope had reported, and the army Lincoln handed to McClellan represented, both in numbers and morale, a formidable battle force of more than 113,000 men. In later years Little Mac claimed he had assumed command without orders or communication from the administration and that he had prepared for battle "with a halter around [his] neck." Both claims were false. A letter to his wife on September 7 left a different impression: "I leave here this afternoon to take command of the troops in the field. The feeling of the Government towards me, I am sure is kind and trusting." Several days later Lincoln questioned his own decision to restore McClellan to command after the general took four days to get the army ten miles into Maryland in pursuit of the invading Confederates.[1]

Lee explained his strategy for invading Maryland as soon as Pope withdrew to Washington. In addition to inflicting further harm on the enemy, he hoped to entice more Marylanders to adopt the Confederate cause and follow him into Pennsylvania. He also wanted to strengthen the antiwar movement in the North, draw Federal troops from areas where they were menacing the South, and relieve Virginia temporarily from the ravages of war so crops could be harvested. When Lee learned McClellan had been reinstated to command, he expected the twelve thousand–man garrison at Harpers Ferry to be withdrawn because of Little Mac's insatiable appetite for reinforcements. When Halleck did nothing, Lee decided to capture the town so he could shift his communications to the more protected Shenandoah Valley. On September 9 he issued Special Orders № 191, splitting his forces into two wings. The order called for Jackson, with six divisions, to converge on Harpers Ferry, while Longstreet's three divisions moved toward Hagerstown. If McClellan followed slowly, as Lee anticipated, Jackson and Longstreet would link up and move into Pennsylvania, thus forcing McClellan to fight on a field favorable to the Confederates.[2]

True to his practice of unaggressive pursuit, McClellan moved with a force of men and wagons so enormous he claimed it occupied fifty miles of road. Nevertheless, he paused on September 10 to beg Halleck for more reinforcements, asking that the entire Washington garrison of 72,500 troops be put at his disposal. He said the capture of Washington would be a trifling affair compared with the destruction of the Army of the Potomac and asked for Porter's corps. When Lincoln consented, McClellan then asked for Keyes's corps. Little Mac demonstrated no haste in pursuing Lee, whose army he described as "gigantic" and "with large masses of troops operating against our scattered forces." He also ordered his officers to avoid collisions. In a later effort to explain his lackadaisical pursuit, he claimed the administration had held him back to keep him near the capital. Halleck refuted the statement, testifying that his orders to McClellan were to press forward on his left and aid Harpers Ferry, which appeared to be in imminent danger. McClellan, however, reached Frederick on September 13 and seemed disinclined to hurry, after logging about six miles a day since leaving Washington. Even so, Lee had not expected to see McClellan in Frederick so soon. Earlier he had informed Brigadier General John G. Walker that because of the disorganized condition of the Army of the Potomac, McClellan would not be ready for battle "for three or four weeks," adding, "Before that time, I hope to be on the Susquehanna."[3]

On the morning of September 13 McClellan still had no information about the size of Lee's army, its location, or what it was doing. But that morning his luck changed. Nicolay and Hay described the moment as "enough to put a soul of enterprise into the veriest laggard that ever breathed. There never was a general so fruitlessly favored by fortune as

McClellan." A private picked up a wrapper on the ground containing three cigars and a copy of General Lee's Special Orders № 191, accidently lost by a careless Confederate officer. After determining the authenticity of the order, McClellan now knew Lee had divided his army, sending the greater part to capture the Union garrison at Harpers Ferry and the smaller part westward through South Mountain and toward Boonsboro. He instantly grasped the significance of this intelligence. He could interpose the Army of the Potomac between Jackson's force at Harpers Ferry and Longstreet's force at Boonsboro and overpower each one separately. McClellan found Lee's special orders written in such detail that he also knew the location of the enemy's rear guard, cavalry, supply trains, and where the two separated commands intended to march, halt, and reunite. "Here is a paper," McClellan announced cheerfully, "with which if I cannot whip Bobbie Lee I will be willing to go home." The one piece of intelligence eluding Little Mac was the size of Lee's force, which the Army of the Potomac's cavalry commander Alfred Pleasonton routinely reported at 120,000.[4]

The Young Napoleon appreciated the importance of the document, but it was unlike his deliberate nature to act swiftly. Besides, he felt the army had not been properly reorganized to fight and still needed clothing, ammunition, and time to rest. He had, however, divided his force into three wings, with the right wing under Ambrose Burnside, the center wing under Edwin Sumner, and the left wing under William Franklin. He also infused the president with unaccustomed optimism by writing, "I have the whole rebel force in front of me, but am confident, and no time will be lost . . . I have all the plans of the rebels, and will catch them in their own trap if my men are equal to the emergency."[5]

The question was never whether the men would be equal to the emergency but whether McClellan would expediently seize the advantage. Now that Little Mac had reached Frederick, the president predicted: "He can't go ahead. He can't strike a blow." With speed a priority, McClellan faltered, worried once again of staking his army, which now contained some of Pope's demoralized troops, against 120,000 Confederate veterans. Franklin's wing, occupying the most forward position, camped a few hours from South Mountain, beyond which lay three of Longstreet's divisions. Instead of giving Franklin orders to hurry to the rescue of Harpers Ferry, McClellan wrote a long and leisurely letter instructing the general to march the following day. The weather remained perfect, the roads were dry and in good condition, and McClellan knew from Lee's orders there would be no enemy between Franklin's force and Crampton's Gap, which lay at the southern foot of South Mountain. Old Brains worried McClellan by questioning the authenticity of Lee's special orders and warning of a trap. Halleck also erred by not ordering the Harpers Ferry garrison to cross the Potomac bridge into Maryland and join forces with the Army of the Potomac or occupy Maryland Heights, as McClellan had earlier requested. Halleck appeared to have made this error on his own and without any guidance from the president.[6]

Franklin arrived about noon on September 14, pushed away a small Confederate force at Crampton's Gap, and then stalled instead of pressing forward to Harpers Ferry. Had McClellan moved immediately and swiftly on the afternoon of September 13, the Army of the Potomac would have pushed the small Confederate brigade off South Mountain, caught Lee's diminished force unprepared for battle the next day, and possibly relieved Harpers Ferry, which did not surrender to Jackson until the morning of the fifteenth. Six miles to the north, while Franklin stalled at Crampton's Gap, McClellan failed to press his huge numerical advantage at Fox's and Turner's gaps, where some seventeen thousand Confederates checked the Army of the Potomac until midnight. At nightfall McClellan claimed a "glorious victory," but added, "I cannot yet tell whether the enemy will retreat during the night or appear in increased force in the morning." The so-called glorious news electrified Washington, but instead of assaulting a much smaller force, McClellan had been stopped by a delaying action. Based on Lee's special orders, McClellan expected a major battle to be fought at nearby Boonsboro. The sharp engagement at South Mountain came as an unexpected surprise, which made Little Mac more cautious.[7]

Astonished by the Young Napoleon's unanticipated aggressiveness, Lee soon learned the reason from a southern sympathizer who had loitered at Union headquarters before drifting back to Confederate lines—McClellan had discovered the Confederate plans. On the morning of September 15 Lee crossed Antietam Creek and formed a defensive perimeter around Sharpsburg. He thought about joining Jackson, who had not yet captured Harpers Ferry but did so later that morning. As Lee began moving his rear guard through Sharpsburg, he received word of Jackson's success.

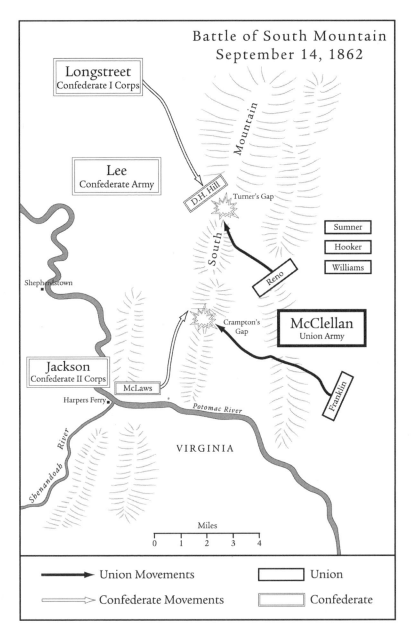

MAP 3. Battle of South Mountain

With this news, coupled with McClellan's patent cautiousness, Lee decided to stand and fight. With only 19,000 men available and another 31,000 possible if Jackson arrived on time from Harpers Ferry, Lee went into a defensive position with the north shore of the Potomac at his back against an army of 112,892 Federals. In a rather bizarre communication to Halleck on the morning of September 15, McClellan claimed he had routed the enemy at South Mountain and described the Confederates as fleeing in "perfect panic." "It is stated," McClellan added, "that Lee gives his loss at fifteen thousand." Lincoln read the dispatch, decided the Confederate army was close to annihilation, and replied: "God bless you, and all with you. Destroy the rebel army." The president must have believed the news because he wrote a friend that McClellan had won a great victory against the rebels in Maryland and was "now pursuing the flying foe." The Young Napoleon, of course, was not pursuing the flying foe because he still believed the rebel army was at least twice its actual size. During the Battle of South Mountain, Lee never had more than 17,000 troops on the field, which was almost all he had at the time, and his actual loss in killed, wounded, and missing totaled 2,685.[8]

Despite self-imposed delays, McClellan had not lost his advantage. On September 15 Lee had only three of Longstreet's already bloodied divisions at Sharpsburg, and Jackson was still south of the Potomac at Harpers Ferry. Jackson never hesitated to march day or night and began doing so after making arrangements to collect more than twelve thousand Harpers Ferry prisoners, along with tons of supplies and munitions. McClellan thus had the balance of the day to bring his army forward to strike Lee. After writing his wife, "How glad I am for my country that it is delivered from immediate peril," he then found Lee's small force waiting for him at Sharpsburg. Instead of attacking, McClellan stopped when he reached Antietam Creek, placed his troops in defensive positions, and rode from end to end of his battle line enjoying one of the grandest ovations ever given by an army to its commander. Morale soared. His men were ready to be led and to fight.[9]

As General Joseph Johnston often observed on the Peninsula, time seemed of no special importance to McClellan. The Young Napoleon refused to attack on the afternoon of September 15, when Lee was weakest. He did nothing the following day other than throw part of his right wing across the Antietam. As each hour passed, more of Jackson's troops from Harpers Ferry filed into Sharpsburg. Never had McClellan's habitual procrastination cost the Union so many casualties. He wasted the whole of the sixteenth in ineffectually approaching the emerging battlefield and meticulously getting troops into position. Lee's error of dividing his force should have been fatal. McClellan only had to advance in force, but he waited. By the next morning Lee had all of Jackson's force at Sharpsburg but A. P. Hill's division, which was still at Harpers Ferry. By then McClellan had sacrificed some of the best topographical features of the battlefield and given the Confederates forty-eight hours to strengthen them. Lee's slight advantage in position partially offset McClellan's advantage in numbers, but not entirely. The difference depended on the execution of McClellan's well-developed tactical plan, which with a superior force gave Little Mac distinct advantages if he and his corps commanders used good generalship.

McClellan intended to attack both of Lee's flanks simultaneously, and he had the troops to do it. The heaviest thrust would fall on Lee's left by Joseph Hooker's First Corps, followed immediately by an assault on the Confederate right by Burnside's Fourth Corps. McClellan then planned to release his considerable reserves on the Confederate center as soon as one of Lee's flanks collapsed. The plan would have worked brilliantly on September 16, even if poorly executed, and could have still worked the following morning. Battle plans never come off as planned. McClellan launched a series of poorly coordinated piecemeal attacks on the seventeenth, first on the Confederate left, next on the center, and then on the right. During late afternoon A. P. Hill met and repulsed Burnside's belated attack on Lee's right flank, having arrived with his division from Harpers Ferry at an opportune moment. Whatever McClellan might have accomplished at Sharpsburg on the seventeenth began falling apart early in the morning, when Burnside failed to cross the Antietam bridge—which today bears his name—to assault Lee's right flank.

McClellan blamed Burnside for failing to execute the battle plan on schedule, but the Young Napoleon created multiple mistakes through procrastination and by failing to use his reserves. He fought a drawn battle he should have won against an army half the size of his own. McClellan ineptly gave Lee forty-eight hours of unbroken leisure to study the ground

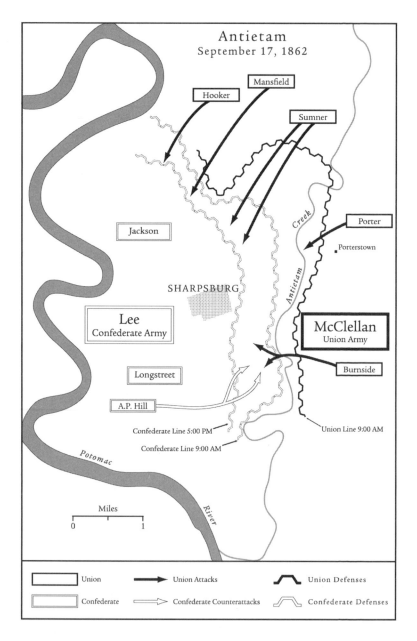

MAP 4. Battle of Antietam

and make dispositions, which he did, as McClellan watched with increasing anxiety. When the battle began early on September 17, the opponents were on closer to even terms because of Lee's defensive arrangement. The higher ground occupied by Lee provided adequate cover for artillery, defense, and the movement of reinforcements. Little maneuvering could be done on the battlefield, and little was attempted. Once the battle began, McClellan's plan collapsed. He piecemealed brigade after brigade into the fight without ever using his advantage in manpower. McClellan could have cracked Lee's line more than once, but he never put 24,000 reserves into the fight. Had he used one corps to follow up a temporary breach on Lee's weakened right flank, he might have swept the Confederates from the field. At the crowning moment of his career he doomed Lee's movement into Pennsylvania but hesitated and lost the opportunity to end the war in the East. Like his tactics on the Peninsula, McClellan always kept several divisions in reserve to cover the possibility of retreat, and this cautionary trait prevented him from ever winning a decisive battle. Part of the blame could be shifted to Halleck, who constantly badgered McClellan to safeguard the routes to the capital. McClellan later testified to having had 94,000 effectives, but he had only used some 70,000 during the battle. By sending men into battle in stages, he gave Lee the ability to move brigades from one section of the Confederate defensive line to another. On the bloodiest single day of the Civil War, the Battle of Antietam resulted in a draw. McClellan's casualties totaled 12,410 (2,108 killed, 9,549 wounded, and 753 missing). Lee suffered 13,724 casualties (2,700 killed, 9,024 wounded, and about 2,000 missing). By mishandling the coverage at Harpers Ferry, McClellan lost another 12,737 Federals at a time when he might have rescued them and augmented his army.[10]

Despite closely watching Lee's defensive preparations on September 16, McClellan still believed Lee had the larger army. He had personally scanned the enemy camp that day and after the battle informed Halleck that "200,000 men and five hundred pieces of artillery were for fourteen hours engaged in this memorable battle," meaning some 70,000 Federals had fought up to 120,000 Confederates. There were never more than 50,000 Confederates engaged, and the 120,000 men McClellan attributed to Lee never existed. Throughout the day he informed Halleck of being in the most "terrible battle of the war—perhaps of history." He had great odds stacked against him, and he hoped to gain a glorious victory, adding, "Hurry up all the troops possible." Lincoln tried to follow the reports coming from the battlefield, all of which were going to either Halleck or to Mrs. McClellan. After declaring victory, McClellan added: "The night . . . brought with it grave responsibilities. Whether to renew the attack on the eighteenth or to defer it, even with the risk of the enemy's retirement, was the question before me." His letter to his wife on the eighteenth, written after he had decided not to force the fighting, reflected his concerns about being attacked by Lee. Yet he claimed the fight the previous day had been his personal "masterpiece of art." While complaining of being in a high state of anxiety, he worried about exposing Washington, Baltimore, Philadelphia, and New York if he fought and lost a battle on the eighteenth, so he deferred his decision another day. Lee quietly withdrew that night, so on the nineteenth McClellan jubilantly announced: "Our victory complete. Enemy has left his dead and wounded on the field. Our people now in pursuit." Victory was far from complete, and McClellan should never have made that statement. Although relieved to find the Confederates gone from the field, he made no effort to impede their withdrawal or pursue their retreat. Nor was his conviction true a day later, when he advised his wife, "I believe I have done all that can be asked in twice saving the country." His reasons for failing to assault Lee on the eighteenth occurred because he doubted the "certainty of success" and worried about being attacked. By the time he submitted his battle report in mid-October, he had rationalized his gutlessness by filling pages with excuses.

The Battle of Antietam threw McClellan completely out of his comfort zone of fighting defensively. He disliked fighting on open ground and found every excuse to avoid doing it again. The unprecedented amount of bloodshed horrified him. The historian William Swinton, who excused McClellan when he could, nevertheless admitted, "If he had thrown forward his army with the vigor used by Jackson . . . he could have relieved Harpers Ferry, which did not surrender until the 15th." Francis Palfrey, in his history on Antietam and Fredericksburg, minced no words: "[McClellan] was not equal to the occasion. He threw away his chance, and a precious opportunity of making a great name passed away . . . He fought his battle *one day too late, if not two,*" nor did he do much "in the way of compelling the execution of his orders" because on the Peninsula and at

Antietam "he never made his personal presence felt on the battle-field" and was never close enough to the action to animate his men.[11]

Stanton believed McClellan had achieved a great victory and acceded to the general's demands for reinforcements. He ordered a special train to transport fresh brigades from Washington on the assumption they would be used to pursue Lee. By September 20 all of McClellan's losses had been replaced, and the Army of the Potomac in Maryland numbered 93,149 effectives. Two days later McClellan asked for more officers and more enlisted men to fill vacancies caused by the fighting. A few days later Lincoln did the math and concluded that McClellan was shading his returns as he had done on the Peninsula to goad the administration into sending more men. Looking up from his tabulation, Lincoln gave a grotesque smile and told his two secretaries, "Sending men to that army is like shoveling fleas across a barnyard; not half of them get there."[12]

Lincoln became suspicious of McClellan's complete victory when Halleck showed him a report dated September 19, which read: "Pleasonton is driving the enemy across the river. Our victory was complete. The enemy is driven back into Virginia. Maryland and Pennsylvania are now safe." Lincoln wondered why Pleasonton's cavalry and not McClellan's army was driving Lee across the Potomac. McClellan's emphasis on pushing the enemy army back into Virginia rather than destroying it also bothered him. Lincoln's entreaty to McClellan, dating from September 12, had been, "Please do not let him [Lee] get off without being hurt." Nevertheless, he accepted McClellan's promise to pursue Lee and seemed satisfied the Young Napoleon would keep his word, follow up with final victory, and end the fighting in the East. In a cabinet meeting on the nineteenth he gave Little Mac the benefit of the doubt, saying, "I rejoice in this success for many public reasons and I am also happy on account of McClellan." Lincoln seemed pleased, believing that his general had finally learned how to fight.[13]

On September 22 the first of two unrelated events occurred. Allan Pinkerton arrived at the White House to spy on Lincoln on behalf of McClellan, who wanted his victory at Antietam promoted as "complete." Always concerned about new conspiracies being hatched against him, McClellan also wanted Pinkerton to evaluate the president's thoughts while selling the general's complete victory hypothesis. During the interview

Lincoln used his prosecutorial skills to learn far more about the general than Pinkerton did about the president. The president became skeptical when the detective estimated Lee's army at one hundred and forty thousand, though he did not say so. He also did not accept Pinkerton's explanation of why McClellan did not fight on September 18 and let Lee escape across the Potomac. As the meeting ended, Lincoln expressed his gratification for McClellan's victory without accepting it as complete.[14]

Later in the day Lincoln capitalized on McClellan's ostensible success by announcing the Emancipation Proclamation, which he had held in abeyance, awaiting a victory. Adding emancipation as a cause for the war infuriated McClellan, who had consistently opposed fighting for the abolition of slavery. He became outraged again on September 24, when Lincoln suspended the writ of habeas corpus. Ironically, Lincoln might have delayed both proclamations had McClellan not declared complete victory. The action of the president enraged the general, who visualized himself as an unwitting tool of the administration. Little Mac had many high-ranking friends within the Army of the Potomac who opposed emancipation, and he naively believed the war should not be fought for political purposes. Instead of pursuing Lee, as promised, McClellan sulked and confided to his wife, "I cannot make up my mind to fight for such an accursed doctrine . . . it is too infamous." He also mentioned another complaint. Believing he had saved the country twice entitled him to demand the removal of Stanton and Halleck. "The continuation of Stanton & Halleck in office," McClellan wrote, "render it almost impossible for me to retain my commission & self respect at the same time." Both problems continued to fester, and the general remained idle. By September 20 Welles observed a rise in sneering remarks within the cabinet, writing, "There is no abatement of hostility to McClellan."[15]

Even though the Confederate army had been shattered at Antietam and paralyzed by a huge number of stragglers during the withdrawal, Lee was less affected by his defeat than McClellan by his victory. Little Mac, however, was almost alone in his decision not to renew the engagement on September 18. Burnside wanted the attack resumed on the Confederate right, and Franklin reported weaknesses on the Confederate left and suggested a dawn assault. Despite being wounded, Hooker agreed with Franklin. McClellan wavered and said he would wait for reinforcements.[16]

While stocks declined, volunteering lagged, and fine autumn days wore away, McClellan stalled and clamored for reinforcements, warning of a new Confederate buildup in Virginia. "This army is not now in condition to undertake another campaign," he complained, though he agreed to attack the enemy if it crossed the river. From dispatches Lincoln observed that while McClellan would defend Maryland, the general had no interest in invading Virginia. Sick at heart by these delays, the president decided to visit McClellan's camp to see whether a personal interview might inspire the general to fight. Before departing, Lincoln checked returns for September 30 and found another 10,000 men had been added to McClellan's force, bringing it to 101,756 effectives.[17]

Lincoln arrived at McClellan's camp during the first days of October and emphatically urged, consistent with his habitual courtesy, the importance of destroying what remained of Lee's army. McClellan met all the president's suggestions with amiable inertia. The day before Lincoln's arrival, McClellan had informed his wife, "I do not yet know what are the military plans of the gigantic intellects at the head of government," and on the following day, after parrying with the president, added, "His ostensible purpose is to see the troops and the battlefield; I incline to think that the real purpose of his visit is to push me into a premature advance into Virginia." McClellan soon realized the president had come on a friendly visit in an effort to be helpful, but when the general tried to discuss his opposition to emancipation, the president changed the subject and got to the point. He mildly criticized the general's habit of wanting everything in perfect order before moving forward. Lincoln knew if he commenced the conversation with the criticism he deeply felt, McClellan would become resistant and nothing would be accomplished by the visit, so he spent three days tactfully trying to prod the general into advancing.[18]

On October 2 Lincoln spent the entire day with McClellan, reviewing troops and discussing possible ways of ending the war in the East. Disturbed by his general's cautiousness, he returned to his tent and went to bed. Early the following morning he walked with a friend, Oziah M. Hatch, to the crest of a hill overlooking the vast Army of the Potomac. The rising sun shone brightly on miles and miles of white tents still shedding the morning dew. Gazing silently on the scene, Lincoln turned to Hatch and said, "Do you know what this is?" Hatch, looking puzzled, replied, "It is the Army of the Potomac." Lincoln appeared amused. "So it is called," he replied, "but that is a mistake; it is only McClellan's body-guard."[19]

Before departing for Washington on October 4, Lincoln believed he had wrung a commitment from McClellan to lead the army into Virginia and strike Lee before the rebels withdrew to the Rappahannock and became stronger. Meanwhile, said Union general Carl Schurz, "the government as well as the Northern people fairly palpitated with impatience." Schurz controlled the German wing of the Republican Party. He also proved to be a capable officer and could get Lincoln's attention. When McClellan continued to stall, Lincoln authorized Halleck on October 6 to issue orders summarizing a plan he had discussed with the general four days earlier. The order instructed the army to move now while the roads were good and as an incentive promised thirty thousand reinforcements if McClellan followed an interior line between the Blue Ridge and Washington but only half that number if the army moved up the Shenandoah Valley. Although the order read, "The president directs that you cross the Potomac and give battle to the enemy or drive him south," Halleck gave McClellan the option of choosing the route, ordered the movement to commence "as soon as possible," and asked for a timetable. Halleck should have known that McClellan never obeyed any direct order if it involved fighting. Four days later Confederate cavalry commander Jeb Stuart delivered another stinging insult by riding completely around the Army of the Potomac. Instead of evoking embarrassment, McClellan used the incident as a reason to delay offensive operations because his cavalry and their mounts were fatigued from chasing Stuart, whose cavalry logged ninety miles while performing the reconnaissance.[20]

Grasping at any excuse to avoid marching into Virginia, McClellan demanded more horses, claiming his mounts had been reduced to a thousand. Quartermaster Meigs refuted the general's claim, showing 8,754 cavalry horses had been delivered to the Army of the Potomac since September 1, along with several thousand mules. "Is there an instance on record," asked Meigs, "of such a drain and destruction of horses in a country not a desert?" When McClellan blamed the scarcity of horses on the administration, Halleck rummaged through reports and requisitions and on October 14 reported thirty-one thousand animals in McClellan's command. "It is believed," wrote Halleck, "that your present proportion of cavalry and of animals is much larger than that of any other of our armies." McClellan admitted not knowing the number of horses assigned but insisted they were exhausted and had sore tongues. Ten days later Lincoln injected a sharp rejoinder, writing the general: "I have just read your dispatch about sore-tongued and fatigued horses. Will you pardon me for asking what the horses of your army have done since the battle of Antietam that fatigues anything?"[21]

Three weeks had passed since Lincoln's visit to Antietam, and although McClellan felt compelled to have the last word on horses to justify his complaining, he did agree to cross the Potomac without exactly saying when. Horses had not been the only cause of McClellan's self-inflicted delay. He had requisitioned forty-eight thousand pairs of boots and shoes and wanted more clothing, tents, knapsacks, and blankets. McClellan now had every item he had requested and far more than he actually needed. He had the best-dressed army on the planet, while Lee's troops remained barefoot and, except for articles of clothing captured at Harpers Ferry, clad in shreds. When Lincoln asked why the army had not crossed the Potomac, Halleck replied that for four weeks there had been no want of supplies to prevent McClellan's advance. The general "is a good 'engineer,'" Lincoln grumbled, "but he seems to have a special talent for developing a 'stationary' engine."[22]

Having exhausted his patience, and furious after Stuart's latest stunt, Lincoln wrote the general: "You remember my speaking to you of what I called your over-cautiousness. Are you not over-cautious when you assume that you cannot do what the enemy is constantly doing? Should you not claim to be at least his equal in prowess, and act upon the claim?" The president then answered his own questions and summarized what McClellan must do to defeat Lee. He even suggested the route, writing, "You are now nearer Richmond than the enemy is by the route that you *can,* and must *take.*" This route was one he had mentioned earlier, being east of the Blue Ridge and closest to Washington. McClellan had a straight line to travel, while Lee, at Winchester, had to swing on a wider arc through the Shenandoah Valley. Lincoln then challenged McClellan by asking, "Why can you not reach there [Richmond] before him, unless you admit that he is more than your equal on a march." McClellan acknowledged receiving the letter without specifically replying to it other than to say he would consider the president's views with the "fullest & most unprejudiced consideration." Lincoln's letter took McClellan by surprise. He had just placed Darius Couch in charge of the Second Corps and told him, "I may not have command of the army much longer." Pulling the president's letter from his pocket, he added, "Lincoln is down on me."[23]

On hearing that Lincoln had pressed McClellan to pursue Lee on October 6, Congressman George S. Boutwell spoke for radicals in the House when he grumbled: "It is difficult to reconcile the continued inactivity of General McClellan with the claim of his friends that he was a patriot, not to say an active, supporter of the cause of the Union. With that letter in hand, a patriotic and sensitive commander would have acted at once upon one of the alternatives presented by the President, or he would have formed a plan of campaign for himself and ordered a movement without delay, or he would have asked the President to relieve him from duty." Boutwell, however, did not understand the mind and motivations of General McClellan.[24]

Why McClellan refused to fight when on October 20 he had 144,662 troops fit for duty is inexplicable, but during this period he had been communicating with friends in New York and condemning the Emancipation Proclamation. Nicolay and Hay concluded that McClellan "believed, and thought the army believed, the president's anti-slavery policy was ill-advised and might prove disastrous," and this sentiment might have factored into the general's hesitation to force the fighting.[25]

McClellan could not keep silent about his opposition to emancipation. After telling his wife on September 25 how he doubted whether he could "fight for such an accursed doctrine," he made no effort to engage the enemy. After calling the document "infamous," he condemned Stanton as a great villain and called Halleck a great fool who "has no brains whatever." Clearly on a collision course with the administration, McClellan remained preoccupied and confused over what course to take, if any, in opposition to the proclamation. He invited a number of generals, many of whom had been politicians before the war, to dinner. In this setting he asked their advice on opposing the emancipation before it went into effect on January 1, 1863. He mentioned that a number of conservative supporters had urged him to endorse the proclamation because the war would inevitably destroy the institution. If McClellan had an ulterior purpose in mind by convening his generals, it remains speculative, but he mentioned that unnamed others believed the entire army would follow him in opposition to emancipation. The dinner guests recoiled at the suggestion and urged him to support the president's proclamation. McClellan finally agreed and closed the session.[26]

On October 7 McClellan kept his word and, referring to the president's "proclamation of September 22" without mentioning the word *emancipation,* defined the relationship "borne by all persons in the military service . . . toward the civil authorities of the Government." Most soldiers already understood this relationship. He then deprecated any intemperate discussion of public measures that might destroy the discipline and efficiency of the army. What caught Lincoln's attention was a sentence that read, "The remedy for political errors, if any are committed, is to be found only in the action of the people at the polls." Whether McClellan was looking ahead to the presidential election in 1864 remains unclear, but Republicans interpreted it as such. He certainly wanted Democrats to regain congressional control in the 1862 elections, and he believed the army felt the same way. He also naively believed that by personally resisting the proclamation, the army would too. Although he had occasionally told his wife the nation needed a dictator, it was all talk. While McClellan might be criticized for having an overactive ego, he lacked the ruthless credentials men must have to become dictators. McClellan's failure had always been his inability to be ruthless enough on the battlefield when men's lives were at stake.[27]

After another twenty days of procrastination, McClellan accepted Lincoln's plan of pursuing Lee by using the route east of the Blue Ridge because, according to his own statement, "it would secure [him] the largest accession of force." He tentatively set November 1 as the earliest date to commence the campaign, and on October 26 the first units began crossing the Potomac. Lincoln vigilantly monitored the movement as McClellan dribbled the men into Virginia and down to Warrenton. Stanton asked Halleck why everything was taking so long. Old Brains replied that McClellan wanted more shoes. On the back of the report Stanton scribbled, "Having waited 3 weeks after receiving peremptory orders to move, it is strange that he [McClellan] should have just now discovered that his army wanted shoes & could not move until supplied." Stanton took the report to Lincoln and said McClellan should be dismissed. The president calmed the secretary, as if to say, "Be patient." Annoyed by the loss of six weeks of fine marching weather, Lincoln kept pressure on the general. "When you get entirely across the river let me know," he ordered, asking, "What do you know of the enemy?" McClellan could provide only vague reports to the effect that Lee was "not far distant" and Stuart was "within an hour's march." When the last units crossed the Potomac on November 1, the army began marching toward the Rappahannock River without setting any records for speed. As Nicolay observed, the president "kept poking sticks into McClellan's ribs."[28]

By then McClellan had lost all his friends in the administration and most of his support within Congress. Lincoln had long ago come to understand the general's strength as an organizer and his weakness as a field commander. He also understood McClellan's ego, which demanded deference from others coupled with a resentment of higher authority. For the exigencies in the East, the president considered Little Mac the best man in the service. He wanted McClellan's talents, even though the general behaved badly. He had overlooked McClellan's insolent dispatches and closed his ears to complaints from those who wanted the Young Napoleon sacked. The general's political prejudices annoyed Lincoln most because they influenced officers under his command.[29]

After the Battle of Antietam, Lincoln tried to control his impatience over McClellan's inactivity until an incident surfaced within the general's inner sanctum. Major John J. Key—the brother of Colonel Thomas M. Key, who served on McClellan's staff—had been asked by another officer why the rebel army had not been bagged immediately after the battle at Antietam. The major replied, "That is not the game; the object is that neither army shall get much advantage of the other; that both shall be kept in the field till they are exhausted, when we will make a compromise and save slavery." The president sent a note to Major Key citing the alleged statement and invited him to disprove it within twenty-four hours. Key arrived at the White House with Major Levi C. Turner, to whom he had made the remark. The president held court in his office and, after listening, ruled, "If there was a game even among Union men to have our army not take any advantage of the enemy when it could, it was his object to break up the game." He summarily dismissed Key from the service, commenting later, "I thought his silly, treasonable expressions were 'staff talk' and I wished to make an example." Certain Key had been influenced by gossip in staff meetings, Lincoln began to see a pattern developing.[30]

The incident, coupled with McClellan's inexplicable lethargy in every campaign, at last provoked the president's distrust of his general's motives. He began to wonder whether McClellan had ever intended to defeat the enemy or had only been focused on driving Lee back into Virginia. In less than a year he would suspect Major General George Gordon Meade, commanding the Army of the Potomac at Gettysburg, of doing the same. Historian Ethan S. Rafuse called this malady McClellan's penchant for fighting a war of "moderation." Lincoln also found himself once more involved in day-to-day operations because of Halleck's inability to make decisions. In October the president reached the limit of forbearance regarding McClellan, but he discussed it with no one until later. Lincoln privately resolved to replace McClellan if he allowed Lee to cross through the Blue Ridge and interpose the Confederate army between Richmond and the Army of the Potomac. Stanton alone understood the arrangement. On November 5, after Lee and Longstreet crossed through the passes of the Blue Ridge and reached Culpepper, Stanton queried Lincoln, "Mr. President, what do you think now?" Lincoln replied, "As you do," and sent instructions to Halleck to replace McClellan with General Burnside. Halleck jubilantly issued the orders and, in an effort to keep McClellan away from Washington, instructed him to go to Trenton, New Jersey, and wait there for orders. Stanton chose Trenton because of the city's proximity to Orange, where the Marcys and Mrs. McClellan lived.[31]

After first persuading Burnside to accept the command, Brigadier General Catharinus P. Buckingham delivered the orders to McClellan during a late night snowstorm on November 7. McClellan had been penning his nightly letter to his wife when Buckingham and Burnside entered the tent. He read the orders, turned to his successor, and said, "Well, Burnside, I turn the command over to you." After a brief discussion McClellan bid his visitors good night and returned to the letter. "I am sure that not a muscle quivered nor was the slightest expression of feeling visible on my face," he wrote, referring to the moment he had read his orders. "They shall not have that triumph—alas for my poor country." Lincoln made a bad mistake promoting Burnside, and McClellan suspected as much. "Poor Burn . . . I am sorry for him," he confided to Mary Ellen. Little Mac knew far more about his replacement's military aptitude than the president did.[32]

In closing the letter to his wife, and perhaps as an epitaph to his own military career, McClellan did what he had always done and shed blame: "I have done the best I could for my country—to the last I have done my duty as I understand it. That I must have made many mistakes I cannot deny—I do not see any great blunder—but no one can judge of himself. Our consolation must be that we have tried to do what was right—if we have failed it was not our fault." When news of Little Mac's removal made the circuit through the camps, a few rumbles of mutiny occurred, and some officers threatened to resign. Most Army of the Potomac generals accepted it as long overdue, but they questioned the choice of Burnside as McClellan's replacement.[33]

On November 10 McClellan boarded a train for home. After taking leave of his men, he sent a letter to his wife, writing: "I did not know before how much they loved me nor how dear they were to me. Gray-haired men came to me with tears streaming down their cheeks. I never before had to exercise so much control. The scenes of today repay me for all that I have endured." Little Mac did care for his men and always had, and though he failed as a fighting general, he departed loved and not hated. Thus ended the military career of George Brinton McClellan but not his political career.[34]

Over time Lincoln responded to many questions regarding the removal of McClellan. In an informal meeting with war correspondent Albert D. Richardson, the president referred to the aftermath of Antietam, saying: "I directed McClellan peremptorily to move on Richmond. It was eleven days before he crossed the first man over the Potomac; it was eleven days after that before he crossed the last man. Thus he was twenty-two days in passing the river at a much easier and more practicable ford than that where Lee crossed his entire army between dark one night and daylight the next morning. That was the last grain of sand that broke the camel's back." Lincoln erred slightly on the math but made his point. He probably summed up his reasons for cashiering McClellan best when he informed Francis Blair Sr., one of the general's supporters: "I said I would remove him if he let Lee's army get away from him, and I must do so. He has got the 'slows,' Mr. Blair."

Lincoln had other reasons for removing McClellan. He concluded that Major Key might have been right. Perhaps McClellan never intended to fight but hoped to drag out the war until both sides became exhausted and quit. Was that the game? Lincoln doubted it but remained uncertain. As George Julian noted, "Mr. Lincoln had clung to General McClellan with great pertinacity and in the face of much popular clamor, but his patience was now completely exhausted, and his passions carried him by storm." Lincoln's passion had nothing to do with cashiering McClellan. The general was a courteous gentleman with outwardly amiable and respectable personal characteristics. McClellan simply would not fight, and somebody had to be found who would. Lincoln said so himself when he grumbled that McClellan "thinks he is going to whip the rebels by strategy: and the army has got the same notion." "They have no idea that the war is to be carried on and put through by hard, tough fighting, that will hurt somebody," he contended, "and no headway is going to be made while this delusion lasts . . . General McClellan is responsible for the delusion that is intoning the whole army—that the South is to be conquered by strategy."[35]

McClellan did not exit the scene of war without leaving indelible marks of accomplishment, though fewer on the battlefield. There had never been a conflict in American history quite like the Civil War. McClellan experienced personal difficulty dealing with massive bloodshed, leaving his battlefield performance less than perfect. He made the mistake of believing that fighting with moderation would win the war and reunite the country. Lincoln knew better. To Little Mac's credit, in 1861 he conceived a sensible military strategy consistent with the president's goals but failed to execute it successfully. He built an exceptionally well-trained and equipped Federal army fully capable of overwhelming Confederate positions in the autumn of 1861 but failed to launch an offensive because of faulty intelligence. He also masterminded the ring of defenses that protected Washington throughout the war. He then fought two major battles in 1862, which created a veteran army that won few laurels. One hundred and fifty years later some historians still praise McClellan, while others consider him hesitant and indecisive. Little Mac was certainly a little of each, but one must not forget the president's interference. Both were novices, and novices make mistakes.[36]

15

"It is the people's business"

ELIEVING MCCLELLAN AND REPLACING him with General Burnside did not improve the president's problems with the Army of the Potomac. Burnside demonstrated his unfitness on December 13, 1862, at Fredericksburg, which resulted in what McClellan had always tried to avoid—a slaughter of Federal troops. General Hooker succeeded Burnside and on May 1 through 4, 1863, mismanaged the Battle of Chancellorsville. After the second disaster many in the country began petitioning for the reinstatement of McClellan. Lincoln ignored their pleas, commenting, "Do we gain anything by opening one leak to stop another?" On the eve of the Battle of Gettysburg, Lincoln replaced Hooker with Major General George Gordon Meade, who also did not want the job but obeyed the president's orders. On July 1 through 3 Meade repulsed Lee at Gettysburg, which took public pressure off the president for a spell. When Meade failed to pursue the Confederates, Lincoln grumbled, "This is a dreadful reminiscence of McClellan." Without expecting an answer, he asked Gideon Welles, "What can I do with such generals as we have?"[1]

When on July 4 Major General Ulysses S. Grant accepted the unconditional surrender of Vicksburg, Lincoln took notice because he saw in Grant a general who believed in winning battles by fighting. He also began to realize that his meddling in earlier campaigns, beginning with McClellan's Peninsular Campaign, might have been overly disruptive. Although some members of Lincoln's inner circle, in particular the Blairs, believed McClellan would have made a better general-in-chief than a field commander, and certainly one better than Halleck, Lincoln wanted nothing more to do with Little Mac. On March 9, 1864, he named Grant supreme commander and demoted Halleck to Grant's chief of staff. Lincoln placed great responsibility on Grant, and though frustrated at times, he stopped interfering. He needed victories in 1864, an election year, and his re-nomination depended on progress in the war. Assistant Secretary of War Charles Dana summed up the political landscape, writing: "The country is deeply discouraged and the party for peace at any price very active. Still more active, if possible, is the anti-Lincoln party among Republicans, composed of all the elements of discontent that a four-year administration could produce."[2]

After reorganizing the Army of the Potomac for the fifth time, the conflict in Virginia did not progress as well as Lincoln hoped. Grant pushed Lee back as far as Petersburg without ending the war. Instead, prospects for a lengthy and unpopular siege mounted. Democrats referred to the setback as "Grant's failure or seeming failure," and this perceived disappointment strengthened the peace sentiment among a war-weary public, who believed McClellan could solve the divided nation's differences and restore peace faster than Lincoln. Little Mac, who had become the most electable Democrat in the country, could not decide whether to be a peace Democrat or a war Democrat and confused both factions of the party by his statements. He shocked peace Democrats on June 15, when he declared the rebellion "cannot be justified upon ethical grounds, and the only alternatives . . . are its suppression or the destruction of our nationality." Democrats decided they needed more time to resolve issues within the party, so after the Petersburg stalemate began, they saw an opportunity to improve their candidate's popularity by postponing their July 4 convention in Chicago to August 29. McClellan objected to the delay, warning that the army might strike a fatal blow in Virginia or Georgia, but the committee remained adamant and extended the convention date.[3]

Lincoln experienced internal problems within his own party. A group of ultra-abolitionists tried to form the Radical Democracy Party around a common hatred of Lincoln. They convened in Cleveland on May 31 and chose Major General John C. Frémont, who despised Lincoln, as their presidential nominee. Frémont also hated McClellan and gladly accepted the nomination. "But if Mr. Lincoln should be nominated," he said in his acceptance speech, "there will remain no other alternative but to organize against him every element of conscientious opposition with the view to prevent his reelection." There were, however, many abolitionists in the Radical Democracy who still believed in Lincoln, and there were others who preferred Grant to Frémont. None of the ultra-abolitionists actually believed Frémont could beat Lincoln or McClellan but went ahead with their program despite having doubts.[4]

Lincoln made no overt measures to promote his own presidency and to others appeared to be ambivalent about his prospects for renomination. He did tell Senator Elihu B. Washburne, a personal friend, "A second term would be a great honor and a great labor, which together perhaps I would not decline if tendered." To another congressman he replied, "I do not desire renomination, except for the reason that such action on the part of the Republican party would be the most emphatic indorsement which could be given to the policy of my administration." When asked about Grant as a candidate, Lincoln replied: "If Grant could be more useful than I in putting down the rebellion, I would be quite content. He is fully committed to the policy of emancipation." Lincoln had already explored Grant's interest in the presidency and knew the general had none. "If he [Grant] takes Richmond," Lincoln quipped, "let him have it." When reporters asked Grant for comments, the general replied, "Lincoln is just the man of all others whom the country needs, and his defeat would be a great national calamity." On the eve of the Republican convention both men received sharp criticism when the press revealed that on June 3 the Army of the Potomac had suffered seven thousand casualties in twenty minutes at Cold Harbor.[5]

Despite grim news from Virginia and Lincoln-haters among Republicans, the convention opened for business on June 7 in Baltimore's Front Street Theater. By then most issues had been discussed beforehand, and Lincoln won nomination on the first ballot. Although he had pledged not to interfere in the balloting, he wanted a war Democrat as a running mate and on several occasions mentioned this to Alexander McClure and others. Simon Cameron, Lincoln's former secretary of war, and fiery Senator James H. Lane, of Kansas, swung the nomination of vice president from incumbent Hannibal Hamlin to Andrew Johnson, the military governor of Tennessee and Lincoln's personal choice. Pennsylvania congressman Thaddeus Stevens, one of the radical ultra-abolitionists, complained to McClure after Johnson's nomination, "Can't you find a candidate for

Vice-President of the United States, without going down to one of those damned rebel provinces to pick one?" The Republican platform also made Lincoln's life easier. While war Democrats and peace Democrats continued to bicker among themselves, Republicans endorsed the president's management of the war, called for the suppression of the rebellion by force of arms, and approved Lincoln's call for a thirteenth amendment to the Constitution to end slavery. The delegates went home convinced they had acted in the best interest of the country, while the Democrats, who had postponed their convention, muddled through the next two months seeking common ground.[6]

SINCE BEING RELIEVED FROM DUTY in November 1862, McClellan had spent several days in Washington testifying before the Joint Committee on the Conduct of the War. He complained about suffering through "quite an inquisition" and reminded his wife of how he despised "this wretched place," meaning Washington. "I have many—very many—bitter enemies here—they are making their last grand attack. I *must & will* defeat them." Yet McClellan's ambitions seemed to be less focused on a political career and more focused on spending time with his family and enjoying life on a senior general's salary in New York's Fifth Avenue Hotel. He learned from friends that the administration had no interest in assigning him to duty, despite Burnside's disaster at Fredericksburg, Hooker's defeat at Chancellorsville, and Halleck's ineptness as general-in-chief. His only duty, aside from occasional trips to Washington to testify before Congress, involved the preparation of reports covering his fifteen months of service.[7]

Radicals on the Committee on the Conduct of the War had several reasons for bringing McClellan to Washington other than setting the war record straight. They conspired with Stanton to discredit Little Mac's generalship, shed light on his incompetence, and publish unfavorable fragments from his testimony for public consumption. Stanton had already disposed of McClellan's two "pets," Fitz-John Porter and William Franklin. Rumors appeared in the press that Stanton and the Committee on the Conduct of the War intended to drive eighty generals from the service because they supported McClellan and were Democrats. Senator Zachariah Chandler notified his wife: "McClellan is deader than the prophets. He will *never* be heard from again." Democrats countered by releasing McClellan's self-serving reports for operations on the Peninsula and in Maryland, which he submitted in August 1863, after dexterously refuting damaging testimony made by others in the committee's report. Counterbalancing unfavorable testimony in the congressional publication later became the basis for *McClellan's Own Story,* published in 1887. Little Mac's partisans continued to advance their own views on the general's leadership credentials because they had no other commanding public figure to rally behind as their presidential candidate.[8]

McClellan waited twelve months before complaining to the president about not being assigned to duty. "It is evident that my services are no longer desired by your Excellency," he wrote, "and I am unwilling longer to receive pay while performing no service. It is now my duty to consult my private interests." It may have then occurred to McClellan that General Winfield Scott had run for president in 1852 while retaining his commission and no custom would be violated if he did the same, but Little Mac was not thinking about the presidency of the United States. He had in mind the presidency of the New Jersey Railroad and Transportation Company, which had been mentioned to him on November 19, 1863. When nothing materialized, McClellan retained his commission and his six thousand–dollar annual salary and never sent the letter to Lincoln. What changed his mind may have been the prospect of a bigger job. Democrats had been courting him as their presidential nominee, and though he wrote his mother of "being very indifferent about the White House," he reverted to his military habit of letting Providence decide his future. Despite efforts by friends, reporters, and influential Democrats to extract a commitment from McClellan, he refused to make a statement regarding his availability as a presidential candidate or to allow any comments he made to be quoted. The publication and circulation of his report in early 1864, however, acted as the unofficial commencement of his presidential campaign. The national press had been waiting for this moment and sprang into action, one faction touting the general for president and the other faction exposing him for military incompetence and opposing emancipation. McClellan's correspondence and public rejoinders became increasingly political, especially in the context of responding to attacks from Republicans. Acknowledging the inevitability of running for president, he finally admitted to his mother on March 16, 1864, of being "quite willing to accept what I cannot avoid."[9]

In May 1864, when General Grant pressed into the Wilderness, McClellan took great interest in the progress of his old command. "I have implicit faith in the ability of my poor old army to accomplish anything that troops can affect, but there is such a thing as expecting impossibilities," he informed his mother, "and such may have been the task now set before it." In early June Grant suffered staggering losses at Cold Harbor and a week later initiated the unpopular siege of Petersburg. Peace Democrats construed the setback as an opportunity to postpone their convention from July 4 to August 29. They also needed time to resolve their differences with war Democrats. McClellan opposed the delay but, according to his correspondence, refrained from stating his views publicly.[10]

After Grant placed Petersburg under siege, Lincoln became alarmed that the war would drag on another year, thus improving the opposition's efforts to capture the White House. He saw many unresolved issues between peace Democrats and war Democrats, but he also expected McClellan to be their candidate. Lieutenant General Jubal A. Early's raid on Washington, D.C., on July 11 and 12, 1864, suggested the war was far from over when rebels reached the outskirts of the capital. Any disaster on the battlefield merely improved McClellan's prospects. Lincoln became concerned and summoned Grant to Fort Monroe on July 31 to discuss command problems in the East. One way to stultify McClellan politically would be to reassign him to active duty. Alternatives included command of the upper Potomac to press Early out of the Shenandoah Valley or replacing Meade as commander of the Army of the Potomac. Grant actually preferred McClellan to Meade, and the discussion leaked back to Francis Blair Sr., who still supported the Young Napoleon. There were strings attached to the scheme. An offer would be made to McClellan only if he turned down the presidential nomination. Blair put the offer in McClellan's hands to accept, reject, or negotiate. Because this negotiation was all handled through intermediaries, Little Mac never explained his reaction to the offer. In a later letter he confided to Major Charles A. Whittier that the deepest wish his "heart ever realized" was "to command the Army of the Potomac in one more great campaign."[11]

By August the long, bitter war favored Democrats, and McClellan remained the frontrunner. Diarist George Templeton Strong wrote, "The great election of next November more and more obscure, dubious, and muddled every day." Lincoln also read the signs. On August 23 he wrote a brief note: "This morning, as for some days past, it seems exceedingly probable that this Administration will not be re-elected. Then it will be my duty to so co-operate with the President elect, as to save the Union between the election and the inauguration; as he will have secured his election on such ground that he cannot possibly save it afterwards." Lincoln folded the note, pasted the edges together so the message could not be read, and during the morning cabinet meeting instructed each member to endorse the back without reading the message. The president's action had been prompted by men of influence, such as Thurlow Weed, the New York powerbroker, who characterized Lincoln's reelection as "an impossibility," and Henry J. Raymond, chairman of the Republican National Committee, who said, "The people are wild for peace," and "unless some prompt and bold step be now taken, all is lost." Raymond also ran the *New York Times* and said if the election were held now, Illinois, Indiana, New York, and Pennsylvania would go to the Democrats. Nicolay, writing Hay from New York, said: "Hell is to pay. The N.Y. politicians have got a stampede on that is about to swamp everything," by which he meant that Richmond had to fall to save the election. "R[aymond] thinks a [peace] commission to Richmond is about the only salt to save us," he added.[12]

Democrats needed no help bungling their own convention. Lincoln observed the paradox, commenting, "They must nominate a Peace Democrat on a war platform, or a War Democrat on a peace platform." The war situation also showed a glimmer of improvement when in August Admiral David Farragut captured Mobile Bay, thus closing the Confederacy's last key port in the Gulf of Mexico.[13]

Sagacious Democrats also saw dangers in their platform, as did McClellan's close friends. Samuel Barlow, who acted as McClellan's political manager, knew the general was a war Democrat. He warned that peace Democrats thought, despite risks, they could have their way at the convention and win the national election with whomever they chose. When George W. Morgan, a peace man, suggested McClellan call for an immediate armistice because it would double the general's chances at the polls, Little Mac informed William C. Prime of the *Journal of Commerce,* "If these fools will ruin the country, I won't help them." Although McClellan admitted a willingness to be the Democrats' candidate, he opposed a platform not predicated on reuniting the country. When he considered withdrawing from consideration, Barlow and others appealed to the general's vanity, promising him control of the party. On August 28, as the delegates convened in Chicago, McClellan wrote Barlow, "Things are just as I would have them—if we win we win everything and are free as air." The Young Napoleon waited impatiently at home in Orange, New Jersey, for the outcome of the convention. He thought about going to Chicago to accept the nomination, but Barlow warned him off, writing: "I do not see how you can safely come to town at all, just now, if you are nominated. You will be *crowded* out of sight." So McClellan waited, and so did Lincoln.[14]

On August 29 the Democrat convention opened with remarks from New York financier August Belmont, who attempted to unify the forthcoming platform debate by saying, "We are here, not as war Democrats or peace Democrats, but as citizens of the great Republic." Belmont remembered how the Democrats had split in 1860 and tried to prevent another catastrophe by pulling the party together. He knew the war Democrats would have no candidate other than McClellan, but he also worried because most of the general's backers came from New York, which raised questions about Little Mac's popularity outside the Empire State. What Belmont may not have clearly understood was McClellan's position on the war. As far back as June 1863, McClellan had written Thurlow Weed, "The war must be prosecuted to save the Union and the Government, at whatever cost of time and treasure and blood."[15]

War Democrats wanted McClellan as the party's nominee because most of the North still wanted the South defeated and the country unified. Barlow believed a military commander in the White House would draw Republican votes. Lincoln had lost support within his own party after being renominated, which Barlow believed would help McClellan. Many delegates outside New York still wanted a peace candidate, prompting Barlow to warn, "I fear there will be trouble as to the platform." Clement L. Vallandigham, a fiery peace Democrat from Ohio, became a member of the platform committee, and Governor Horatio Seymour of New York became the permanent chairman of the convention. After declaring, "This Administration cannot now save the Union if it would" and "If the Administration cannot save this Union, we can," Seymour began showing interest in becoming the presidential nominee as a moderate compromise candidate. Barlow could not allow his hope for McClellan's nomination to trickle away by factional infighting. The general had stated his political position to Lincoln on July 7, 1862, in his Harrison Bar letter, and war Democrats printed those remarks together with others and ceremoniously distributed copies to the delegates. They claimed no other candidate but McClellan could win the army vote and that if Little Mac gained the presidency, Democrats would return to power and control the decisions regarding the war.[16]

The sensible approach brought war and peace Democrats together in an effort to design a platform satisfactory to both. Work progressed smoothly until confronting the big issue—the plank defining the party's position on the war. Vallandigham had once been deported to the South for making treasonous statements, but he was back from exile and just as voluble as ever. After calling the war a failure and denigrating the administration, he also articulated grievances that differentiated Democrats from Republicans. His resolution became known as the "war failure" plank. Vallandigham tried to have it both ways by calling the war an "experiment" conceived "under the pretense of military necessity, or war power higher than the Constitution," and appealed to war and peace Democrats alike by adding, "The public welfare demands that immediate efforts be made for a cessation of hostilities . . . at the earliest practicable moment peace may be restored on the basis of the Federal Union of the States."

Vallandigham's remarkable resolution condemned the war on one hand but sustained the war on the other and created the open-ended peace platform Lincoln had predicted. Knowing McClellan stood for reunification and believing he would accept the plank, war Democrats adopted the resolution without debate. Despite opposition from peace Democrats, McClellan won the nomination on the first ballot.[17]

Democrats enjoyed a few hours of lively but fleeting triumph. As the streets of Chicago blazed with torches carried by merry peace men and bands played Dixie, General William Tecumseh Sherman's army marched into Atlanta. The national press could not decide how to fashion its morning headlines. While Democrats were declaring the war a failure and lobbying for peace, Federal troops captured the great manufacturing metropolis of Georgia. Guns saluted the victory in Chicago, as disillusioned conventioneers packed their bags. Democrats had their ticket, but they also had Vallandigham's war failure plank. Delegates returned home, few of them jubilating. Thus began the political campaign of 1864, with McClellan's nomination on August 31 and the surrender of Atlanta on September 1.[18]

McClellan read the war news while composing his letter of acceptance. Stephen W. Sears found six drafts that had been written before the general selected the one sent to the nominating committee. It was not what peace Democrats expected. True to form and entirely consistent with his beliefs, McClellan wrote, "The reestablishment of the Union in all its integrity is, and must continue to be, the indispensible condition of any settlement." If the South refused to accept peace "upon the basis of the Union," the war would continue. He also stated that "the Union must be preserved at all hazards" and that southern states must be brought back into the Union with full constitutional rights, which meant that, while he disagreed with Republican radicals, he did agree with Lincoln on reconstruction. McClellan left no question on where he stood. His policy was the same as Lincoln's with one exception. Perhaps in an appeal to southerners and indifferent northerners, he did not demand abolition and never mentioned the word *slavery* in an acceptance letter massaged by Barlow. After Democrats had worked so assiduously differentiating themselves from Republicans, McClellan's acceptance letter read like a commentary, minus emancipation, crafted by Lincoln. After repudiating the part of the platform on which he had been nominated, McClellan closed by adding, "Believing that the views here expressed are those of the Convention . . . I accept the nomination."

Delegates read their nominee's statements and cringed, but they could not stop the letter from being published. Quite proud of his missive, McClellan informed his wife that the effect of his letter had thus far "been electric—the peace men are the only ones that squirm—but all the good men are delighted with it." McClellan accomplished in a single letter what Lincoln could not have accomplished in a rejoinder. Slavery was already beyond saving, and the South paid no attention to McClellan's implied tolerance. As in 1861, the general completely missed the point. The South was fighting for independence, not slavery. Lincoln had sagaciously added slavery to the equation as a moral and political issue, which McClellan stubbornly and with flawed reason resisted.[19]

Gideon Welles studied news reports covering the Chicago convention and decided, after reading the resolutions, that the Democrats had deceived themselves. "It is whether a war shall be made against Lincoln to get peace with Jeff Davis," he concluded. He found it ironic that Democrats would nominate a general committed to war on a peace platform. "I think the president will be reelected," he wrote, "and I shall be surprised if he does not have a large majority."[20]

Even radicals who had once sought to depose Lincoln as the presidential nominee changed their minds after Sherman captured Atlanta. "The fall of Atlanta," wrote one conspirator, "puts an entirely new aspect upon the face of affairs." Not one governor believed Lincoln should be deserted. Thurlow Weed, who had been deeply involved in the New York plot, notified Seward, "The conspiracy against Mr. Lincoln collapsed on Monday, last." Horace Greeley, another instigator, admitted the whole scheme had been a mistake. He used the *New York Tribune* to support the Republican Party but seldom mentioned Lincoln by name. He pledged, however, to "fight like a savage in this campaign," adding, "I hate McClellan."[21]

On September 1, 1864, the battle for the presidency began. Neither candidate actively participated in the campaign. "I cannot run the political machine," Lincoln quipped when urged to do something on his own behalf. "I have enough on my hands without *that*. It is the *people's* business." The comment made good rhetoric, but barely an hour passed without Lincoln becoming engaged in the so-called people's business. His cabinet members did not feel the same restraints as the president. Stanton had already conceived and activated a full-blown propaganda machine supported by the radical element in Congress. Zachariah Chandler had also released a report designed to "kill McClellan as dead as a herring." On September 3 he went to the White House intent on bringing the radicals together in support of the president and laid before Lincoln his plan for restoring harmony within the party. Lincoln agreed, and as a concession to the radicals, he removed Montgomery Blair from his cabinet.[22]

Seward returned to his home in Auburn on September 3 and unofficially commenced the president's campaign in New York. He expressed exactly what Lincoln would have said had campaign protocol allowed the president to make political speeches: "While the rebels continue to wage war against the Government of the United States, the military measures affecting slavery, which have been adopted from necessity to bring the war to a speedy and successful end, will be continued . . . with a view to the same end. When insurgents shall have disbanded their armies and lain down their arms the war will instantly cease, and all war measures then existing . . . whether they arose before the civil war began, or whether they grew out of it, will, by force of the constitution, pass over the arbitrament of courts of law and to the councils of legislation." Seward built every speech around the same theme, telling others: "Sherman and Farragut have knocked the bottom out of the Chicago nominations . . . The issue is squarely made up—McClellan and disunion, or Lincoln and Union."[23]

After misinterpreting Seward's comments, a new round of rumors spread among Democrats that Lincoln intended to overthrow the government if his reelection failed. As a countermove, Democrats considered reconvening and nominating someone other than McClellan who would at once seize control of the government. Although the president felt barred from making public statements, he cleared the air on the evening of October 19, when serenaders from Maryland appeared on the White House lawn. Knowing they would ask for a speech, he prepared one: "I am struggling to maintain government, not overthrow it. I am struggling especially to prevent others from overthrowing it. I therefore say, that if I shall live, I shall remain President until the fourth of next March, and whoever shall be constitutionally elected . . . shall be duly installed as President . . . and that in the interval I shall do my utmost that whoever is to hold the helm for the next voyage, shall start with the best possible chance to save the ship."[24]

October 19 was also a good day for the president because Major General Philip H. Sheridan, after driving General Early's Confederates up the Shenandoah Valley, shattered the rebels at Cedar Creek. With the election little more than two weeks away, the victory improved Lincoln's prospects at the polls. Democrats no longer had their war failure issue. McClellan's odds at the polls might have improved had Lincoln's supporters not spent two months convincing the public that the general was bound to upholding the Chicago peace platform.

While McClellan spent the campaign season secluded in his home at
Orange processing correspondence with the help of a single secretary,
Lincoln used his official capacity as president to steer the campaign while
appearing to be removed from it. When Republicans across the country
descended on the White House to urge the president to help himself at the
polls by suspending the draft, Lincoln refused to deny the army its men
and said, "What is the Presidency worth to me if I have no country?"[25]

Stanton appreciated the support and worked assiduously behind the
scenes to capture the soldiers' vote. When he learned some of McClellan's
former officers were destroying boxes of Republican leaflets sent to army
camps, he dismissed twenty quartermaster clerks working on the general's behalf. When Democrats howled, Stanton replied, "When a young
man receives his pay from an administration and spends his evenings
denouncing it in offensive terms, he cannot be surprised if the administration prefers a friend on the job." The pilfering stopped. As Election
Day approached, some officers faithful to McClellan tried to obstruct the
soldiers' vote. Lincoln took personal interest and said, "Whenever the law
allows soldiers to vote, their officers must also allow it." He left the rest
to Stanton, who set rules for voting in the field and planted agents to spy
on political gatherings. Several colonels supporting McClellan spent the
balance of the war serving as captains in remote commands.[26]

Stanton became Lincoln's unofficial election strongman. "All the power
and influence of the War Department was employed to secure the reelection of Mr. Lincoln," Charles Dana recalled. The government provided
no funds for political campaigns, but Dana observed "vast expenditures"
being made from Stanton's war chest without the knowledge of the president. When Governor Seymour planned to order out the National Guard to
supervise the polls on Election Day, Stanton sent forty-three hundred infantry to New York City to interdict any misconduct at the polls. John Hay
reported that during the November 8 election New York became "the qui-
etest city ever seen," adding, "The president had nothing to do with it."[27]

Behind the scenes Lincoln did take steps to secure his reelection. He
no longer viewed the war as a conflict only for the salvation of the Union
but for the American form of government. In his opinion "the weal or woe
of this great nation will be decided in the approaching canvas." Although
restrained from publicly campaigning, Lincoln pressed Stanton and

Welles to find ways for every soldier and sailor to vote. Stanton emptied hospitals and sent recovering soldiers home to vote. Welles dispatched special steamers through blockading squadrons in the Atlantic and the Gulf to collect the sailors' vote. Stanton made arrests after agents found several boxes of Lincoln's ballots replaced by McClellan's ballots. When charges of fraud appeared in the press, Democrats drummed up accusations of their own. Most of the disputes involved the military vote, which in some states proved to be decisive. Balloting in the field gave Lincoln 119,754 votes and McClellan 34,291. Soldiers voting at home merely added to the count. Stanton's efforts to bring home the soldiers' vote mattered. In the final balloting Lincoln won New York by a slim margin of 6,000 votes and Connecticut by 2,406 votes.[28]

Unlike Lincoln, McClellan did virtually nothing to bolster his own prospects at the polls aside from devoting his efforts to secure the army vote, for which Stanton had the inside track. Little Mac deluded himself into believing fighting men and veterans still idolized him. He communicated with few supporters other than his closest friends, those being Samuel Barlow, Samuel Cox, Manton Marble, William Prime, and Robert C. Winthrop. While Lincoln would speak with anyone, including members of the opposition, McClellan informed Prime, "Don't send any politicians out here—I'll snub them if they come—confound them!" When Democrats sent Hiram Ketchum to speak to McClellan about writing endorsements to help with the distribution of campaign literature, the general appealed to Prime, "Can't you invent some way of getting me out of the scrape?" After Barlow warned McClellan that snubbing campaign workers could be fatal, the general agreed to compose a series of letters to those seeking interviews, commenting, "It don't make much difference if I don't see them provided I don't avoid them." McClellan did write his army friends and asked for their help in distributing campaign literature, but he isolated himself from the public and left campaign matters in the hands of his managers and a network of volunteers.[29]

Barlow kept McClellan informed on campaign progress and in a footnote to a letter dated October 27 said: "All the news I hear is *very* favorable. There is every reason to be most hopeful." Prime promised McClellan New York and Pennsylvania, which accounted for half the electoral votes. Barlow complained of Stanton's agents stopping boxes "containing our ballots" and warned of a conspiracy reported by Allan Pinkerton that some of the general's friends intended to assassinate the president. Mc-Clellan said none of his friends would consider such extremes. Had he disputed Pinkerton's intelligence during the war with the same decisiveness, he might have ended the rebellion in 1862 and vaulted himself into the presidency without trouble.[30]

On November 7, the day before the national election, war came to a standstill. Northerners waited for the polls to open. Southerners also waited, but they had abdicated their right to vote. With nothing more to do, Lincoln went to bed, and so did McClellan. It was time for the "people's business" to begin.

ON ELECTION DAY, November 8, 1864, a cold drizzle fell from leaden skies and soaked the streets of Washington. From the windows of the White House, Hay observed a column of men hunched under black umbrellas strolling to polling centers. He found the president sitting quietly in his office, obviously reflecting on some troubling matter. Lincoln looked up as Hay entered and said, "It is a little singular that I, who am not a vindictive man, should have always been before the people for election in canvasses marked for their bitterness." Hay remembered the moment as "one of the most solemn days" of Lincoln's life. Noah Brooks joined the president at noon, but Lincoln could not relax. "About this thing," he told his friend, "I am very far from certain. I wish I were certain." Lincoln expected to lose the popular vote but during the morning recalculated the electoral vote and thought he might win by a small margin. McClellan also anticipated winning a close election and on November 7 wrote William Prime, asking, "What do you & Barlow think about my resigning my commission tomorrow?" He expected to win in Connecticut, Illinois, New York, and Pennsylvania because his handlers and friends told him so, and those states would carry him into the White House.[31]

Neither man accurately estimated the actual outcome of the election. Returns showed the president polling 2,213,665 votes to McClellan's 1,802,237. Lincoln won every state but Delaware, Kentucky, and New Jersey, giving him an electoral majority of 212 to 21. Seventy-eight percent of the military vote went to Lincoln.[32]

On Election Day the Young Napoleon tendered his resignation as "Major General in the Army of the U.S.A.," which Lincoln accepted without comment. Two days later McClellan wrote Barlow: "For my country's sake I deplore the result—but . . . feel that a great weight is removed from my mind. I can imagine no combination of circumstances that can ever induce me to enter [public life] again." On November 26 Abram S. Hewitt offered McClellan the presidency of New Jersey's Morris & Essex Railroad at an annual salary of eight thousand dollars, and Little Mac accepted. It was a new beginning for the former general, who in 1878, despite his disdain for public service, became New Jersey's governor and served one four-year term. He died in 1885 after finishing his autobiography, *McClellan's Own Story*, which provides a most interesting defense of his military record. McClellan remains a military enigma, a talented organizer, a better-than-average strategist, but an ineffective implementer of his own strategy. His admirers will say he was never given a fair chance, which may have been partly true, at least until Antietam. His chronic overestimates of the opposition's strength and his many lost opportunities to achieve military success led to his failure in the field and his eventual removal.[33]

Had Lincoln not been mortally wounded by an assassin on April 14, 1865, his second term might have been as difficult as his first term but for different reasons. The war quickly ended after his election, giving his second term the momentum he needed to reconstruct the South humanely as it returned to the Union. His death put radical Republicans in control of the nation, and their reconstruction views embittered the South for decades to come. His assassination cut short a great man's life and passed on to men far less capable the future and fate of the nation.

NOTES

Introduction

1. Frederick W. Seward, *Reminiscences of a War-Time Statesman and Diplomat, 1830–1915* (New York, 1916), 167.

2. Hugh McCulloch, *Men and Measures of Half a Century* (New York, 1888), 301.

3. Howard Beale, ed., *Diary of Edwin Bates, 1859–1866* (Washington, D.C., 1930), 200, 218–20 (hereafter cited as Beale, *Bates Diary*).

4. John B. Alley in *Reminiscences of Abraham Lincoln by Distinguished Men of His Time,* ed. Allen Thorndike Rice (New York, 1888), 588.

5. Beale, *Bates Diary,* 249.

6. McCullough, *Men and Measures,* 311–12.

Chapter 1. "It is impossible for him to lead"

1. Carl Sandburg, *Abraham Lincoln: The Prairie Years,* 2 vols. (New York, 1926), 1:155; Roy P. Basler, *The Collected Works of Abraham Lincoln,* 9 vols. (New Brunswick, N.J., 1953), 4:64 (hereafter cited as Basler, *Works*); Ida M. Tarbell, *The Life of Abraham Lincoln,* 4 vols. (New York, 1903), 1:75.

2. Sandburg, *Prairie Years,* 1:155, 156.

3. Basler, *Works,* 1:10; Tarbell, *Life of Lincoln,* 80.

4. Tarbell, *Life of Lincoln,* 87–88; Basler, *Works,* 1:10n; Ward Hill Lamon, *The Life of Abraham Lincoln: From His Birth to His Inauguration* (Boston, 1872), 118. Lincoln's experiences in the Black Hawk War can be traced in Earl Schenck Miers, *Lincoln Day by Day* (Dayton, 1991), 17–29; and Stephen B. Oates, *With Malice Toward None: The Life of Abraham Lincoln* (New York, 1977), 23.

5. Basler, *Works,* 1:13, 4:64–65.

6. John G. Nicolay and John Hay, eds., *Complete Works of Abraham Lincoln,* 12 vols. (New York, 1905), 6:32, 2:96–100 (hereafter cited as Nicolay and Hay, *Works*).

7. George Fort Milton, *The Eve of Conflict: Stephen A. Douglas and the Needless War* (Boston, 1934), 230.

8. Albert J. Beveridge, *Abraham Lincoln, 1809–1858,* 2 vols. (Boston, 1928), 2:395; Henry C. Whitney, *Life on the Circuit with Lincoln* (Boston, 1892), 95–96.

9. John J. Nicolay and John Hay, *Lincoln: A History (10 volumes, New York, 1914),,* 2:136–37, hereinafter Nicolay and Hay, Lincoln. See also Basler, *Works,* 2:461.

10. George B. McClellan, *McClellan's Own Story* (New York, 1887), 36 (hereafter cited as *McClellan's Own Story*); Stephen W. Sears, *George B. McClellan: The Young Napoleon* (New York, 1988), 58–59; John M. Douglas to McClellan, January 26, 1861, McClellan MSS, Library of Congress (LC).

11. Basler, *Works,* 4:45.

12. Warren W. Hassler Jr., *General George B. McClellan* (Baton Rouge, 1957), 21.

13. Gideon Welles, *Diary of Gideon Welles,* 3 vols. (Boston, 1911), 1:6 (hereafter cited as Welles, *Diary*); Basler, *Works,* 6:192–220; Montgomery Blair to Andrew Johnson, August 9, 1865, Gist-Blair MSS, LC; Chase to Elihu Burritt, October 6, 1862, Chase MSS, Historical Society of Pennsylvania (HSP).

14. Nicolay and Hay, *Lincoln,* 3:388; Basler, *Works,* 4:423–26.

15. Basler, *Works,* 4:331–32, 333, 353–54; Mark Mayo Boatner III, *The Civil War Dictionary* (New York, 1959), 169 (hereafter cited as Boatner, *CWD*).

16. J. G. Randall, *Lincoln the President,* 4 vols., (New York, 1997), 1:355.

17. Basler, *Works,* 4:338–39; Ellis to Cameron, April 15, 1861, and Rector to Cameron, April 22, 1861, *Official Records of the Union and Confederate Armies,* ser. 3, 1:72, 99 (hereafter cited as *ORA*). All references to *ORA* are to series 1 unless otherwise specified.

18. Jackson to Cameron, April 17, 1861, *ORA,* 1:82–83; Nicolay and Hay, *Lincoln,* 4:208–210.

19. Magoffin to Cameron, April 15, 1861, *ORA,* ser. 3, 1:70.

20. Scott to McClellan and General Orders № 1, both May 13, 1861, *ORA,* 51, pt. 1, 369–70, 376; Stephen W. Sears, ed., *The Civil War Papers of George B. McClellan: Selected Correspondence, 1860–1865* (New York, 1989), 7, 11, 16 (hereafter cited as Sears, *McClellan Papers*); Gabor S. Boritt, ed., *Lincoln's Generals* (New York, 1994), 7.

21. McClellan to Townsend, May 10, 1861, *ORA,* 51, pt. 1, 374; Basler, *Works,* 370.

22. Frank Moore, ed., *The Rebellion Record: A Diary of American Events,* 10 vols. (New York, 1977), 1:74.

23. McClellan to Townsend, May 17, 1861, *ORA,* 51, pt. 1, 380–81.

Chapter 2. *"Come hither without delay"*

1. Sears, *George B. McClellan,* 6, 10.

2. Ibid., 16–17, 18.

3. McClellan to John H. B. McClellan, September 9, 1855, McClellan MSS, LC.

4. *McClellan's Own Story,* 2.

5. Ibid.

6. Sears, *George B. McClellan,* 48–49.

7. *McClellan's Own Story,* 36; Sears, *George B. McClellan,* 57, 58.

8. Sears, *George B. McClellan,* 64–65.

9. Welles, *Diary,* 107.

10. Sears, *McClellan Papers,* 7–9; Townsend to McClellan, April 30, 1861, *ORA,* 51, pt. 1, 342–43; Ulysses S. Grant, *Personal Memoirs of U. S. Grant,* 2 vols. (New York, 1885–86), 1:241.

11. Robert U. Johnson and Clarence C. Buell, *Battles and Leaders of the Civil War,* 4 vols. (New York, 1887–88) 1:89, 94–95 (hereafter cited as *B&L*).

12. *McClellan's Own Story,* 43–47; Townsend to McClellan, April 30, 1861, and McClellan to Scott, May 2, 1861, *ORA,* 51, pt. 1, 339, 342–43.

13. McClellan to Scott, April 27, 1861, *ORA,* 51, pt. 1, 338–39; Basler, *Works,* 4:532; T. Harry Williams, *Lincoln and His Generals* (New York, 1952), 27.

14. Scott to McClellan, May 3, 1861, *ORA,* 51:369–7.

15. Basler, *Works,* 4:370; John Niven, *Salmon P. Chase: A Biography* (New York, 1995), 254–55.

16. Allan Pinkerton, *The Spy of the Rebellion* (New York, 1883), chap. 12; McClellan to Lincoln, June 10, 1861, Lincoln MSS, LC.

17. McClellan to Townsend, May 17, 1861, and Scott to McClellan, May 21, 1861, *ORA,* 51, pt. 1, 381, 387.

18. Scott to McClellan, May 24, 1861, and McClellan to Scott, May 27, 1861, *ORA,* 2:648, 653; Sears, *McClellan Papers,* 1989), 24.

19. Address to the Soldiers of the Expedition and Proclamation to the People of Western Virginia, both May 26, 1861, *ORA,* 2:48, 49.

20. McClellan to Lincoln, May 30, 1861, Lincoln MSS, LC; William Howard Russell, *My Diary North and South* (New York, 1954), 194.

21. Scott to McClellan, May 24, 1861, and McClellan to Scott, June 10, 1861, *ORA,* 2:648, 65; *B&L,* 1:127–28.

22. Lee to Garnett, July 1, 1861, Garnett's Report, June 25, 1861, and McClellan's Report, July 14, 1861, *ORA,* 2:239, 236–37, 205–6.

23. McClellan to the Soldiers of the Army of the West, June 25, 1861, *ORA,* 2:196–97.

24. McClellan to Morris, July 3, 1861, *ORA,* 2:208–9.

25. McClellan to Townsend, July 5, 1861, and McClellan's Report, July 14, 1861, *ORA,* 2:198, 205–8; *B&L,* 1:130–34.

26. McClellan to Soldiers of the Army of the West, July 16, 1861, and McClellan to Townsend, July 14, 1861, *ORA,* 2:236, 208.

27. Scott to McClellan, July 13, 1861, *ORA,* 2:204; McClellan to Scott, April 27, 1861, *ORA,* 51, pt. 1, 338.

28. Thomas to McClellan, July 22, 1861, *ORA,* 2:753.

Chapter 3. *"The people trust him"*

1. Basler, *Works,* 4:431–32.

2. Scott to McClellan, May 3, 1861, *ORA,* 51, pt. 1, 369–70.

3. E. D. Townsend, *Anecdotes of the Civil War in the United States* (New York, 1884), 55–56.

4. James Harrison Wilson, *Under the Old Flag,* 2 vols. (New York, 1912), 1:66; Russell, *My Diary,* 389.

5. Heintzelman's Journal, June 8, 1861, LC; Townsend, *Anecdotes,* 57.

6. Colin R. Ballard, *The Military Genius of Abraham Lincoln* (New York, 1952), 49–50.

7. McDowell's Testimony, *Report of the Joint Committee on the Conduct of the War,* 8 vols. (Washington, D.C., 1863–66), 2:35–38, hereafter cited as *JCCW;* Townsend, *Anecdotes,* 57; Ballard, *Military Genius of Lincoln,* 49–50.

8. Nicolay and Hay, *Lincoln,* 4:352–54; McDowell to Townsend, July 21, 1861, *ORA,* 2:316.

9. Nicolay and Hay, *Lincoln,* 4:358; Thomas to McClellan, July 22, 1861, *ORA,* 2:753.

10. *McClellan's Own Story,* 55; Basler, *Works,* 4:457–58.

11. Sears, *George B. McClellan,* 93, 101; Carl Schurz, *Reminiscences of Carl Schurz,* 3 vols. (New York, 1907–8), 2:333.

12. Charles W. Elliott, *Winfield Scott: The Soldier and the Man* (New York, 1937), 733; *McClellan's Own Story,* 66; Sears, *McClellan Papers,* 70; Boritt, *Lincoln's Generals,* 14.

13. General Orders № 1, July 27, 1861, *ORA,* 2:766; McClellan's Report, August 4, 1863, *ORA,* 2:5:11; Sears, *McClellan Papers,* 70.

14. Russell, *My Diary,* 480; Sears, *McClellan Papers,* 71, 60; *McClellan's Own Story,* 68.

15. Russell, *My Diary,* 521, 479; McClellan's Report, August 4, 1863, *ORA,* 5:12; Nicolay and Hay, *Lincoln,* 4:443; Sears, *McClellan Papers,* 71.

16. William Swinton, *Campaigns of the Army of the Potomac* (Secaucus, N.J., 1988), 65–66.

17. Sears, *McClellan Papers,* 76; Margaret Leech, *Reveille in Washington, 1860–1865* (New York, 1941), 110.

18. Sears, *McClellan Papers,* 75; Randall, *Lincoln the President,* 3: 353–54.

19. McClellan Memorandum to Lincoln, August 2, 1861, *ORA,* 5:6–8; McClellan to Scott, April 27, 1861, *ORA,* 51, pt. 1, 338–39; Leech, *Reveille in Washington,* 108.

20. Sears, *McClellan Papers,* 75.

21. Edwin C. Fishel, "Pinkerton and McClellan: Who Deceived Whom?" *Civil War History* 34 (1988): 116–17; McClellan to Scott, August 8, 1861, *ORA,* 11, pt. 3, 3–4; McClellan to Cameron, September 13, 1861, Cameron MSS, LC.

22. McClellan to Cameron, September 13, 1861, Cameron MSS, LC; Scott to Cameron, August 9, 1861, *ORA,* 11, pt. 3, 4.

23. McClellan to Lincoln, August 10, 1861, and Scott to Cameron, August 12, 1861, *ORA,* 11, pt. 3, 4–5, 6–7.

24. Sears, *McClellan Papers,* 81, 82; Elliott, *Winfield Scott,* 725, 731–32; William Ernest Smith, *The Francis Preston Blair Family in Politics,* 2 vols. (New York, 1993), 2:125–26.

25. William T. Sherman, *Memoirs of General William T. Sherman,* 2 vols. (New York, 1875), 1:191, 192.

Chapter 4. "I can do it all"

1. Nicolay and Hay, *Lincoln,* 4:444; Sears, *McClellan Papers,* 84, 95.

2. Nicolay and Hay, *Lincoln,* 4:446.

3. Sears, *McClellan Papers,* 60, 87, 89; *McClellan's Own Story,* 87.

4. General Orders № 15, August 17, 1861, and General Orders № 1, August 20, 1861, *ORA,* 5:567, 575.

5. T. Harry Williams, *Lincoln and the Radicals* (Madison, Wis.: 1941), 48; McClellan's Report, August 4, 1863, *ORA,* 5:23; Cameron to McClellan, September 7, 1861, McClellan MSS, LC.

6. McClellan to Cameron, September 8, 1861, *ORA,* 5:588–89.

7. Sears, *McClellan Papers,* 95.

8. Welles, *Diary,* 1:242; Sears, *McClellan Papers,* 103–4.

9. Beale, Bates *Diary,* 194; McClellan's Report, August 4, 1863, *ORA,* 5:8.

10. Basler, *Works,* 4:544–45.

11. Sears, *McClellan Papers,* 105.

12. Pinkerton to McClellan, October 4, 1861, McClellan MSS, LC; Heintzelman's Testimony, *JCCW* (1863), 1:127; Confederate Field Returns, October, 1861, *ORA,* 5:932.

13. Cameron to Dix, September 11, Banks to Ruger, September 16, and Copeland to Banks, September 18 and 16, 1861; *ORA,* ser. 2, 1:678, 681, 682–83.

14. Sears, *McClellan Papers,* 105–6.

15. Tyler Dennett, ed., *Lincoln and the Civil War in the Diaries and Letters of John Hay* (New York, 1939), 27 (hereafter cited as *Hay Diary*).

16. Sears, *McClellan Papers,* 106–7.

17. Dennett, *Hay Diary,* 27.

18. Sears, *McClellan Papers,* 107.

19. Dennett, *Hay Diary,* 31; *McClellan's Own Story,* 171.

20. *McClellan's Own Story,* 170; Coburn to Stone, October 20, 1861, *ORA,* 5:290.

21. Stone's Testimony, *JCCW* (1863), 2:488–89; McClellan to Stone, October 21, 1861, *ORA,* 51, pt. 1, 500.

22. Stone to Baker, October 21, 1861, *ORA,* 5:303; McClellan to Stone, October 21, 1861, *ORA,* 51, pt. 1, 500; McClellan to Banks, October 21, 1861, McClellan MSS, LC.

23. Dennett, *Hay Diary,* 30.

24. Richard B. Irwin, "Ball's Bluff and the Arrest of General Stone," in *B&L,* 2:123–34.

25. Sears, *McClellan Papers,* 111; Williams, *Lincoln and the Radicals,* 48.

26. McClellan to Cameron, October 31, 1861, *ORA,* 5:9–11; George C. Gorham, *Life and Public Service of Edwin M. Stanton,* 2 vols. (Boston, 1899) 1:223–24.

27. Sears, *McClellan Papers,* 113–14.

28. Basler, *Works,* 5:9–10; Leech, *Reveille in Washington,* 17; Dennett, *Hay Diary,* 32–33.

Chapter 5. "All quiet on the Potomac"

1. General Orders № 19, November 1, 1861, *ORA,* ser. 3, 1:613–14; Sears, *McClellan Papers,* 126; *McClellan's Own Story,* 173–74.

2. Russell, *My Diary,* 56; *McClellan's Own Story,* 161–62.

3. Heintzelman's Journal, November 11, 1861, LC.

4. Nicolay and Hay, *Lincoln,* 4:468–69; Dennett, *Hay Diary,* 34–35; Williams, *Lincoln and His Generals,* 46.

5. Sears, *McClellan Papers,* 127; Hugh McCulloch, *Men and Measures of Half a Century* (New York, 1888), 302.

6. McClellan's Report, August 4, 1863, *ORA,* 5:41; McClellan's Testimony, February 28, 1863, *JCCW* (1863), 1:422.

7. Sherman's Testimony, in Nicolay and Hay, *Lincoln,* 5:19.

8. Chester G. Hearn, *Admiral David Dixon Porter: The Civil War Years* (Annapolis, 1996), 68–72; Sears, *McClellan Papers,* 135.

9. McClellan to Buell, November 7, 1861, *ORA,* 4:342; General Orders № 97, November 9, 1861, *ORA,* 4:349.

10. General Orders № 97, November 9, 1861, *ORA*, 567; McClellan to Halleck, November 11, 1861, *ORA*, 3:568–69.

11. Ballard, *Military Genius of Lincoln*, 177; Sears, *McClellan Papers*, 132, 128.

12. McClellan to Cameron, October 31, 1861, *ORA*, 5:11; Sears, *McClellan Papers*, 128.

13. Leech, *Reveille in Washington*, 114–15; Nicolay and Hay, *Lincoln*, 4:469.

14. *McClellan's Own Story*, 77, 78, 79; Joseph E. Johnston, *Narrative of Military Operations* (New York, 1874), 81; E. J. Allen (Pinkerton) to McClellan, October 4 and 28, November 15, 1861, McClellan MSS, LC; Allan Nevins, *War for the Union*, 4 vols. (New York, 1959–71), 2:44.

15. *McClellan's Own Story*, 177; McClellan to Buell, November 29, 1861, *ORA*, 7:457–58; Johnston, *Narrative*, 81.

16. Buell to McClellan, November 22, 1861, *ORA*, 7:444; Nicolay and Hay, *Lincoln*, 154–55.

17. Nicolay and Hay, *Lincoln*, 5:151; quotes from Sears, *George B. McClellan*, 132.

18. Henry J. Raymond, *Life and Public Services of Abraham Lincoln* (New York, 1865), 773; Basler, *Works*, 5:34–35.

19. McClellan to Lincoln, December 10, 1861, McClellan MSS, LC; *McClellan's Own Story*, 79, 155; Hassler, *General George B. McClellan*, 47.

20. *McClellan's Own Story*, 155.

21. Lincoln to Buell and Halleck, December 31, 1861, *ORA*, 7:524; Buell to Lincoln, January 1, 1862, *ORA*, 7:526; Alexander Howard Meneely, *The War Department, 1861* (New York, 1928), 359.

22. Halleck to Buell, January 2, 1862, *ORA*, 7:527; Halleck to Lincoln January 1 and 6, 1862, *ORA*, 7:526, 532–33; Nicolay and Hay, *Works*, 7:78; Beale, *Bates Diary*, 223.

23. McClellan to Cameron, October 31, 1861, *ORA*, 5:10–11; *McClellan's Own Story*, 202–3; John G. Barnard, *The Peninsula Campaign and Its Antecedents* (Charleston, S.C., 2008), 51.

24. *McClellan's Own Story*, 203; Jacob W. Schuckers, *Life and Public Services of Salmon P. Chase* (New York, 1874), 445; David Donald, *Inside Lincoln's Cabinet: The Civil War Diaries of Salmon P. Chase* (New York, 1954), 74.

25. Montgomery C. Meigs, "General M. C. Meigs on the Conduct of the War," *American Historical Review* 26 (January 1921): 292.

26. Raymond, *Life of Lincoln*, 772–74; McDowell's Journal, in Swinton, *Campaigns*, 84.

27. McDowell's Journal, in Swinton, *Campaigns*, 84–85; A. K. McClure, ed., *Annals of the War* (1879; rpt., Edison, N.J., 1996), 79; Meigs, "General Meigs," 292–93; *McClellan's Own Story*, 156–58.

28. Joseph T. Glatthaar, *Partners in Command: The Relationships between Leaders in the Civil War* (New York, 1994), 67–68.

29. Basler, *Works*, 5:98.

30. *McClellan's Own Story*, 155.

31. Williams, *Lincoln and the Radicals*, 86; McClellan's Report, August 4, 1863, *ORA*, 5:9–11; Benjamin P. Thomas and Harold M. Hyman, *Stanton: The Life and Times of Lincoln's Secretary of War* (New York, 1962), 126; *McClellan's Own Story*, 152.

32. Thomas and Hyman, *Stanton*, 128–29. For the McCormick Reaper case, see Randall, *Lincoln the President*, 1: 33, 38–39.

33. Thomas and Hyman, *Stanton*, 131, 132, 133. For the *Trent* Affair, see Nevins, *War for the Union*, 1:384–94, 400–404, 412–14.

34. Sears, *George B. McClellan,* 140, 142; Sears, *McClellan Papers,* 154; George W. Julian, *Political Recollections, 1840 to 1872* (Chicago, 1884), 204.

35. Malcolm Ives to James Gordon Bennett, January 15, 1862, James Gordon Bennett MSS, LC; Sears, *George B. McClellan,* 142–43.

36. Thomas and Hyman, *Stanton,* 146.

37. Charles A. Dana, *Recollections of the Civil War: With the Leaders at Washington and in the Field in the Sixties* (Lincoln, Neb., 1966), 5; Leech, *Reveille in Washington,* 128; Sears, *McClellan Papers,* 160; Williams, *Lincoln and the Radicals,* 91–92.

38. Julian, *Political Recollections,* 211–12; Alexander McClure, *Lincoln and Men of War-Times* (Philadelphia, 1892), 171.

Chapter 6. "He doesn't intend to do anything"

1. David Homer Bates, *Lincoln in the Telegraph Office* (New York, 1939), 42.

2. Basler, *Works,* 5:98–99; McClellan to Halleck, January 13, 1862, McClellan to Buell, January 13, 1862, Halleck to McClellan, January 31, 1862, and Buell to McClellan, January 31, 1862, *ORA,* 7:547, 571, 572, 573.

3. See exchanges between McClellan, Halleck, and Buell, January 30–February 21, 1862, *ORA,* esp. 7:584–646.

4. Dennett, *Hay Diary,* 36; Welles, *Diary,* 1:61; Basler, *Works,* 111–12, 115.

5. John Codman Ropes, *The Story of the Civil War,* 2 vols. (New York, 1895–98), 1:226.

6. Lincoln to McClellan, February 3, 1862, *ORA,* 5:41–42.

7. McClellan to Stanton, January 31 [February 3], 1862, *ORA,* 5:41–45; Stanton to John Tucker, February 27, 1861, *ORA,* 5:46; *McClellan's Own Story,* 237.

8. E. J. Allen [Pinkerton] to McClellan, March 8, 1862, *ORA,* 5:736–37; Confederate Returns, January 22, 1862, *ORA,* 5:1040.

9. McClellan to Lincoln, February 22, 1862, Lincoln MSS, LC; Sears, *George B. McClellan,* 143.

10. Ruth Painter Randall, *Lincoln's Sons* (Boston, 1955), 131; Thomas and Hyman, *Stanton,* 176–77, 211; Sears, *McClellan Papers,* 187.

11. McClellan to Stanton, February 26, 1862, *ORA,* 5:727.

12. Ibid., February 27, 1862, 728.

13. Helen Nicolay, *Lincoln's Secretary: A Biography of John G. Nicolay* (New York, 1949), 142–44; Thomas and Hyman, *Stanton,* 142; Marcy to McClellan and Horace White to Joseph Medill, March 3, 1862, Charles H. Ray Papers, Huntington Library (HL); Marsena Patrick Diary, February 28 and March 6, 1862, LC.

14. Beale, *Bates Diary,* 253; William D. Kelley, *Lincoln and Stanton* (New York, 1885), 6–7; Salmon P. Chase, *Diary and Correspondence of Salmon P. Chase,* 2 vols. (Washington, D.C., 1902–3), 1:50, 51; *Congressional Globe,* 37th Cong., 2d Sess., 59; Basler, *Works,* 5:92.

15. Nevins, *War for the Union,* 2:44–45; Committee Journal, *JCCW* (1863): 1:84; Wilmer C. Harris, *Public Life of Zachariah Chandler* (Lansing, Mich., 1917), 227–28; McClellan to Halleck, March 3, 1862, *ORA,* 11, pt. 3, 7, 8; Isaac Newton Arnold, *The Life of Abraham Lincoln* (Lincoln, Neb., 1994), 281.

16. Beale, *Bates Diary,* 253; Samuel P. Heintzelman's Diary, March 8, 1862, LC; *McClellan's Own Story,* 196; Theodore C. Pease and James G. Randall, eds., *The Diary of Orville*

Hickman Browning, 2 vols. (Springfield, Ill., 1925, 1933), 1:537; Robert B. Warden, *Account of the Private Life and Public Services of Salmon Portland Chase* (Cincinnati, 1874), 498–99.

17. *JCCW,* Reports and Testimony (1863), 1:270, 360, 387, 425, 597, 681; Frank A. Flower, *Edwin McMasters Stanton: The Autocrat of Rebellion, Emancipation, and Reconstruction* (New York, 1905), 138–39; Heintzelman's Diary, March 8, 1862, LC.

18. Stephen W. Sears, *To the Gates of Richmond: The Peninsula Campaign* (New York, 1992), 7–8; *McClellan's Own Story,* 196; Glatthaar, *Partners in Command,* 70.

19. Sears, *George B. McClellan,* 159–60; Heintzelman's Diary, March 8, 1862, LC; Barnard, *Peninsular Campaign,* 94; Rowena Reed, *Combined Operations of the Civil War* (Annapolis, 2005), 125–38, 189; Stanton's Notes, March 8, 1862, Stanton MSS, LC; Dennett, *Hay Diary,* 36.

Chapter 7. *"McClellan seems not to value time especially"*

1. Basler, *Works,* 5:149–50; *McClellan's Own Story,* 226.

2. Erasmus D. Keyes, *Fifty Years' Observation of Men and Events* (New York, 1884), 438; McClellan to Stanton and Stanton to McClellan, March 9, 1862, *ORA,* 5:739; Heintzelman's Journal, March 8, 1862, LC.

3. Williams, *Lincoln and the Radicals,* 120–21.

4. Basler, *Works,* 5:151; William B. Franklin, "The First Great Crime of the War," *Annals of the War,* 81; *McClellan's Own Story,* 162–63.

5. Welles, *Diary,* 1:63–65; Pease and Randall, *Diary,* 1:532–33; Nicolay and Hay, *Lincoln,* 5:173; Stanton to McClellan, March 12, 1862, McClellan MSS, LC.

6. *McClellan's Own Story,* 224; McClellan to Samuel L. M. Barlow, Barlow Papers, HL; McClellan to Stanton and Stanton to McClellan, March 10, 1862, *ORA,* 5:740–41.

7. Schurz, *Reminiscences,* 2:337; Sears, *To the Gates of Richmond,* 17; McClellan's Report, August 4, 1863, *ORA,* 5: 51; Johnston, *Narrative,* 102–6; Johnston to Whiting, March 15, 1862, *ORA,* 5:1101; Francis Fessenden, *Life and Public Services of William Pitt Fessenden,* 2 vols. (Boston, 1907), 1:261.

8. Julian, *Political Recollections,* 205; Dennett, *Hay Diary,* 37; Nevins, *War for the Union,* 2:47; McClellan to Banks, March 16, 1862, *ORA,* 5:56.

9. Nevins, *War for the Union,* 2:47.

10. Beale, *Bates Diary,* 239, 240.

11. Basler, *Works,* 5:155; Jacob Dolson Cox, *Military Reminiscences of the Civil War,* 2 vols. (New York, 1900), 1:195; Dennett, *Hay Diary,* 37–38; Julian, *Recollections,* 208–9; Emory Upton, *The Military Policy of the United States* (Washington, D.C., 1916), 291–92.

12. William A. Croffut, ed., *Fifty Years in Camp and Field: the Diary of Major-General Ethan Allen Hitchcock* (New York, 1909), 437–40; Pease and Randall, *Diary,* 1:537–39.

13. Dennison to McClellan, March 14, 1862, in *McClellan's Own Story,* 250; Randolph Marcy to McClellan, March 12, 1862, McClellan MSS, LC; Sears, *McClellan Papers,* 201, 202, 206, 207, 213; Beale, *Bates Diary,* 240; Julian, *Recollections,* 210.

14. McClure, *Lincoln and Men of War-Times,* 204–5; *McClellan's Own Story,* 224–25; Thomas J. Rowland, *George B. McClellan and Civil War History: In the Shadow of Grant and Sherman* (Kent, Ohio, 1998), 97.

Chapter 8. *"The stride of a giant"*

1. McClellan to Fox, March 12, 1862, and Fox to McClellan, March 13, 1862, *ORA,* 9:27; McClellan to Lincoln, February 3, 1862, *ORA,* 5:45.

2. McClellan's Report, August 4, 1863, *ORA,* 5:50, 55–56; Fox to McClellan, March 13, 1862, *ORA,* 9:27; Heintzelman's Diary, March 13, 1862, LC; *JCCW,* Barnard's Testimony (1863), 1:386–90.

3. Stanton to McClellan, March 13, 1862, *ORA,* 5:750; McClellan to Stanton, March 13, 1862, *ORA,* 51, pt. 1, 551; McClellan's Report, August 4, 1863, *ORA,* 5:56.

4. Stanton to McClellan, March 22, 1862, McClellan Papers, LC; Alexander S. Webb, *The Peninsula* (New York, 1882), 28–29; *JCCW,* Reports, 1:12.

5. Wilson, *Under the Old Flag,* 1:123; McClellan's Report, August 4, 1863, *ORA,* 5:63.

6. Swinton, *Campaigns,* 99–100; John Tucker's Report, April 5, 1862, *ORA,* 5:46.

7. Sears, *Civil War Papers,* 211; Sears, *George B. McClellan,* 166.

8. Prince de Joinville, *The Army of the Potomac: Its Organization, Its Commander, and Its Campaign* (New York, 1862), 34.

9. Swinton, *Campaigns,* 100; Nicolay and Hay, *Lincoln,* 5:182.

10. McClellan's Report, August 4, 1863, *ORA,* 5:57–58; Daniel Woodbury to McClellan, March 19, 1862, *ORA* 11, pt. 3, 22–24.

11. McClellan's Report, March 19, 1862, *ORA,* 5:57–58; Fox to McClellan, March 13, 1863, *ORA,* 9:27; *JCCW,* Reports (1863), 1:628–34.

12. Nicolay and Hay, *Works,* 7:138; *McClellan's Own Story,* 164–65, 252; Sears, *McClellan Papers,* 219; Hitchcock Journal, March 23, 1863, LC.

13. Swinton, *Campaigns,* 100; Porter to McClellan, March 30, 1862, *ORA,* 51, pt. 1, 564.

14. *JCCW,* Reports, 1:260–61; *McClellan's Own Story,* 306.

15. Pease and Randall, *Diary,* 1:537–59.

16. Wadsworth to Stanton, April 2, 1862, *ORA,* 11, pt. 3, 60–61; Barnard, *Peninsular Campaign,* 73; Nicolay and Hay, *Lincoln,* 5:183–84.

17. McClellan to Thomas, April 1, 1862, *ORA,* 5:60–61; Ballard, *Military Genius of Abraham Lincoln,* 74–75.

18. McClellan to Stanton, April 7, Lincoln to McClellan, April 9, 1862, *ORA,* 11, pt. 1, 11–12, 15; McClellan to Winfield Scott, April 11, 1862, McClellan MSS, LC; Army of the Potomac Returns, April 13, 1862, *ORA,* 11, pt. 3, 97.

Chapter 9: *"But you must act"*

1. Nicolay and Hay, *Lincoln,* 5:183.

2. Ballard, *Military Genius of Abraham Lincoln,* 75–76.

3. McClellan to Thomas, April 1, 1862, *ORA,* 5:60–61; *JCCW,* Reports, 1:304–5.

4. Pease and Randall, *Diary,* 1:537–39; Basler, *Works,* 5:179; Army of the Potomac Returns, March 31, April 13, 1862, *ORA,* 11, pt. 3, 53, 97; Upton, *Military Policy,* 292.

5. Franklin, "The First Great Crime of the War," 81; *McClellan's Own Story,* 241; Heintzelman's Journal, April 3, 1862; Welles, *Diary,* 1:349.

6. Heintzelman's Journal, April 2, 1862, LC.

7. Magruder's Report, May 3, 1862, *ORA,* 11, pt. 1, 405–6; Magruder to Randolph, April 11, 1862, *ORA,* 11, pt. 3, 436.

8. *McClellan's Own Story,* 307; *Official Records of the Union and Confederate Navies in the War of the Rebellion,* 30 vols. (Washington, D.C., 1894–1922), 12:195–96.

9. McClellan to McDowell and Thomas to McClellan, April 4, 1862, *ORA* 11, pt. 3, 68, 66; Sears, *McClellan Papers,* 228; McClellan to Lincoln, April 5, 1862, *ORA,* 11, pt. 3, 71.

10. Basler, *Works,* 182; *B&L,* 2:171–72; McClellan's Report, August 4, 1862, *ORA,* 11, pt. 1, 10; Dennett, *Hay Diary,* 39.

11. McClellan's Report, August 4, 1862, *ORA,* 11, pt. 1, 10; *B&L,* 2:170; Sears, *To the Gates of Richmond,* 29.

12. Missroon to McClellan, April 5 and 6, 1862, Goldsborough to McClellan, April 6, 1862, *ORA,* 11, pt. 3, 80–81; *JCCW* (1863), 1:630–32.

13. Sears, *McClellan Papers,* 230; McClellan to Lincoln, April 6, 1862, and McClellan to Stanton, April 7, 1862, *ORA,* 11, pt. 3, 73–74, 81–81; Nicolay and Hay, *Lincoln,* 5:366; Magruder's Returns, April 23, 1862, *ORA,* 11, pt. 3, 460; Army of the Potomac Returns, April 13, 1862, *ORA,* 11, pt. 3, 97.

14. Basler, *Works,* 184; Hitchcock's Testimony, January 16, 1863, *ORA,* 12, pt. 1, 220; McClellan to Lincoln, April 14, 1862, *ORA,* 11, pt. 3, 98.

15. Basler, *Works,* 184; Army of the Potomac Returns, April 13, 1862, *ORA,* 11, pt. 3, 97; Sears, *McClellan Papers,* 244; McClellan to Lincoln, April 18, 1862, *ORA,* 51, pt. 1, 578; *McClellan's Own Story,* 283.

16. Basler, *Works,* 185.

17. Johnston to Lee, April 22, 1862, *ORA,* 11:456; McClellan to Ripley, April 26, 1862, and McClellan to Lincoln, May 1, 1862, *ORA,* 51, pt. 1, 584, 589; Basler, *Works,* 203.

18. Webb, *Peninsula,* 59, 63–66; Heintzelman's Testimony, *JCCW* (1863), 1:346, 347; William F. Barry's Report, May 5, 1862, *ORA,* 11, pt. 1, 130; Nicolay and Hay, *Lincoln,* 5:367–68, 372.

Chapter 10. *"I shall aid you all I can"*

1. Sears, *McClellan Papers,* 245.

2. Warden, *Life of Chase,* 428.

3. Ibid., 431–32.

4. Webb, *Peninsula,* 69; Sears, *McClellan Papers,* 255; *B&L,* 2:172; *McClellan's Own Story,* 327.

5. Hooker's Report, May 10, 1862, Hancock's Report, May 11, 1862, *ORA,* 11, pt. 1, 468, 540–41; McClellan to Stanton, May 5 and 6, 1862, *ORA,* 11, pt. 1, 448, 449; *McClellan's Own Story,* 328, 330; Joinville, *Army of the Potomac,* 55.

6. Johnston's Report, May 18, 1862, *ORA,* 11, pt. 1, 276; McClellan to Stanton, May 7, 1862, *ORA,* 11, pt. 3, 146.

7. J. H. Stine, *History of the Army of the Potomac* (Washington, D.C., 1893), 57–58; McClellan to Stanton, May 8 and 10, 1862, and McClellan to Lincoln, May 14, 1862, *ORA,* 11, pt. 3, 151, pt. 1, 26, 27.

8. McClellan to Stanton, May 9, 1862, *ORA,* 11, pt. 3, 153–54; *McClellan's Own Story,* 354.

9. Stanton to McClellan and Lincoln to McClellan, May 9, 1861, *ORA,* 11, pt. 3, 154–55.

10. Sears, *McClellan's Papers*, 262; *McClellan's Own Story*, 357; Stine, *Army of the Potomac*, 58.

11. McClellan to Lincoln, May 14, 1862, *ORA*, 11, pt. 1, 26–27; Lincoln to McClellan, May 15, 1862, *ORA*, 11, pt. 3, 173; Stanton to McClellan, May 18, 1862, *ORA*, 11, pt. 1, 27.

12. McClellan to Lincoln, May 21, 1862, *ORA*, 11, pt. 1, 29; *McClellan's Own Story*, 359; Stanton to McDowell, May 17, 1862, *ORA* 11, pt. 1, 28.

13. McClellan's Report, August 4, 1863, *ORA*, 11, pt. 1, 28; Webb, *Peninsula*, 87.

14. John G. Barnard's Report, January 26, 1863, *ORA*, 11, pt. 1, 110–11; Joel Cook, *The Siege of Richmond: A Narrative of the Military Operations of Major-General George B. McClellan during . . . May and June, 1862* (Ann Arbor, Mich., 2005), 118–21.

15. McClellan to Burnside, May 21, 1862, *ORA*, 9:392.

16. *JCCW*, Reports (1863), 1:262–67; Peter Watson to Stanton, May 9, 1862, Stanton MSS, LC.

17. Lincoln to McClellan, May 24, 1862, *ORA*, 11, pt. 1, 30; Lincoln to Frémont, May 24, 1862, *ORA*, 12, pt. 1, 643.

18. Lincoln to McDowell and McDowell to Stanton and to Lincoln, May 24, 1862, *ORA*, 12, pt. 3, 219, 220.

19. Basler, *Works*, 5:235–36; McClellan to Lincoln, May 25, 1862, *ORA*, 11, pt. 1, 32.

20. Basler, *Works*, 5:237, 239; Sears, *McClellan Papers*, 275–76.

21. Basler, *Works*, esp. 5:243–52; Stanton to McDowell and Frémont, June 2, 1862, *ORA*, 12, pt. 3, 321.

22. Basler, *Works*, 5:235–36, 232; *JCCW*, Testimony, 1:272.

23. William H. Powell, *The Fifth Army Corps* (Dayton, Ohio, 1984), 61; Sears, *McClellan Papers*, 275.

24. John Tucker to Stanton, May 22, 1862, Stanton MSS, LC.

25. McClellan to Stanton, May 28, 1862, and McClellan to Lincoln, May 26, 1862, *ORA*, 11, pt. 1, 35, 33; Basler, *Works*, 5:236.

26. McClellan to Stanton, May 28 and 30, 1862, *ORA*, 11, pt. 1, 35, 37; *B&L*, 2:320–23; Webb, *Peninsula*, 96.

27. McClellan to Stanton, May 28, 1862, *ORA*, 11, pt. 1, 35; Basler, *Works*, 5:245; *McClellan's Own Story*, 397.

28. E. P. Alexander, *Military Memoirs of a Confederate* (New York, 1907), 74–75; Army of the Potomac Returns, May 31, 1862, *ORA*, 11, pt. 3, 204; *B&L*, 2:211, 219; Webb, *Peninsula*, 97.

29. Basler, *Works*, 5:255; Ropes, *Story of the Civil War*, 2:150; Sears, *McClellan Papers*, 287, 306–7.

30. Joinville, *Army of the Potomac*, 132–33; Barnard's Report, January 26, 1863, *ORA*, 11, pt. 1, 130–31.

Chapter 11. "I almost begin to think we are invincible"

1. General Orders № 57, June 1, 1862, *ORA*, 11, pt. 3, 207; McDowell to McClellan, June 8, 1862, and Dix to Stanton, June 9, 1862, *ORA*, 11, pt. 3, 221; McClellan to Stanton, June 7, 1862, *ORA*, 11, pt. 1, 46.

2. Statement of Reinforcements, June 15, 1862, *ORA*, 11, pt. 3, 230; McClellan to Stanton, June 14, 1862, *ORA*, 11, pt. 1, 48.

3. Basler, *Works,* 5:272–73; McClellan's Report, August 4, 1863, *ORA,* 11, pt. 1, 46; Army of Potomac Returns, June 20, 1862, *ORA,* 11, pt. 3, 238–39.

4. McClellan to Stanton, Lincoln to McClellan, and McClellan to Lincoln, June 18, 1862, *ORA,* 11, pt. 3, 232, 233; Basler, *Works,* 5:277–78; Sears, *McClellan Papers,* 301.

5. McClellan's Report, August 4, 1863, *ORA,* 11, pt. 1, 47; Stine, *Army of the Potomac,* 75; Upton, *Military Policy,* 274–75; Johnston, *Narrative,* 145–46.

6. *B&L,* 2:325; McClellan to Rodgers, June 24, 1862, and Marcy to Heintzelman and Sumner, June 25, 1862, *ORA,* 11, pt. 3, 250, 252.

7. McClellan's Report, August 4, 1863, *ORA,* 11, pt. 1, 50; Return of Casualties, June 25, 1862, *ORA,* 11, pt. 2, 38; Cook, *Siege of Richmond,* 294–99.

8. McClellan to Stanton, June 25, 1862, McClellan Papers, LC; McClellan's Report, August 4, 1863, *ORA,* 11, pt. 1, 51; Basler, *Works,* 5:286.

9. Webb, *Peninsula,* 119; Army of the Potomac Returns, June 20, 1862, *ORA,* 11, pt. 3, 238; Johnston, *Narrative,* 145–46.

10. Lee to Jackson, June 16, 1862, and McClellan to Lincoln, June 18, 1862, *ORA,* 11, pt. 3, 602, 233.

11. Jefferson Davis, *Rise and Fall of Confederate Government,* 2 vols. (New York, 1881), 2:132; Swinton, *Army of the Potomac,* 146–47; *McClellan's Own Story,* 410–11.

12. *B&L,* 2:330, 352; Webb, *Peninsula,* 129.

13. *B&L,* 2:331, 398; McClellan's Report, August 4, 1863, *ORA,* 11, pt. 1, 51; McClellan to Stanton, June 26, 1862, *ORA,* 11, pt. 3, 260.

14. Marcy to Porter, June 23, 1864, *ORA,* 11, pt. 3, 247; Heintzelman's Journal, June 27, 1862, LC; Webb, *Peninsula,* 187.

15. McClellan to Stanton, June 26, 1862, *ORA,* 11, pt. 1, 52; Barnard's Report, January 26, 1863, *ORA,* 11, pt. 1, 131; Sears, *McClellan Papers,* 317.

16. Webb, *Peninsula,* 130–35; Powell, *Fifth Army Corps,* 83–107; *B&L,* 2:335.

17. Webb, *Peninsula,* 187; Swinton, *Army of the Potomac,* 153.

18. Webb, *Peninsula,* 188; Magruder's Report, *ORA* 11, pt. 2, 662.

19. McClellan to Stanton and McClellan to Goldsborough, June 27, 1862, *ORA* 11, pt. 3, 266, 267; *B&L,* 2:361.

20. *McClellan's Own Story,* 442, 443.

21. Ibid., 423; McClellan to Stanton, June 27, 1863, *ORA,* 11, pt. 3, 264–65; McClellan to Stanton, June, 28, 1862, *ORA,* 11, pt. 1, 61; Basler, *Works,* 5:290–91n; Bates, *Lincoln in the Telegraph Office* (New York, 1939), 109–10.

22. Stanton to Halleck, June 30, 1862, *ORA,* 16, pt. 2, 69–70; Sears, *McClellan Papers,* 318, 324.

23. McClellan's Report, August 4, 1863, *ORA,* 11, pt. 1, 62–65; Lee's Report, March 6, 1863, *ORA,* 11, pt. 2, 494; Stine, *Army of the Potomac,* 65–66.

24. *B&L,* 2:375, 369; *JCCW,* Testimony (1863), 1:436.

25. *B&L,* 2:375–82; McClellan's Report, August 4, 1863, *ORA* 11, pt. 1, 65–67; Lee's Report, March 6, 1863, *ORA,* 11, pt. 2, 495.

26. *B&L,* 2:391–95.

27. *JCCW,* Testimony (1863), 1:436–37; *B&L,* 4:414, 422–23; Webb, *Peninsula,* 154; *McClellan's Own Story,* 434, 435.

28. Robert L. Dabney, *Life and Campaigns of Lieutenant General Thomas J. Jackson* (New York, 1866), 473; *McClellan's Own Story,* 440; Ropes, *Story of the Civil War,* 2, 208–9.

29. H. J. Eckenrode and Bryan Conrad, *George B. McClellan: The Man Who Saved the Union* (Chapel Hill, N.C., 1941), 98–99; Rowland, *George B. McClellan,* 75.

30. Sears, *McClellan Papers,* 330.

Chapter 12. *"I have no reinforcements to send you"*

1. Schuckers, *Life of Chase,* 447; Basler, *Works,* 5:289–90.

2. McClellan to Stanton, June 28, 1862, *ORA,* 11, pt. 1, 61; Basler, *Works,* 5:287, 292; McClellan to Lincoln, June 26, 1862, *ORA,* 11, pt. 3, 259.

3. *JCCW,* Testimony (1863), 1:276–82; Pope to the Officers and Soldiers of the Army of Virginia, July 14, 1862, *ORA,* 12, pt. 3, 473–74; Cox, *Military Reminiscences,* 1:222–23.

4. *B&L,* 2:453–56.

5. McClellan to Stanton, July 1, 1862, McClellan to Thomas, July 1, 1862, and Lincoln to McClellan, July 2, 1863, *ORA,* 11, pt. 3, 280, 281, 282, 286; Basler, *Works,* 296–97, 298, 305–6.

6. Marcy to McClellan, July 4, 1862, McClellan MSS, LC; Sears, *McClellan Papers,* 334.

7. McClellan to Lincoln and McClellan to Stanton, July 3, 1862, *ORA,* 11, pt. 3, 287–88, 291–92; *McClellan's Own Story,* 484–85.

8. Meigs's Diary, July 4 and 5, 1862, Meigs MSS, LC; Dennett, *Hay Diary,* 176.

9. Basler, *Works,* 5:305–6, 307; Marcy to McClellan, July 4, 1862, McClellan MSS, LC.

10. McClellan to Lincoln, June 20, 1862, and Lincoln to McClellan, June 21, 1862, *ORA,* 11, pt. 1, 48; Powell, *Fifth Army Corps,* 181; George Templeton Strong, *The Diary of George Templeton Strong: The Civil War, 1861–1865,* ed. Allan Nevins and Milton H. Thomas (New York, 1952), 237, 244.

11. Stanton to Dix, July 7, 1862, *ORA,* 51, pt. 1, 717; Sears, *McClellan Papers,* 344–45, 346n; Nicolay and Hay, *Lincoln,* 5:447–49; Williams, *Lincoln and His Generals,* 133; *McClellan's Own Story,* 446.

12. Chase, *Diary and Correspondence,* 2:47–48; Gideon Welles, *Lincoln and Seward* (Freeport, N.Y., 1969), 191.

13. Heintzelman's Journal, July 8–9, 1862, LC; *JCCW,* Testimony, 1:613; Basler, *Works,* 5:310; Sears, *McClellan Papers,* 348.

14. McClellan to Samuel L. M. Barlow, July 15, 1862, Barlow Papers, HL.

15. Nicolay to Therena Bates, July 13, 1862, Nicolay MSS, LC; Lincoln to McClellan, July 13, 1862, and McClellan to Lincoln, July 15, 1862, *ORA,* 11, pt. 3, 319, 321–22; Sears, *McClellan's Papers,* 345.

16. Chase, *Diary and Correspondence,* 2:46–47.

17. Halleck to McClellan, July 30, 1862, *ORA,* 11, pt. 3, 343; Halleck to Lincoln, July 10, 15, and 19, 1862, Lincoln MSS, LC; Basler, *Works,* 5:323; Welles, *Diary,* 1:373; Boatner, *CWD,* 367.

18. Sears, *McClellan Papers,* 364, 365, 371; Barlow to McClellan, July 18, 1862, Barlow Papers, HL; Chandler to Mrs. Chandler, July 6, 1862, Chandler MSS, LC; *Congressional Globe,* 37th Cong., 2d Sess., 3149–50, 3219, 3220–21, 3390; Welles, *Diary,* 1:108.

19. Pease and Randall, *Diary,* 1:563.

20. Basler, *Works,* 5:318, 336–37; F. B. Carpenter, *Six Months in the White House with Abraham Lincoln* (New York, 1866), 20–21.

21. Sears, *McClellan Papers*, 351, 354–55, 368; *McClellan's Own Story*, 452–53.

22. Halleck's Memorandum, July 27, 1863, *ORA*, 11, pt. 3, 337–38; Heintzelman's Journal, July 26, 28, and 29, 1862, LC; *McClellan's Own Story*, 454.

23. Keyes to Meigs, July 27, 1863, *ORA*, 11, pt. 3, 338–39; Meigs to Halleck, July 28, 1862, *ORA*, 11, pt. 3, 340–41; McClellan's Returns, August 10, 1862, *ORA*, 11, pt. 3, 367; *McClellan's Own Story*, 465.

24. *JCCW*, Reports, 1:452–56; William Marvel, *Burnside* (Chapel Hill, N.C., 1991), 99–100.

25. *McClellan's Own Story*, 490, 491; Halleck to McClellan, July 30, August 3 and 6, 1862, *ORA*, 11, pt. 1, 76–77, 80–81, 83–84; McClellan to Halleck, August 5, 1862, *ORA*, 11, pt. 1, 77–78, 82; Halleck to McClellan, August 5, 1862, *ORA*, 11, pt. 3, 359; Upton, *Military Policy*, 331.

26. McClellan to Halleck, August 6 and 12, 1862, *ORA*, 11, pt. 1, 79, 88; Basler, *Works*, 5:359.

27. Halleck to McClellan, August 12, 1862, *ORA*, 11, pt. 1, 87; Heintzelman's Journal, August 11, 1862, LC.

28. McClellan to Halleck and Halleck to McClellan, August 24, 1862, *ORA*, 11, pt. 1, 93, 94.

Chapter 13. "He is troubled with the 'slows'"

1. Schuckers, *Life of Chase*, 448.

2. Pope to McClellan, July 4, 1862, and McClellan to Pope, August 7, 1862, *ORA*, 11, pt. 1, 295–97; McClellan to Halleck, August 12, 1862, *ORA*, 11, pt. 1, pt. 3, 372–73; Halleck to McClellan, August 3, 9, and 12, 1862, *ORA*, 11, pt. 1, pt. 1, 80–81, 85, 87.

3. Lorenzo Thomas to Stanton, August 16, 1862, *ORA*, 12, pt. 3, 578–79; Welles, *Diary*, 1:83.

4. Halleck's Report, November 25, 1862, *ORA*, 12, pt. 2, 6.

5. Sears, *McClellan Papers*, 388, 389–90; Fitz-John Porter to Manton Marble, August 10, 1862, Manton Marble MSS, LC.

6. Halleck to McClellan, August 21, 1862, and McClellan to Halleck, August 12, 1862, *ORA*, 11, pt. 1, 92, 87; Sears, *McClellan Papers*, 395, 397, 400.

7. Halleck to McClellan, August 7, 1862, *ORA*, 11, pt. 3, 359–60; McClellan to Halleck, August 17, 1862, *ORA*, 11, pt. 3, 378; *McClellan's Own Story*, 466, 468, 470, 471, 474.

8. Halleck to Buell, August 18, 1862, *ORA*, 16, pt. 2, 360.

9. McClellan to Halleck, August 24, 1862, and Halleck to McClellan, August 24 and 26, 1862, *ORA*, 11, pt. 1, 93–94; Halleck to McClellan, August 27, 1862, *ORA*, 11, pt. 3, 691; Stine, *Army of the Potomac*, 123.

10. *McClellan's Own Story*, 509–10, 511–13; Fitz-John Porter Court-Martial, *ORA*, 12, pt. 2 supp., 1003; McClellan to Halleck, August 27, 1862, *ORA*, 11, pt. 1, 96–97.

11. Sears, *McClellan Papers*, 406.

12. Lincoln to McClellan and McClellan to Lincoln, August 29, 1862, *ORA*, 11, pt. 1, 98; Upton, *Military Policy*, 354.

13. Townsend's Order, August 30, 1862, McClellan's Papers, LC; *McClellan's Own Story*, 525–26, 534. See exchange of correspondence between McClellan and Halleck in *ORA*, 11, pt. 1, 96–104.

14. Halleck to Stanton, November 25, 1862, *ORA* 12, pt. 2, 7–8; Pope to Halleck, August 30 and 31, 1862, *ORA* 12, pt. 3, 741, pt. 2, 80, 82–83; Dennett, *Hay Diary,* 46; Sears, *McClellan Papers,* 422, 423; William E. Doster, *Lincoln and the Episodes of the Civil War* (Whitefish, Mont., 2007), 155–56; *McClellan's Own Story,* 525.

15. *McClellan's Own Story,* 531; Sears, *McClellan Papers,* 395, 406; Moore, *Rebellion Record,* Documents, 12:616.

16. McClellan to Halleck, August 28 and 30, 1862, *ORA,* 11, pt. 1, 97, 111; *B&L,* 2:548–49; Sears, *McClellan's Papers,* 419.

17. Townsend's Order, August 30, 1862, *ORA,* 11, pt. 1, 103; Sears, *McClellan Papers,* 424, 423.

18. Dennett, *Hay Diary,* 45, 46; Thomas L. Livermore, *Numbers and Losses in the Civil War in America, 1861–1865* (Boston, 1901), 88–89; McClellan to Halleck, August 29, 1862, *ORA,* 11, pt. 1, 100.

19. McClellan to Porter, September 1, 1862, *ORA,* 12, pt. 3, 787–88; *McClellan's Own Story,* 534; Pope to Lincoln, September 5, 1862, Lincoln MSS, LC; Pope to Halleck and Halleck to Pope, September 5, 1862, *ORA,* 12, pt. 3, 812, 813.

20. Boatner, *CWD,* 662–63.

21. *McClellan's Own Story,* 535–36; Halleck to McClellan, August 29, 1862, *ORA,* 12, pt. 3, 722; McClellan to Lincoln, August 29, 1862, *ORA,* 11, pt. 1, 98; Nicolay and Hay, *Lincoln,* 6:16, 17; Herman Haupt, *Reminiscences of General Herman Haupt* (Milwaukee, 1901), 82–83; General Orders № 122, *ORA* 12, pt. 2, 807. See *ORA,* 11, pt. 1, 94–98, and pt. 3, 707–10.

22. Chase Dairy, September 2, 1862, LC; Welles, *Lincoln and Seward,* 193–94; Flower, *Stanton,* 176–77; Donald, *Inside Lincoln's Cabinet,* 110–12.

23. Sears, *McClellan Papers,* 423–24, 428; *McClellan's Own Story,* 532–33, 535; Nicolay and Hay, *Lincoln,* 6:26–27, 28.

24. Dennett, *Hay Diary,* 47; Leach, *Reveille in Washington,* 194; Nicolay and Hay, *Lincoln,* 6:23, 24, 25.

25. *Welles Diary,* 1:106; Marvel, *Burnside,* 110–11; Stanton to Curtin, September 8, 1862, *ORA,* 19, pt. 2, 217; Williams, *Lincoln and the Radicals,* 180.

26. *McClellan's Own Story,* 567.

Chapter 14. "If I cannot whip Bobbie Lee . . ."

1. Dennett, *Hay Diary,* 47; *McClellan's Own Story,* 551, 567; Welles, *Diary,* 1:124.

2. Lee to Cooper, August 19, 1863, *ORA,* 19, pt. 1, 144–45.

3. Special Orders № 4, September 7, 1862, and McClellan to Halleck, September 11, 1862, *ORA,* 19, pt. 2, 202, 254–55; McClellan's Report, August 4, 1863, *ORA,* 19, pt. 1, 41; *JCCW,* Testimony (1863), 1:452; John G. Walker, "Jackson's Capture of Harper's Ferry," in *B&L,* 2:605–6.

4. Nicolay and Hay, *Lincoln,* 6:135; Special Orders № 191, September 9, 1862, *ORA,* 19, pt. 1, 42–43; John Gibbon, *Personal Recollections of the Civil War* (New York, 1928), 73; Silas Colgrove, "The Finding of Lee's Lost Order," *B&L,* 2:603; McClellan to Halleck, September 8 and 9, 1862, *ORA,* 19, pt. 2, 211, 219.

5. *McClellan's Own Story,* 551–52; Swinton, *Army of the Potomac,* 197, 202; McClellan to Lincoln, September 13, 1862, *ORA,* 19, pt. 2, 281.

6. Welles, *Diary,* 1:124; Halleck to McClellan, September 13, 1862, *ORA,* 19, pt. 2, 280–81; *JCCW,* Testimony (1863), 1:479; Ropes, *Story of the Civil War,* 2:333; *McClellan's Own Story,* 549–50, 559.

7. McClellan to Halleck, September 14, 1862, *ORA,* 19, pt. 2, 289; *B&L,* 2:585; Ruggles to Franklin, September 15, 1862, *ORA* 19, pt. 1, 47.

8. Alexander, *Military Memoirs,* 230; McClellan to Halleck, September 15, 1862, *ORA,* 19, pt. 2, 294–95; Basler, *Works,* 5:425, 426.

9. Sears, *McClellan's Papers,* 463; Nicolay and Hay, *Lincoln,* 6:138.

10. *JCCW,* Testimony (1863), 1:441; Livermore, *Numbers and Losses,* 92–93; *B&L,* 2:603, 630–58.

11. McClellan to Halleck, September 17 and 18, 1862, *ORA,* 19, pt. 2, 312, 322; McClellan's Report, August 4, 1863, *ORA,* 19, pt. 1, 65–67; *B&L,* 2:658; Sears, *McClellan Papers,* 469, 476; Swinton, *Campaigns of the Army,* 202; Francis A. Palfrey, *The Antietam and Fredericksburg* (New York, 1882), 41, 119, 133–34. Swinton served as a war correspondent with the Army of the Potomac, and Brigadier General Palfrey served under McClellan and suffered a wound at Antietam.

12. Army of the Potomac Returns, September 20, 1862, *ORA,* 19, pt. 2, 336; McClellan to Halleck, September 22, 1862, *ORA,* 19, 342–43; Nicolay and Hay, *Lincoln,* 6:142.

13. McClellan to Halleck, September 19, 1862, *ORA,* 19, pt. 2, 330; Lincoln to McClellan, September 12, 1862, *ORA,* 19, 270; Montgomery Blair to McClellan, September 19, 1862, McClellan MSS, LC.

14. James D. Horan and Howard Swiggert, *The Pinkerton Story* (New York, 1951), 111–19.

15. Basler, *Works,* 433–36, 436–37; Sears, *McClellan Papers,* 481; *McClellan's Own Story,* 615; Welles, *Diary,* 1:142.

16. Lee's Report, August 19, 1863, *ORA,* 19, pt. 1, 151; Burnside's and Franklin's Testimony, *JCCW* (1863), 1:627.

17. McClellan to Halleck, September 23, 27, 1862, *ORA,* 19, pt. 2, 346, pt. 1, 70; Army of the Potomac Returns, September 30, 1862, *ORA,* 19, pt. 2, 374.

18. *McClellan's Own Story,* 617, 627, 654, 655.

19. Nicolay and Hay, *Lincoln,* 6:175.

20. Schurz, *Reminiscences,* 2:397; Halleck to McClellan, October 6, 1862, *ORA,* 19, pt. 1, 72; McClellan's Report, August 4, 1863, *ORA,* 19, 73.

21. Meigs to Stanton, October 14, 1862, *ORA,* 19, pt. 2, 422–23; *McClellan's Own Story,* 638; Basler, *Works,* 474–75; McClellan to Lincoln, October 25, 1862, *ORA,* 19, pt. 2, 485.

22. *McClellan's Own Story,* 630–33; Halleck to Stanton, October 28, 1862, *ORA,* 19, pt. 1, 8–9; Rufus Ingalls to Meigs, October 26, 1862, *ORA,* 19, pt. 2, 492–93; Nicolay to Therena Bates, October 26, 1862, Nicolay MSS, LC; F. B. Carpenter, *Six Months at the White House with Abraham Lincoln* (New York, 1866), 255.

23. Nicolay to Therena Bates, October 13, 1863, Nicolay MSS, LC; Basler, *Works,* 5:460–61; McClellan to Lincoln, October 17, 1862, *ORA,* 19, pt. 1, 18.

24. George S. Boutwell, *Reminiscences of Sixty Years of Public Affairs,* 2 vols. (New York, 1968), 2:305–6.

25. *McClellan's Own Story,* 655; Nicolay and Hay, *Lincoln,* 6:181.

26. Sears, *McClellan Papers,* 481; Francis Blair Sr. to McClellan, September 30, 1862, McClellan MSS, LC; Cox, *Military Reminiscences,* 1:355–61.

27. General Orders № 163, October 7, 1862, *ORA,* 19, pt. 2, 395–96.

28. McClellan's Report, August 4, 1863, *ORA,* 19, pt. 1, 83; *McClellan's Own Story,* 641; Halleck to Stanton, October 28, 1862, Stanton MSS, LC; Basler, *Works,* 5:481; McClellan to Lincoln, October 29, 1862, Lincoln MSS, LC; John Nicolay to John Hay, October 26, 1862, Nicolay MSS, LC.

29. Welles, *Lincoln and Seward,* 195–96.

30. Basler, *Works,* 5:442–43; Dennett, *Hay Diary,* 219.

31. Dennett, *Hay Diary,* 218–19; Flower, *Stanton,* 194; Ethan S. Rafuse, *McClellan's War: The Failure of Moderation in the Struggle for the Union* (Bloomington, Ind., 2005), 395; Lincoln to Halleck and Halleck to McClellan, November 5, 1862, *ORA,* 19, pt. 2, 545.

32. *McClellan's Own Story,* 651–52; Sears, *McClellan Papers,* 520.

33. *McClellan's Own Story,* 660; Henry Villard, *Memoirs of Henry Villard, Journalist and Financier, 1835–1900,* 2 vols. (Boston, 1904), 1:337.

34. *McClellan's Own Story,* 661.

35. Albert D. Richardson, *The Secret Service, the Field, the Dungeon, and the Escape* (Hartford, Conn., 1865), 324; Smith, *Blair Family,* 2:144–45; see also Pease and Randall, *Diary,* 1:619–20; Julian, quoted in Rice, *Reminiscences of Abraham Lincoln,* 53; Lincoln, quoted in Rafuse, *McClellan's War,* 374–75.

36. Palfrey, *Antietam and Fredericksburg,* 134–35; Rowland, *George B. McClellan,* 197.

Chapter 15. "It is the people's business"

1. Basler, *Works,* 6:311; Dennett, *Hay Diary,* 67; Welles *Diary,* 1: 345, 440.

2. Rowland, *George B. McClellan,* 237; Dana to J. S. Pike, August 8, 1864, quoted in Thomas and Hyman, *Stanton,* 321.

3. Samuel S. Cox to Manton Marble, June 20, 1864, Manton Marble MSS, LC; John C. Waugh, *Reelecting Lincoln: The Battle for the 1864 Presidency* (New York, 1997), 205–8.

4. Charles M. Segal, *Conversations with Lincoln* (New York, 1961), 321–22.

5. Basler, *Works,* 6:540; Nicolay and Hay, *Lincoln,* 9:59; Albert D. Richardson, *A Personal History of Ulysses S. Grant, and Sketch of Schuyler Colfax* (Hartford, Conn., 1868), 407, 434.

6. Randall, *Lincoln,* 4:133–34; McClure, *Lincoln and Men of War-Times,* 281–82, 457–63; Basler, *Works,* 7:381.

7. Sears, *George B. McClellan,* 344–49; Sears, *McClellan Papers,* 540.

8. Sears, *George B. McClellan,* 352; Williams, *Lincoln and the Radicals,* 228; Zachariah Chandler to his wife, March 31, 1863, Chandler MSS, LC; McClellan's Report, August 4, 1863, *ORA,* 19, pt. 1, 36–94.

9. Sears, *McClellan Papers,* 560–62, 563, 571.

10. Ibid., 575, 579.

11. Sears, *George B. McClellan,* 366; Sears, *McClellan Papers,* 585–87, 605.

12. Strong, *Diary,* 473; Basler, *Works,* 7:514–15; Nicolay, *Lincoln's Secretary,* 212.

13. Noah Brooks, *Washington in Lincoln's Time* (New York, 1896), 187.

14. Barlow to McClellan, August [?], 1864, Barlow Papers, HL; Sears, *McClellan Papers,* 580, 586, 587.

15. Nicolay and Hay, *Lincoln,* 9:255; Rice, *Reminiscences,* xxxv.

16. Barlow to McClellan, August 29, 1862, McClellan Papers, LC; Nicolay and Hay, *Lincoln,* 9:256; McClellan to Lincoln, July 7, 1862, *ORA,* 11, pt. 1, 73–74.

17. Nicolay and Hay, *Lincoln,* 9:257; Brooks, *Washington in Lincoln's Time,* 187.

18. Nicolay and Hay, *Lincoln,* 9:351–52.

19. Sears, *McClellan Papers,* 592, 595–96, 597.

20. Welles, *Diary,* 2:132, 135, 136.

21. H. S. Eliot to Welles, September 3, 1864, Welles MSS, LC; Governor James T. Lewis to Greeley et al., September 7, 1864, Weed to Seward, September 10, 1864, and Nicolay to Lincoln, August 30, 1864, Lincoln MSS, LC.

22. Emanuel Hertz, *Abraham Lincoln: A New Portrait,* 2 vols. (New York, 1931), 2:941; Zachariah Chandler to Mrs. Chandler, January 22, 1863, Chandler MSS, LC; Harris, *Life of Chandler,* 273–74.

23. Nicolay and Hay, *Lincoln,* 9:353–54, 354n.

24. Basler, *Works,* 8:52–53.

25. Sears, *George B. McClellan,* 379; Kenneth M Stampp, *Indiana Politics during the Civil War* (Indianapolis, 1949), 250–51.

26. G. W. Adams to Manton Marble, September 27, 1864, Manton Marble MSS, LC; Basler, *Works,* 8:24; Thomas and Hyman, *Stanton,* 328–31.

27. Dana, *Recollections,* 261; Dennett, *Hay Diary,* 233.

28. Basler, *Works,* 7:506–7; William F. Zornow, *Lincoln and The Party Divided* (Norman, Okla., 1954), 201; William B. Hesseltine, *Lincoln and the War Governors* (New York, 1955), 381.

29. Sears, *McClellan Papers,* 586, 606, 610; Sears, *George B. McClellan,* 381.

30. Sears, *McClellan Papers,* 617.

31. Dennett, *Hay Diary,* 232–33; Brooks, *Washington in Lincoln's Time,* 216; Sears, *McClellan's Papers,* 617.

32. Edward McPherson, *The Political History of the United States of America during the Great Rebellion* (Washington, D.C., 1865), 623.

33. Sears, *McClellan Papers,* 618.

BIBLIOGRAPHY

Documents, Letters, and Manuscripts

Historical Society of Pennsylvania, Philadelphia
    Chase, Salmon P., Manuscripts
Huntington Library
    Barlow, Samuel L. M., Papers
    Ray, Charles H., Papers
Library of Congress
    Bennett, James Gordon, Manuscripts
    Blair, Montgomery, Manuscripts in Gist-Blair Manuscripts
    Cameron, Simon, Manuscripts
    Chandler, Zachariah, Manuscripts
    Chase, Salmon P., Diary and Manuscripts
    Dana, Charles A., Manuscripts
    Heintzelman, Samuel P., Journal
    Hitchcock, Ethan Allen, Journal and Manuscripts
    Lincoln, Abraham, Manuscript, Robert Todd Lincoln Collection
    Marble, Manton, Manuscripts
    McClellan, George Brinton, Manuscripts
    Meigs, Montgomery, Manuscripts
    Nicolay, John G., Manuscripts
    Patrick, Marsena, Diary
    Stanton, Edwin McMasters, Manuscripts
    Welles, Gideon, Manuscripts

Official Records

Congressional Globe, 37th Cong., 2d sess., May 20, 1862.
Official Records of the Union and Confederate Navies in the War of the Rebellion. 30
    vols. Washington, D.C.: Government Printing Office, 1894–1922.

Report of the Joint Committee on the Conduct of the War. 8 vols. Washington, D.C.: Government Printing Office, 1863–66.

War of the Rebellion: Official Records of the Union and Confederate Armies. 130 vols. Harrisburg, Pa.: National Historical Society, 1971.

Books

Alexander, E. P. *Military Memoirs of a Confederate.* New York: Charles Scribner's Sons, 1907.

Ambrose, Stephen E. *Halleck: Lincoln's Chief of Staff.* Baton Rouge: Louisiana State University Press, 1962.

Arnold, Isaac Newton. *The Life of Abraham Lincoln.* Lincoln: University of Nebraska Press, 1994.

Ballard, Colin R. *The Military Genius of Abraham Lincoln.* New York: World Publishing Co., 1952.

Barnard, John G. *The Peninsular Campaign and Its Antecedents.* Charleston, S.C.: BookSurge, 2008.

Basler, Roy P., ed. *The Collected Works of Abraham Lincoln.* 9 vols. New Brunswick, N.J.: Rutgers University Press, 1953–55.

Bates, David Homer. *Lincoln in the Telegraph Office.* New York: D. Appleton-Century, 1939.

Beale, Howard, ed. *Dairy of Edward Bates, 1859–1866.* Washington, D.C.: Annual Report of American Historical Association, 1930.

Beveridge, Albert J. *Abraham Lincoln, 1809–1858.* 2 vols. Boston: Houghton Mifflin, 1928.

Boatner, Mark Mayo, III. *The Civil War Dictionary.* New York: David McKay Co., 1959.

Boritt, Gabor S., ed. *Lincoln's Generals.* New York: Oxford University Press, 1994.

Boutwell, George S. *Reminiscences of Sixty Years of Public Affairs.* 2 vols. New York: Greenwood, 1968.

Brooks, Noah. *Washington in Lincoln's Time.* New York: Century Co., 1896.

Carpenter, F. B. *Six Months in the White House with Abraham Lincoln.* New York: Hurd & Houghton, 1866.

Chase, Salmon P. *Diary and Correspondence of Salmon P. Chase.* 2 vols. Washington, D.C.: Annual Report of the American Historical Association, 1902–3.

Cook, Joel. *The Siege of Richmond: A Narrative of the Military Operations of Major-General George B. McClellan during . . . May and June, 1862.* Ann Arbor: University of Michigan Library, 2005.

Cox, Jacob Dolson. *Military Reminiscences of the Civil War.* 2 vols. New York: Scribner's, 1900.

Croffut, William A., ed. *Fifty Years in Camp and Field: The Diary of Major-General Ethan Allen Hitchcock.* New York: G. P. Putnam's Sons, 1909.

Dabney, Robert L. *Life and Campaigns of Lieutenant General Thomas J. Jackson.* New York: Blelock & Co., 1866.

Dana, Charles A. *Recollections of the Civil War: With the Leaders at Washington and in the Field in the Sixties.* Lincoln: University of Nebraska Press, 1996.

Davis, Jefferson. *Rise and Fall of Confederate Government.* 2 vols. New York: D. Appleton, 1881.

Dennett, Tyler, ed. *Lincoln and the Civil War in the Diaries and Letters of John Hay.* New York: Dodd, Mead, 1939.

Donald, David Herbert. *Inside Lincoln's Cabinet: The Civil War Diaries of Salmon P. Chase.* New York: Longmans, Green & Co., 1954.

———. *Lincoln.* New York: Simon & Schuster, 1995.

Doster, William E. *Lincoln and the Episodes of the Civil War.* Whitefish, Mont.: Kessinger Publishing, 2007.

Eckenrode, H. J., and Bryan Conrad. *George B. McClellan: The Man Who Saved the Union.* Chapel Hill: University of North Carolina Press, 1941.

Elliott, Charles W. *Winfield Scott: The Soldier and the Man.* New York: Macmillan, 1937.

Fessenden, Francis. *Life and Public Services of William Pitt Fessenden.* 2 vols. Boston: Houghton Mifflin, 1907.

Flower, Frank A. *Edwin McMasters Stanton: The Autocrat of Rebellion, Emancipation, and Reconstruction.* New York: Saalfield, 1905.

Gibbon, John. *Personal Recollections of the Civil War.* New York: G. P. Putnam's, 1928.

Goodwin, Doris Kearns. *Team of Rivals: The Political Genius of Abraham Lincoln.* New York: Simon & Schuster, 2005.

Gorham, George C. *Life and Public Service of Edwin M. Stanton.* 2 vols. Boston: Houghton Mifflin, 1899.

Grant, Ulysses S. *Personal Memoirs of U. S. Grant.* 2 vols. New York: Charles L. Webster & Co., 1885–86.

Gurowski, Adam. *Diary.* 3 vols. Boston: Lee & Shephard, 1862–64.

Harris, Wilmer C. *Public Life of Zachariah Chandler.* Lansing: Michigan Historical Commission, 1917.

Hassler, Warren B. *General George B. McClellan: Shield of the Union.* Baton Rouge: Louisiana State University Press, 1957.

Haupt, Herman. *Reminiscences of General Herman Haupt.* Milwaukee: Wright & Joys, 1901.

Hearn, Chester G. *Admiral David Dixon Porter: The Civil War Years.* Annapolis: Naval Institute Press, 1996.

Hertz, Emanuel. *Abraham Lincoln: A New Portrait.* 2 vols. New York: Horace Liveright, 1931.

Hesseltine, William B. *Lincoln and the War Governors.* New York: Knopf, 1955.

Horan, James D. *The Pinkertons: The Detective Dynasty That Made History.* New York: Crown, 1967.

Horan, James D., and Howard Swiggert. *The Pinkerton Story*. New York: G. P. Putnam's Sons, 1951.

Johnson, Robert U., and Clarence C. Buell. *Battles and Leaders of the Civil War*. 4 vols. New York: Century Co., 1886–90.

Johnston, Joseph E. *Narrative of Military Operations*. New York: D. Appleton, 1874.

Joinville, Prince de. *The Army of the Potomac: Its Organization, Its Commander, and Its Campaign*. New York: Anson D. F. Randolph, 1862.

Julian, George W. *Political Recollections, 1840 to 1872*. Chicago: Jansen, McClurg & Co., 1884.

Kelley, William D. *Lincoln and Stanton*. New York: G. P. Putnam's Sons, 1885.

Keyes, Erasmus D. *Fifty Years' Observation of Men and Events*. New York: Charles Scribner's Sons, 1884.

Lamon, Ward Hill. *The Life of Abraham Lincoln: From His Birth to His Inauguration*. Boston: Osgood & Co., 1872.

———. *Recollections of Abraham Lincoln, 1847–1865*. Lincoln: University of Nebraska Press, 1994.

Leech, Margaret. *Reveille in Washington, 1860–1865*. New York: Harper & Bros., 1941.

Livermore, Thomas L. *Numbers and Losses in the Civil War in America, 1861–1865*. Boston: Houghton Mifflin, 1901.

Marvel, William. *Burnside*. Chapel Hill: University of North Carolina Press, 1991.

McClellan, George B. *McClellan's Own Story*. New York: Charles L. Webster & Co., 1887.

———. *Report on the Organization of the Army of the Potomac, and of Its Campaigns in Virginia and Maryland*. Washington, D.C.: Government Printing Office, 1864.

McClure, Alexander K. *Lincoln and Men of War-Times: Some Personal Recollections of War and Politics during the Lincoln Administration*. Philadelphia: Times Publishing Co., 1892.

———, ed. *Annals of the War*. Edison, N.J.: Blue & Grey Press, 1996.

McCulloch, Hugh. *Men and Measures of Half a Century*. New York: Charles Scribner's Sons, 1888.

McPherson, Edward. *The Political History of the United States of America during the Great Rebellion*. Washington, D.C.: Philip & Solomons, 1865.

Meneely, Alexander Howard. *The War Department, 1861*. New York: Columbia University Press, 1928.

Miers, Earl Schenck, ed. *Lincoln Day by Day*. Dayton, Ohio: Morningside Press, 1991.

Milton, George Fort. *The Eve of Conflict: Stephen A. Douglas and the Needless War*. Boston: Houghton Mifflin, 1934.

Moore, Frank, ed. *The Rebellion Record: A Diary of American Events*. 10 vols. New York: Arno Press, 1977.

Myers, William Starr. *A Study in Personality: General George Brinton McClellan.* New York: D. Appleton-Century, 1934.

Nevins, Allan. *War for the Union.* 4 vols. New York: Charles Scribner's Sons, 1959–71.

Nicolay, Helen. *Lincoln's Secretary: A Biography of John G. Nicolay.* New York: Longmans, Green & Co., 1949.

Nicolay, John G., and John Hay. *Abraham Lincoln: A History.* 10 vols. New York: Century Co., 1914.

———. *The Complete Works of Lincoln.* 12 vols. New York: Century Co., 1905.

Niven, John. *Salmon P. Chase: A Biography.* New York: Oxford University Press, 1995.

Oates, Stephen B. *With Malice toward None: The Life of Abraham Lincoln.* New York: Harper & Row, 1977.

Palfrey, Francis A. *The Antietam and Fredericksburg.* New York: Scribner's, 1882.

Pease, Theodore C., and James G. Randall, eds. *The Diary of Orville Hickman Browning.* 2 vols. Springfield: Illinois State Historical Library, 1925, 1933.

Piatt, Donn. *Memories of the Men Who Saved the Union.* New York: Belford, Clarke & Co., 1887.

Pinkerton, Allan. *The Spy of the Rebellion: Being a True History of the Spy System of the United States Army during the Late Rebellion.* New York: G. W. Carleton & Co., 1883.

Powell, William H. *The Fifth Army Corps.* Dayton, Ohio: Morningside Bookshop, 1984.

Rafuse, Ethan. *McClellan's War: A Failure of Moderation in the Struggle for the Union.* Bloomington: Indiana University Press, 2005.

Randall, J. G. *Lincoln the President.* 4 vols. in 2. New York: Da Capo Press, 1997.

Randall, Ruth Painter. *Lincoln's Sons.* Boston: Little, Brown, 1955.

Raymond, Henry J. *Life and Public Services of Abraham Lincoln.* New York: Derby & Miller, 1865.

Reed, Rowena. *Combined Operations in the Civil War.* Annapolis: Naval Institute Press, 2005.

Rhodes, James Ford. *History of the United States from the Compromise of 1850.* 7 vols. New York: Macmillan, 1910.

Rice, Allen Thorndike, ed. *Reminiscences of Abraham Lincoln by Distinguished Men of His Time.* New York: North American Review, 1888.

Richardson, Albert D. *A Personal History of Ulysses S. Grant, and Sketch of Schuyler Colfax.* Hartford, Conn.: American Publishing Co., 1868.

———. *The Secret Service, the Field, the Dungeon, and the Escape.* Hartford, Conn.: American Publishing Co., 1865.

Ropes, John Codman. *The Story of the Civil War.* 2 vols. New York: G. P. Putnam's Sons, 1895–98.

Rowland, Thomas. *George B. McClellan and Civil War History: In the Shadow of Grant and Sherman.* Kent, Ohio: Kent University Press, 1998.

Russell, William H. *My Diary, North and South.* New York: Harper's Bros., 1954.

Sandburg, Carl. *Abraham Lincoln: The War Years.* 4 vols. New York: Charles Scribner's Sons, 1943.

Schuckers, Jacob W. *Life and Public Services of Salmon Portland Chase.* New York: D. Appleton, 1874.

Schurz, Carl. *Reminiscences of Carl Schurz.* 3 vols. New York: McClure Co., 1907–8.

Sears, Stephen W., ed. *The Civil War Papers of George B. McClellan: Selected Correspondence, 1860–1865.* New York: Ticknor & Fields, 1989.

———. *George B. McClellan: The Young Napoleon.* New York: Ticknor & Fields, 1988.

———. *Landscape Turned Red: The Battle of Antietam.* New York: Ticknor & Fields, 1983.

———. *To the Gates of Richmond: The Peninsula Campaign.* New York: Ticknor & Fields, 1992.

Segal, Charles M., ed. *Conversations with Lincoln.* New York: G. P. Putnam's Sons, 1961.

Seward, Frederick W. *Reminiscences of a War-Time Statesman and Diplomat, 1830–1915.* New York: G. P. Putnam's, 1916.

Sherman, William T. *Memoirs of General William T. Sherman.* 2 vols. New York: D. Appleton, 1875.

Smith, William Ernest. *The Francis Preston Blair Family in Politics.* 2 vols. New York: Macmillan, 1933.

Stampp, Kenneth M. *Indiana Politics during the Civil War.* Indianapolis: Indiana Historical Bureau, 1949.

Stine, J. H. *History of the Army of the Potomac.* Washington, D.C.: Gibson Bros., 1893.

Strong, George Templeton. *The Diary of George Templeton Strong: The Civil War, 1861–1865.* Ed. Allan Nevins and Milton H. Thomas. New York: Macmillan, 1952.

Swinton, William. *Campaigns of the Army of the Potomac.* Secaucus, N.J.: Blue & Grey Press, 1988.

Tarbell, Ida M. *The Life of Abraham Lincoln.* 4 vols. New York: Lincoln History Society, 1903.

Thomas, Benjamin P. *Abraham Lincoln: A Biography.* New York: Knopf, 1952.

Thomas, Benjamin P., and Harold M. Hyman. *Stanton: The Life and Times of Lincoln's Secretary of War.* New York: Knopf, 1962.

Townsend, E. D. *Anecdotes of the Civil War in the United States.* New York: D. Appleton, 1884.

Upton, Emory. *The Military Policy of the United States.* Washington, D.C.: Government Printing Office, 1916.

Villard, Henry. *Memoirs of Henry Villard, Journalist and Financier, 1835–1900.* 2 vols. Boston: Houghton Mifflin, 1904.

Warden, Robert B. *Account of the Private Life and Public Services of Salmon Port-land Chase.* Cincinnati: Wilstach, Baldwin & Co., 1874.

Waugh, John C. *Reelecting Lincoln: The Battle for the 1864 Presidency.* New York: Crown Publishers, 1997.

Webb, Alexander S. *The Peninsula.* New York: Charles Scribner's Sons, 1882.

Welles, Gideon. *Diary of Gideon Welles.* 3 vols. Boston: Houghton Mifflin, 1911.

———. *Lincoln and Seward.* Freeport, N.Y.: Books for Libraries Press, 1969.

Wheeler, Richard. *Sword over Richmond: An Eyewitness History of McClellan's Peninsula Campaign.* New York: Harper & Row, 1986.

Whitney, Henry C. *Life on the Circuit with Lincoln.* Boston: Estes & Lauriat, 1892.

Williams, T. Harry. *Lincoln and His Generals.* New York: Knopf, 1952.

———. *Lincoln and the Radicals.* Madison: University of Wisconsin Press, 1941.

Wilson, James Harrison. *Under the Old Flag.* 2 vols. New York: D. Appleton, 1912.

Zornow, William Frank. *Lincoln and the Party Divided.* Norman: University of Oklahoma Press, 1954.

Articles

Colgrove, Silas. "The Finding of Lee's Lost Order." In *Battles and Leaders of the Civil War,* by Robert U. Johnson and Clarence C. Buell, 2:603. New York: Century Co., 1886–90.

Fishel, Edwin C. "Pinkerton and McClellan: Who Deceived Whom?" *Civil War History* 34 (June 1988): 115–42.

Franklin, William B. "The First Great Crime of the War." In *Annals of the War,* ed. Alexander. K. McClure, 72–81. Edison, N.J.: Blue and Grey Press, 1996.

Irwin, Richard B. "Ball's Bluff and the Arrest of General Stone." In *Battles and Leaders of the Civil War,* 2:123–34.

McClellan, George B. "The Peninsular Campaign." In *Battles and Leaders of the Civil War,* 2:160–87.

Meigs, Montgomery C. "General M. C. Meigs on the Conduct of the War." *American Historical Review* 26 (January 1921): 285–303.

Walker, John G. "Jackson's Capture of Harper's Ferry." In *Battles and Leaders of the Civil War,* 604–11.

INDEX